More praise for *Why Dogs Hump and Bees Get Depressed*

"Marc Bekoff's wide-ranging books are unfailingly scholarly, entertaining, insightful, and educational."

— Ingrid E. Newkirk, president of PETA

"Dr. Marc Bekoff has, in his characteristically brilliant, accessible, eclectic, and compassionate style, rendered unequivocally clear nothing less than an animal protection manifesto that is likely to resonate for years."

— Michael Charles Tobias, PhD,
president of the Dancing Star Foundation

P9-CSE-206

WHY DOGS HUMP AND BEES GET DEPRESSED

Also by Marc Bekoff

Jasper's Story: Saving Moon Bears
(a children's book with Jill Robinson)

The Animal Manifesto:
Six Reasons for Expanding Our Compassion Footprint

Wild Justice: The Moral Lives of Animals (with Jessica Pierce)

Animals at Play: Rules of the Game (a children's book)

The Emotional Lives of Animals: A Leading Scientist Explores Animal
Joy, Sorrow, and Empathy — and Why They Matter

Animals Matter: A Biologist Explains Why We Should Treat Animals
with Compassion and Respect

Animal Passions and Beastly Virtues:
Reflections on Redecorating Nature

The Ten Trusts (with Jane Goodall)

Minding Animals: Awareness, Emotions, and Heart

Nature's Life Lessons: Everyday Truths from Nature (with Jim Carrier)

Edited by Marc Bekoff

Ignoring Nature No More: The Case for Compassionate Conservation

Encyclopedia of Animal Rights and Animal Welfare

Encyclopedia of Human-Animal Relationships

Encyclopedia of Animal Behavior

The Cognitive Animal:
Empirical and Theoretical Perspectives on Animal Cognition
(with Colin Allen and Gordon Burghardt)

The Smile of a Dolphin: Remarkable Accounts of Animal Emotions

WHY DOGS HUMP AND BEES GET DEPRESSED

The Fascinating Science of
ANIMAL INTELLIGENCE, EMOTIONS, FRIENDSHIP, *and* CONSERVATION

MARC BEKOFF

New World Library
Novato, California

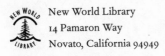 New World Library
14 Pamaron Way
Novato, California 94949

These essays appeared in a different form at *Psychology Today*'s website.

Text design by Tona Pearce Myers

Photo on page 272 by Heather McWilliams Mierzejewski; illustration on page 138 by Lenny Frieling. All other photos by Marc Bekoff.

Library of Congress Cataloging-in-Publication Data
Bekoff, Marc.
[Essays. Selections]
 Why dogs hump and bees get depressed : the fascinating science of animal intelligence, emotions, friendship, and conservation / Marc Bekoff.
    pages   cm
Includes bibliographical references and index.
ISBN 978-1-60868-219-5 (pbk.) — ISBN 978-1-60868-220-1 (ebook)
1. Animal behavior. I. Title.
QL751.B3655 2013
591.5—dc23   2013024533

First printing, November 2013
ISBN 978-1-60868-219-5
Printed in the United States on 100% postconsumer-waste recycled paper

10 9 8 7 6 5 4 3 2 1

CONTENTS

Part 3. Media and the (Mis)representation of Animals 53

Part 4. Why Dogs Hump:
Or, What We Can Learn from Our Special Friends 69

Part 5. Consciousness, Sentience, and Cognition:
A Potpourri of Current Research on Flies, Fish, and Other Animals 107

Part 6. The Emotional Lives of Animals: The Ever-Expanding Circle of Sentience Includes Depressed Bees and Empathic Chickens 147

Part 7. Wild Justice and Moral Intelligence: Don't Blame Other Animals for Our Destructive Ways 193

Part 8. The Lives of Captive Creatures: Why Are They Even There? 211

Part 9. *Who* We Eat Is a Moral Question 237

Part 10. Who Lives, Who Dies, and Why: Redecorating Nature, Peaceful Coexistence, and Compassionate Conservation   265

Part 11. Rewilding Our Hearts: The Importance of Kindness, Empathy, and Compassion for All Beings   307

PREFACE

Sharing and Celebrating
the Fascinating Lives
of Other Animals

IN JUNE 2009 I began writing essays for *Psychology Today* online under the category "Animal Emotions" (see www.psychologytoday.com/blog /animal-emotions). When I was first asked to do this, I emphatically said, "No." I didn't need any more on my desk. However, I thought about this wonderful opportunity a lot over the next week, and then I said, "Sure, why not?" I'm so glad I did. I jumped right in and have written around five hundred essays so far. By doing so I've learned a lot about innumerable topics centering on our relationships with nonhuman animals and the cognitive, emotional, and moral lives of these amazing beings.

During the time I've been writing these essays, several scientific fields devoted to animal studies have grown by leaps and bounds, such as "anthrozoology," the study of human-animal interactions (also called human-animal studies); "ethology," the study of animal behavior (see Lee Dugatkin's book *Principles of Animal Behavior*); and "cognitive ethology," which focuses on the study of animal minds. Studies have expanded to include numerous and diverse animals, and the scientific data show clearly just how smart and emotional other animals really are. And that's the focus of my *Psychology Today* essays. I try to highlight what's hot and new in the fields of scientific research and then ponder what that means for the ways in which we interact with other animals. In our culture today, there is a lot of interest in animals and how we treat them, and indeed, my essays have gotten more than one million hits and numerous comments and personal emails from a wide-ranging audience. I've had the extreme pleasure of having contact with people of all ages from around the world. What I've found is that people are very concerned, and ask hard questions, not only about the emotional and moral lives of other animals, but also about our complicated, challenging, frustrating, and paradoxical relationships with them.

In addition, one thing that always catches my attention is how nonhuman animals are portrayed in the popular media, especially when pictures of other animals are used to make points about human behavior. I'm often frustrated because animals are rarely presented in ways that reflect what we know about them and their capacities. The media often unthinkingly repeat outdated and incorrect stereotypes, and I hope my essays, and this book, are a corrective to that. We must come to understand and appreciate animals for who they are, not for who we want them to be.

One wonderful aspect of writing these essays is the back-and-forth exchanges I've been able to have with readers, which includes scientist colleagues and even other *Psychology Today* experts. These exchanges alone have made writing these essays worthwhile. As you might expect, they range all over the place, but almost invariably, I find that people feel strongly, whether in agreement or disagreement. Most people care deeply about other animals, and nearly everyone recognizes the importance of discussing how humans should care for and treat other animals. Some readers offer stories of their own, while others present additional or sometimes conflicting scientific data. In all these ways, my ongoing dialogue with readers drives home the point that our relationships with other animals and with nature are deeply complex and tell us a lot about who we are as human beings. As such, I've included a few essays that highlight some notable exchanges I've had. I always respect my colleagues' points of view. We don't always agree, but that's not what's important. What is important is that we talk with, and not at, one another, and so come to a greater understanding of the other animals with whom we share our one and only planet.

Overall, I look at these essays as updated editions of some of my previous books, especially *The Emotional Lives of Animals, Animals Matter, Wild Justice: The Moral Lives of Animals*, and *The Animal Manifesto: Six Reasons for Expanding Our Compassion Footprint*. It was difficult to select which essays to reprint, but I tried to choose a representative sampling from the wide array of topics that I typically write about. Many present up-to-the-minute research and scientific theories about animal minds and emotions, while others are more practical and address what each of us can do to improve the lives of other animals — and by doing so, improve our own. There are some fascinating "surprises," such as what we are learning about the cognitive and emotional lives of bees and other invertebrates, and from time to time I get an email from a reader saying, "Oh, I didn't know that." What's nice is that the essays are jargon-free and written to be read by a wide audience, so this collection offers the latest and greatest about the fascinating lives of other animals between two covers. On occasion, essays focus on a specific event or news story, but these highlight ongoing issues or topics that remain relevant today, and will probably remain so into the future.

I organized the essays by theme, rather than chronologically, and each part opens with a brief introduction that frames the topic. These part themes, though, could have been arranged in a number of different ways, for many of the topics overlap, and most issues have multiple aspects to consider. Indeed, many of the essays themselves are related and interconnected, and they can be read in any order, so feel free to jump around. When I post a new essay on *Psychology Today*, I frequently cross-reference previously written essays, in addition to external sources. When cross-referenced essays appear in this book, I've included a page cross-reference in the text. For other essays and sources that don't appear in this book, see the Endnotes for complete website and publication information, and see the Bibliography for book citations. I always maintain the highest standards with respect to "the science," and I try to source every significant claim, study, and news story I mention in my essays.

All the essays that appear here have been revised to some degree. Sometimes this involved simply cleaning up the blog post format for book publication. However, some essays have had more substantial revisions: to avoid repetition, to refocus certain discussions so they read well in a new context, to combine similar topics, and to update information that was not available when they were originally written. Some of the updates clearly show that we are continuing to learn more and more about the fascinating lives of other animals. Steady progress is being made to protect animals and their homes from our destructive ways. This is particularly true for the burgeoning compassionate conservation movement, which is a focus of part 10, and for global efforts to "rewild nature" and "rewild our hearts," which is the focus of part 11. People around the world are working on behalf of many different and diverse animal species, and in my essays I try to highlight just how much we can do to make the lives of all animals, including humans, much better than they currently are. I hope these essays inspire all of us to do all we can to foster local and global compassion and peaceful coexistence. It is not that difficult to do so. We simply need to change our mindless ways of interacting with other animals and with one another to reflect how much we really care about our collective well-being.

I also hope you'll share with others the dire situation in which many different species find themselves and how we must change our ways to make this a more peaceful, safe, compassionate, and empathic place for all animals, human and nonhuman alike. We live in a wounded world that needs deep healing. It's a magnificent place that's filled with awesome animals and awe-inspiring webs of nature that are increasingly fragile and disappearing at unprecedented rates. Most of all, caring about other animals does not mean caring less about humans. Indeed, as I write throughout, compassion begets compassion and readily crosses species lines. We don't have to worry about running out of compassion as we try to provide animals with what they need to live in peace and safety.

You'll also discover that I'm a card-carrying optimist, even though some of the problems with which we're faced are almost incomprehensibly large and daunting. The easiest but wrong route to take would be to run away and pretend all is just fine. Thank goodness people recognize that the problems we face won't go away if we ignore them. Indeed, they'll only get worse. As I travel all over the world, I meet countless people who are trying as hard as they can to make the world a better place, and they give me the hope and the energy I need to keep my dreams alive. Thanks to them and thanks to you for caring and sharing your passions.

It's a wonderful time to be studying other animals, and I hope you share my enthusiasm for who these individuals are — for how bright, emotional, stunning, and charismatic they are — and for trying to provide them what they want and need from us. Online, I end many essays with the invitation "stay tuned for more on the fascinating lives of animals." I'm confident that, no matter how many years I continue writing for *Psychology Today*, this invitation will never get old. We're just on the tip of the iceberg regarding our knowledge of the amazing animals with whom we share Earth. We cannot continue to ignore "Mother Nature," and we do so at our own peril. Please read on.

A special note of thanks is in order. For years I've worked with the fine people at New World Library, especially my editor, Jason Gardner, and also with an outstanding copyeditor, Jeff Campbell. I thank them both for their unrelenting support and going beyond the call of duty in fine-tuning my prose. I also thank Lybi Ma, my editor at *Psychology Today*, for her support of my wide-ranging essays.

PART I

ANIMALS AND US

Reflections on
Our Challenging, Frustrating,
Confusing, and Deep
Interrelationships
with Other Animals

FROM TIME TO TIME, people ask me and the editors at *Psychology Today* why I write for them. I was astounded when these queries first came in, but I came to realize that it's often not clear how the lives and emotions of animals relate to human psychology. In fact, our interactions with animals tell us a good deal about how we perceive ourselves, we who are also animals. Our interactions with animals run deep, and in very direct and pragmatic ways, these interactions affect both ourselves and the animals involved. Simply put, when we harm other animals, we hurt ourselves, and when we protect and nurture other animals, we heal ourselves. Whether we deny or recognize animal emotions and intelligence, this has real-world consequences for everyone. This is why I prefer using the word "interrelationships" rather than "relationships," and why I prefer phrases like "other animals" and "nonhuman animals" rather than "animals," as if humans were somehow separate from or not animals. In these ways I try to emphasize that all animal species share a continuum of being, which includes the way we feel and what we think.

So, in part 1, I've gathered a potpourri of essays that center on our interrelationships with nonhuman animals. I hope these help explain why I feel the human-animal connection is so important and vital for human life and psychology. These essays present some broad, general topics that show up in more specific ways in a range of later essays. I include two essays about kids and animals because they are the future ambassadors for our planet, and we need to teach them well. I also write about the ways in which we say good-bye to our companion animals, a difficult and heart-wrenching topic that I revisit in part 5.

What in the World Do My Essays Have to Do with Psychology?

EVERY NOW AND AGAIN I receive personal emails about my essays asking what if anything my day's subject has to do with human psychology. A few people have not so politely asked me to stop writing because they see no relevance whatsoever to their interests. Presumably, these people must assume all *Psychology Today* readers agree with their views. However, other people write and thank me for making them think more about who other animals are and, consequently, who we are. Yet even positive comments often include the same question — "What in the world do my essays have to do with psychology?"

To me, it's crystal clear that knowing about the incredible lives of nonhuman animals, their emotions and behavior, has everything to do with many aspects of human psychology. One only has to look, for example, at the online comments to my *Psychology Today* essays. These show clearly how our interactions with other animals reflect and affect human attitudes, beliefs, and desires. Essays that sparked a wealth of revealing comments include "Rampant Wolf Killing Makes Some People Happy" (posted November 1, 2011), "Is Eating Dogs Different from Eating Cows and Pigs?" (page 262), "Going 'Cold Tofu' to End Factory Farming" (page 252), and "Tilly's Willy: In the Name of Science?" (page 225), to name a few.

The more we know about how other animals are sentient beings who experience unbounded joy and deep pain and suffering, and even extreme psychological disorders like PTSD, the more it raises human moral and ethical questions. We should really care about what happens to nonhuman animals, but often we don't, or we don't care enough to change our actions. What is the appropriate response when we learn that over 99 percent of animals used in scientific research are not protected by the Federal Animal Welfare Act, or that billions of sentient animals are mercilessly slaughtered for unneeded meals, or that animals are often still terribly abused in the name of entertainment? Urban animals are mercilessly killed when we freely move into their homes and living rooms. To me, recognizing how our intrusions into the lives of animals has made life very tough on them should foster efforts at coexistence. I have a friend, a red fox, who regularly comes by to say hello to me each morning (see photo below). He hangs out near my office and offers deep inspiration. He is just one of the many fascinating animals with whom I share my home.

What we know, think, feel, and believe about animals forms part of our human psychology. Research clearly shows that our attitudes about and relationships with other animals affect us, for good and ill. Consider, for example, the excellent research of my colleague Hal Herzog, who has written the book *Some We Love, Some We Hate, Some We Eat* and also writes for *Psychology Today* online (www.psychologytoday.com/blog /animals-and-us). He's part of the growing field of conservation psychology (http://conservationpsychology.org), which is defined as "the scientific study of the reciprocal relationships between humans and the rest of nature, with a particular focus on how to encourage conservation of the

natural world." Of course, animals are a major component of the natural world. A summary of research in this field can be found in Susan Clayton and Gene Myers's outstanding book *Conservation Psychology: Understanding and Promoting Human Care for Nature*. Changing our attitudes and beliefs about other animals really is a social movement, and that by definition involves human society and psychology. (For more on this, see books by Nick Cooney and Thomas Ryan in the Bibliography, page 357.)

While my *Psychology Today* blog is a constant meditation on why all animals matter, here are three primary reasons why learning about the nature and importance of the human-animal bond is so important to us.

- Gaining knowledge about our interrelationships with animals is incredibly important for learning not only about who they are as individuals but also for learning about who we are as big-brained, big-footed, overproducing, overconsuming, and invasive mammals. I don't mean this description in a pejorative way. That's really who we are as a species. And as our population soars we will interact with other animals even more, even if we don't want to or realize it's happening.
- Whether or not we realize it, and our behavior all too often indicates we don't, animals are a vital part of our daily lives. We are constantly factoring them into decisions about how we choose to live in the world. People all over the world are showing increasing interest in learning how to coexist with other animals — when taking them into our homes as companions, when living in close proximity to them, and when considering how to conserve what little of the precious natural world remains. Recognizing how the well-being of all beings is closely tied together will make it easier for us to choose to coexist. It's a win-win situation. All animals will benefit as we human animals learn more about the common bonds we depend on.
- When we realize how influential and deeply meaningful our close and reciprocal connections with other animals are, and when we accept other animals for who they are — as sentient, intelligent, emotional, and moral beings — we will feel compelled to treat them better. We will offer other animals more compassion and empathy in the numerous venues in which we interact (as food and clothing and in research, education, and entertainment). Mounting evidence shows that we (and they) are basically good and well-meaning individuals, and we must harness these positive traits to develop compassionate regulations and laws. These not only affect their well-being but ours. These practical aspects

associated with learning more about the nature and strength of human-animal bonds are to some the most urgent reason for developing human-animal study programs.   ·

We simply can't go on intruding into the lives of other animals as if they don't matter. We lose when they lose. For all practical purposes, we can do just about anything we want to other animals. They're merely property in the eyes of the law and enjoy little to no legal standing, which varies from one situation to another. *This, in and of itself, tells us lots about human psychology.*

[ORIGINALLY POSTED ON NOVEMBER 11, 2011]

Animals in Our Brain:
Mickey Mouse, Teddy Bears, and "Cuteness"

THERE'S NEVER A SHORTAGE of new studies about nonhuman animals and human-animal interactions. A 2011 study is well worth noting as it bears on a number of very interesting issues concerning how we perceive other animals. The study shows that a specific part of the human brain is hardwired to detect animals, regardless of whether they're cute, ugly, or dangerous, and this reminded me of two older studies that examine "cuteness" itself and the physical features we associate with it.

An article about the 2011 California Institute of Technology and UCLA study said researchers found that "a specific part of your brain...is hardwired to rapidly detect creatures of the nonhuman kind." Most interestingly, "neurons throughout the amygdala — a center in the brain known for processing emotional reactions — respond *preferentially* to images of animals." That is, given a choice of stimuli, we respond first to animals.

There are two other notable aspects of this research: (1) the response of cells in the amygdala is independent of the emotional content of the pictures — we respond first to all animals, whether they are cute, ugly, or dangerous. And (2) only cells in the right amygdala were responsive to seeing animals, which is called hemispheric asymmetry. According to the article, "This striking hemispheric asymmetry helps strengthen previous findings supporting the idea that, early on in vertebrate evolution, the right hemisphere became specialized in dealing with unexpected and biologically relevant stimuli, or with changes in the environment." One researcher said, "In terms of brain evolution, the amygdala is a very old structure, and throughout our biological history, animals — which could represent either predators or prey — were a highly relevant class of stimuli."

This study about how we're hardwired to respond to animals made me think of earlier researchers who found that seeing emotional qualities in certain physical features is also hardwired. Renowned and eclectic scientist Stephen Jay Gould wrote a fascinating essay called "Mickey Mouse Meets

Konrad Lorenz" in which he looked at why we find certain animals cute. In this paper Gould followed up on Nobel Laureate Lorenz's research showing that "humans feel affection for animals with juvenile features: large eyes, bulging craniums, retreating chins. Small-eyed, long-snouted animals do not elicit the same response."

As an example, Gould traced the evolution of Mickey Mouse: "As Mickey became increasingly well behaved over the years, his appearance became more youthful. Measurements of three stages in his development revealed a larger relative head size, larger eyes, and an enlarged cranium — all traits of juvenility." Researchers Robert Hinde and L. A. Barden likewise discovered that during the twentieth century teddy bears went from having long legs and a stubby nose to having stubbier noses and higher foreheads, juvenile traits that Lorenz discovered were called "cute." According to merchants Hinde and Barden spoke with, people increasingly preferred "cute" bears, so teddy bears evolved because of consumer pressure.

This research on how animals are perceived seems directly related to how human babies are perceived. Lorenz called the attractive "cuteness" qualities the "baby schema" (*kindchenschema*), which includes "a set of infantile physical features, such as round face and big eyes, that is perceived as cute and motivates caretaking behavior in the human, with the evolutionary function of enhancing offspring survival." We clearly respond to animals in all sorts of ways. These studies open the door for more fascinating studies into where and how we process animals in our big brains and where the neuroanatomical basis for "cuteness" and other traits lie. This is important because how we treat other animals is related to how we perceive and label them. Perhaps down the road we'll discover differences in how brains process animals when comparing humans who are more or less concerned with the well-being of nonhuman beings. Perhaps there are differences among people who choose to "rewild their heart" and those who don't.

We really have so much still to learn about the nature of human-animal interactions, and that's why this is such an exciting interdisciplinary field of study. Researchers in radically different areas need to talk with one another and share their fascinating findings.

[ORIGINALLY POSTED ON DECEMBER 22, 2011]

Conservation Psychology and Animal and Human Well-Being: Scientists Must Pay Attention to the Social Sciences

OUR RELATIONSHIPS WITH ANIMALS are frustrating, challenging, and paradoxical. They range all over the place. We love animals and harm them in a myriad of ways, and many people wonder not only why we continue to do this but what we can do to treat animals better.

It's rarely a lack of knowledge and concrete data that result in animal abuse and in the unprecedented losses of biodiversity in what is called the "anthropocene," a latter part of the "sixth extinction" — to which we are the major contributors. Massive losses of biodiversity are a form of animal abuse, but few people cash it out this way. Animal abuse and losses in biodiversity are bad for the animals and bad for us.

We know that animals have rich and deep emotional lives and some may be moral beings (see "Wild Justice and Moral Intelligence in Animals," page 195). Abuse is typically due to the inadequate protection of animals as well as to social and cultural factors. Therefore, we must address the important psychological and social/cultural issues that support our poor stewardship of animals (and their habitats). We must learn about the psychological barriers that prevent people from facing and addressing the complex, frustrating, and urgent issues that allow animal abuse to continue in laboratories, classrooms, various forms of entertainment, and in slaughterhouses and the clothing industry. It's here that the social sciences can help us along (the importance of the social sciences in dealing with climate change can serve as a nice model).

A relatively new and rapidly emerging field called conservation psychology (http://conservationpsychology.org) can help us improve our relationships with other animals. Conservation psychology is defined as "the scientific study of the reciprocal relationships between humans and the rest of nature, with a particular focus on how to encourage conservation of the natural world. . . . This applied field uses psychological principles, theories, or methods to understand and solve issues related to human aspects of conservation." A 2009 book by Susan Clayton and Gene Myers called *Conservation Psychology* provides an excellent review of the field.

Here are some important questions and areas that need to be addressed:

- Why do we ignore animal suffering and what nature is telling us?
- What allows us to override innate feelings of biophilia and our love of living systems?
- How do people think about and make personal connections to the natural environment?
- What can we do to improve the attitudes of children toward animals and conservation? It's clear we need to teach the children well.
- What is the relationship between biodiversity and human well-being?
- How can we use psychology to save biodiversity?
- How can humane education be a precursor to attitude change in conservation behavior?

Denver University's Institute for Human-Animal Connection (www .humananimalconnection.org) is a model program that can help to answer these and other questions. It's also the first program of its kind within a human services academic setting.

Part of recognizing that changing how we treat animals is part of a social movement and doesn't only depend on scientific data is to get scientists to act as concerned citizens. As an excellent opinion piece in *New Scientist* said, "We need another kind of scientist to save the world." We as citizens must also act as responsible stewards.

People who care about animals and nature do not have to be apologists for their views. They should not be considered "the radicals" or "bad guys" who are trying to impede "human progress." In fact, they could be seen as heroes who are not only fighting for animals but for humanity.

Biodiversity enables human life; it is imperative that all of humanity reconnects with what sustains the ability of our species to persist. In turn, we should hope that as a species we can act as a collective and fight for our own survival. When animals die, we die, too. Animals are needed for our own psychological well-being, and we can learn a lot from them. We are *that* connected to other beings, and that's why we seek them out when times are tough. Conservation psychology and humane education will surely help figure out the best ways to move forward and to give animals the respect, compassion, and love that they deserve.

[Originally posted on August 12, 2009]

Pets Are Good for Us:
Where Science and Common Sense Meet

PEOPLE AROUND THE WORLD often remark how being around their pets (now usually referred to as companion animals) makes them feel good. Much recent research supports this. Here are a few tidbits from a July 2010 *USA Weekend* article, "Why Pets Are Good for Us," about what we know about the positive effect that companion animals such as dogs, cats, and fish have on us. For more, Marty Becker's *The Healing Power of Pets* and Allen Schoen's *Kindred Spirits* summarize much research that has laid the groundwork for current work on the nature of the human-animal bond, and Michelle Rivera writes about animals in hospice situations and how they can ease human suffering in her recent book *On Dogs and Dying*.

To quote the *USA Weekend* article: "Watch a Lassie movie and spit into a cup. It doesn't sound like it, but this is cutting-edge research. By analyzing saliva, researcher Cheryl Krause-Parello can tell that merely watching a dog in a movie lowers people's stress. In recent years, research has demonstrated the healthful benefits of pets. Now, investigators are trying to figure out why pets are good for us. Krause-Parello, assistant professor and director of the Center for Nursing Research at Kean University in Union, NJ, learned that people feel better after watching a Lassie flick because their levels of cortisol, a hormone associated with stress, take a free fall."

The article continues, "In her book *For the Love of a Dog*, Patricia McConnell, a certified applied animal behaviorist, writes that levels of oxytocin, a mood-affecting neurotransmitter and 'feel-good' hormone in the brain, increase by merely petting a dog." Meg Daley Olmert summarizes recent research on the wide-ranging role of oxytocin in her book *Made for Each Other*.

Fish also help us along. The article says, "After bowls of goldfish were placed in nursing-facility dining rooms, most patients experienced an appetite increase and subsequent weight gain."

Current research also shows cats are very important for preventing death from heart attacks. "Results of a decade-long study suggest cats may have special health-sustaining qualities, which is probably no big surprise to Americans, who own more cats than dogs. For ten years, Adnan Qureshi, professor of neurosurgery and neurology at the University of Minnesota, followed 4,500 people and in 2008 announced his study's intriguing conclusions: Those who owned a cat were 40 percent less likely to die from heart attacks than those who had no feline in their lives. Owning a dog did not appear to convey the same protection. That statistical result is so far unexplained, Qureshi says. Other factors may contribute to the difference."

Children also benefit from the presence of companion animals. "In 2003, Barbara McClasky, a nursing professor at Pittsburg State University in Kansas, studied children seven to fourteen years old. If they lived with a pet — any pet — their self-concept and competence increased, she found."

All in all, according to Mayo Clinic oncologist Edward Creagan, "A pet is a medication without side effects that has so many benefits. . . . I can't always explain it myself, but for years now I've seen how instances of having a pet is like an effective drug. It really does help people."

The future of research in this area is wide open and shows that, when we allow animals into our lives, we, and of course they, can benefit in many different ways.

[ORIGINALLY POSTED ON JULY 23, 2010]

Children and Animals:
Teach the Children Well

CHILDREN ARE INHERENTLY and intuitively curious naturalists. They're sponges for knowledge — absorbing, retaining, and using new information at astounding rates. We all know this, but often we forget when we're helping to develop their roles as future ambassadors with other animals, nature, and ourselves. Some are also future leaders on whose spirit and goodwill many of us will depend. They will be the voices for other animals and, indeed, for the universe. So, it makes good sense to teach children well — to teach them to be role models and to infuse their education with kindness and compassion so that their decisions are founded on a deeply rooted, automatic, reflex-like caring ethic. If we don't, they, we, other animals, human communities, and environments will suffer.

I've been fortunate to teach and have mutually beneficial discussions about animals with young students all over the world. We consider such topics as animal behavior, ecology, conservation biology, and the nature of human-animal interactions. I am astounded by the level of discussion. These classes center on the guiding principles of Jane Goodall's Roots & Shoots program (http://rootsandshoots.org), whose basic tenets are that every individual is important and every individual makes a difference. The program is activity oriented and members partake in projects that have three components: care and concern for animals, human communities, and the places in which we all live together. I work closely with Roots & Shoots groups around the world.

In one recent class, all the students had actively been engaged in projects that fulfilled all three components. They had participated in, or suggested for future involvement, such activities as recycling, being responsible for companion animals, reducing driving, developing rehabilitation centers for animals, helping injured animals, getting companion animals from humane shelters, boycotting pet stores, tagging animals so people could locate lost pets, visiting senior citizen centers and homeless shelters, punishing litterbugs, and punishing people who harmed animals. We discussed how easy it is to do things that make a difference and to develop a compassionate and respectful attitude toward animals, people, and environments. One student noted that by walking the companion dog who lived with his elderly neighbor and cleaning up after the dog, he performed activities that satisfied all three components.

Some students had already developed very sophisticated attitudes about human-animal interactions. We engaged in a classic thought experiment I like to use called "the dog in the lifeboat." I asked the group to solve the following dilemma: There are three humans and one dog in a lifeboat. One of the four has to be thrown overboard because the boat can't hold all of them. Who must go? Generally, when this situation is discussed, most people agree that, all other things being equal, reluctantly, the dog has to go, and these students reached the same conclusion. However, the dilemma's real point is to facilitate a discussion of values. To highlight this, I usually introduce variations. For example, what if the dog is a healthy puppy, two of the humans are healthy youngsters, and one human is an elderly person who is blind, deaf, and paralyzed, without any family or friends, and is likely to die within a week? When tackling this admittedly very difficult situation, the students exhibited some very sophisticated thinking, proposing that perhaps the elderly person had less to lose (having led a full life that was now almost over) and so should be sacrificed. As I stressed with the students, the purpose isn't to devalue any person's or animal's life, but to examine our often-unspoken values.

The level of discussion overwhelmed me. Students raised considerations of quality of life, longevity, value of life, and losses to surviving family and friends. But what really amazed and pleased me was that before we ever got to discuss alternatives, all students wanted to work it out so that no one had to be thrown overboard. Why did any individual have to be thrown over? they asked. Let's not do it. When I said that the thought experiment required that at least one individual had to be tossed, they said this wasn't acceptable! I sat there smiling and thinking: now these are the kinds of people in whom I'd feel comfortable placing my future. Some ideas about how all individuals could be saved included having the dog swim along the side of the boat and feeding her, having them all take turns swimming, taking off shoes and throwing overboard all things that weren't needed to reduce weight and bulk, and cutting the boat in two and making two rafts. All students thought that even if the dog had to leave the boat, she would have a better chance of surviving because more could be done by the humans to save the dog than vice versa. Very sophisticated reasoning, indeed. I've discussed this example many times and never before has a group unanimously decided that everyone must be saved.

I also was thrilled by the commitment of the teachers I met. They were very dedicated, and we should all be grateful that such precious and priceless beings are responsible for educating future adults on whom we will all depend.

The bottom line is pretty simple: teach the children well, treat the teachers well, and treasure all. Nurture and provide the seeds of compassion, empathy, and love with all the nutrients they need to develop deep respect for, and kinship with, the universe. All people, other animals, human communities, and environments — now and in the future — will benefit greatly by developing and maintaining heartfelt compassion that is as reflexive as breathing. Compassion begets compassion — there's no doubt about it.

[ORIGINALLY POSTED ON JULY 1, 2009]

Nature-Deficit Disorder Redux:
Kids Need to Get Off Their Butts

A 2012 SURVEY OF CHILDREN'S BOOKS shows a large decline in the presence of natural environments and animals. Combined with the absence of "wild" play by youngsters, there are serious concerns about the lack of connection of youngsters with nature and increases in nature-deficit disorder. It's pretty simple: kids need to get off their butts and enjoy our magnificent world.

In the survey, researchers looked at 8,100 images in 296 award-winning children's books published between 1938 and 2008. According to a *USA Today* article on the study:

- "Early in the study period, built environments were the primary environments in about 35 percent of images. By the end of the study, they were primary environments about 55 percent of the time.
- "Early in the study, natural environments were the primary environments about 40 percent of the time; by the end, the figure was roughly 25 percent."

The article went on to say, "Images of wild animals and domestic animals declined dramatically over time, says lead author Al Williams of the University of Nebraska–Lincoln: 'The natural environment and wild animals have all but disappeared in these books.'"

The results of this study are bad news in many ways. They can translate into less concern about the environment and also a lack of connection with nature. The article quotes Richard Louv, author of the seminal book *Last Child in the Woods*, who says, "Nature experience isn't a panacea, but it does help children and the rest of us on many levels of health and cognition. I believe that as parents learn more about the disconnect, they'll want to seek more of that experience for their children, including the joy and wonder that nature has traditionally contributed to children's literature."

The article also quotes psychologist Susan Linn, who notes, "Time in green space is essential to children's mental and physical health.... And the health of the planet depends on a generation of children who love and respect the natural world enough to protect it from abuse and degradation."

I was really troubled when I read about this study, and I couldn't agree more about the need to teach children to be environmentally conscious leaders (see "Children and Animals: Teach the Children Well," page 14).

And yet, being the optimist I am, I still feel there's hope. A free online book I published last year called *Kids & Animals*, based on my work with Jane Goodall's Roots & Shoots program, shows that there still are many youngsters around the world who do indeed care about nature and other animals. In 2008, I also wrote another children's book, *Animals at Play*.

It is our goal that *Kids & Animals* will inspire other young people to draw and write about their feelings for animals and to put their own ideas into action to care for animals, protect their habitats, and promote compassion, empathy, coexistence, and peace. It is perfect for classes, discussions, and activities focusing on humane and conservation education. This helps us all expand our compassion footprint.

While it can be an uphill battle, we need to get kids out into nature and away from their desks, couches, computers, and other electronic devices. We need them to have direct experiences with the magnificence of nature, including other animals. The best, and most likely the only, way to do it is to encourage them, or if need be to require them, to get off their butts, as well as to incorporate "nature time" into the curriculum of all schools, not as an after-school option but as part of the main school day. The future of the planet depends on our doing this right now. We should use the results of this study of children's books as an indication of just how important and irreplaceable these direct experiences truly are. We need to rewild our children before it's too late.

[ORIGINALLY POSTED ON FEBRUARY 28, 2012]

Animals and Inmates:
Science Behind Bars

FOR TEN YEARS I've been teaching animal behavior and conservation biology at the Boulder County Jail (in Colorado) as part of Jane Goodall's Roots & Shoots program. The course is one of the most popular in the jail. Students have to earn the right to enroll, and they work hard to get in it.

While there's student turnover, we're all pleasantly surprised at how science connects the inmates to various aspects of nature. Many inmates find it easier to connect with animals than with people. Animals don't judge them, and before being incarcerated, many of the inmates had lived with dogs, cats, and other companions who were their best friends. They trust and empathize with animals in ways they don't with humans.

Nonetheless, there remains a distorted view of how animals treat one another. At one of the first meetings, someone was talking out of turn as I was setting up the curriculum. One of the guys yelled, "Hey, shut up, you're acting like an ass. This guy's here to help us." I responded, "You've just paid him a compliment." I explained that animals could be kind and empathic. While there's competition and aggression, there's also a lot of cooperation, empathy, and reciprocity. I explained that these behaviors are examples of "wild justice," and this idea made them rethink what it means to be an animal. They've had enough of nature red in tooth and claw, and many lament, "Look where that 'I'm behaving like an animal' excuse got me."

Topics we actively discuss include general aspects of animal behavior, the evolution of social behavior, evolution and creationism, biology and religion, sustainability, extinction, animal protection and environmental ethics, eugenics, environmental enrichment, balance in nature, complex webs of nature, cultural views of animals, and who we are in the grand scheme of things — anthropocentric influences on animals and the environment. Our exchanges rival those that I've had at university classes.

Many of the students see the class as building community with animals and people. They yearn to build healthy relationships. I use examples of the social behavior of group-living animals such as wolves as a model for developing and maintaining long-term friendships among individuals who must work together not only for their own good but also for the good of the group.

From time to time I ask the inmates what they get out of the class. Here are some responses:

- The course is healing.
- I've learned a lot about understanding and appreciating animals as individuals.
- The class balances scientific rigor with social consciousness.
- The class gives us a sense of connection to webs of life.
- What I do counts. I now have a vision for the future.
- The class models healthy prosocial ways of living and working in the world.
- The class makes me feel better about myself.

It's clear that science inspires the students and gives them hope. I've been told that because of the class some of their kids are more likely to go into science. I know some students have gone back to school, while others have made contributions in time and money to conservation organizations. Some have gone to work for humane societies. One student went on to receive a master's degree in nature writing.

Science and humane education have helped the inmates connect with values that they otherwise wouldn't have. Science opens the door to understanding, trust, cooperation, community, and hope. There's a large untapped population of individuals to whom science means a lot, but they haven't had the exposure needed to further their education. By the way, I continue to get as much out of the class as the students, and it's made me a better teacher on the outside.

[ORIGINALLY POSTED ON SEPTEMBER 23, 2009]

Animal Cruelty and Antisocial Behavior:
A Very Strong Link

ELEONORA GULLONE'S 2012 BOOK entitled *Animal Cruelty, Antisocial Behaviour, and Aggression: More than a Link*, published as part of the Palgrave Macmillan Animal Ethics Series (www.palgrave.com), shows that there is strong empirical evidence linking different types of abuse. For readers of *Psychology Today* who want to learn more about possible links between how nonhuman animals are treated and how this relates to cruelty to humans, this is an excellent book with which to begin.

Eleonora Gullone is associate professor in the Psychology Department at Monash University in Melbourne, Australia. She brings a strong research background to the topic of her book, and this is highly valuable because it allows her to analyze what we know and don't know about the relationship between animal cruelty and antisocial behavior in general. She notes that what is generally called "the Link" refers to the idea that "acts of interpersonal violence are frequently preceded by, or co-occur with, acts of cruelty to animals, 'red flag' markers that previously were ignored."

Gullone's book is well-organized. It looks at the history of animal cruelty and how it's been conceived, as well as at the development of antisocial behavior and the various risk factors for it. As she notes in her last chapter, one area in which much more research is needed concerns the development of animal cruelty behavior. There still is no study that has looked at its normative development. We also need more cross-cultural studies because, she says, "the conceptualization of animal cruelty as deviant...will have varying validity, depending on that culture's animal treatment standards." We also need more research on animal cruelty itself, and it is essential to remove the property status of animals in legal systems. Currently, animals are considered to be mere property, just like a couch, bicycle, or backpack.

Gullone argues that because animal cruelty is invariably and traditionally trumped by, but strongly linked to, human cruelty, we need to make animal cruelty more worthy of moral concern and a target of intervention.

This helps other animals, but it also helps us learn more about the etiology of human cruelty. Thus: "By positioning acts of animal abuse within the continuum of other antisocial behaviours, rather than as isolated incidents or acceptable childhood rites of passage, we can gain more progress not only in reducing animal abuse but also in improving human safety and lowering tolerance levels for all acts of aggression." There is some movement in this direction already. In America, forty-seven of the fifty states have laws that consider certain acts of animal cruelty to be felonies. Animal cruelty is also getting more attention in public media. The increasing attention is good because, as Gullone notes, "many crimes against humans may well have been prevented had any animal cruelty incidents that preceded them been taken seriously."

All in all, Gullone's convincing case that there are strong empirical links among different types of abuse and violence, particularly between animal and human cruelty, must be taken seriously. She concludes her book by suggesting that we put aside speciesism when it comes to violence: "laws should punish criminals according to the severity of the acts they perpetrate, without discrimination or favour based on the target species of the particular crime." If this were the law of the land, both nonhuman and human animals would greatly benefit.

As someone coming to this field with more than passing interest, I found this book really got me thinking about how, for our own sake, nonhuman animals must be granted much more legal protection and how animal cruelty needs to be taken much more seriously. Someone who abuses an animal today is much more likely to abuse a person tomorrow. Recognizing this, and intervening appropriately, is a win-win situation for all.

[ORIGINALLY POSTED ON DECEMBER 11, 2012]

Dehumanization and
Animal-Human Similarity

I WAS RECENTLY TALKING with Katherine Schrieber, a staff editor for *Psychology Today*, about the rapidly growing field of human-animal studies, and she asked if I'd heard about the research of Gordon Hodson (http://hodson.socialpsychology.org) and his colleagues at Brock University in St. Catherine's, Ontario, Canada. Since I hadn't, Katherine sent me a copy of a 2010 paper by Kimberly Costello and Professor Hodson titled "Exploring the Roots of Dehumanization: The Role of Animal–Human Similarity in Promoting Immigrant Humanization." This paper opened up a new world of ideas for studying not only human-animal relationships but human-human relationships. We still know little about the origins of dehumanization, although it's rather widespread on many fronts.

In a nutshell, Costello and Hodson were interested in what factors led to the humanization of immigrants, and they discovered that "beliefs that animals and humans are relatively similar were associated with greater immigrant humanization, which in turn predicted more favorable immigrant attitudes.... Emphasizing *animals as similar to humans* (versus humans as similar to animals, or the human-animal divide) resulted in greater immigrant humanization (even among highly prejudiced people)" [emphasis added].

A later essay published by Costello, Hodson, and their colleagues confirms this link. In the abstract of this paper, they write: "Comparing animals to humans expands moral concern and reduces speciesism; however, comparing humans to animals does not appear to produce these same effects."

In the 2010 paper, Costello and Hodson also write: "Recognizing that heightened immigrant dehumanization and prejudice follow from an exaggerated human-animal divide, it now becomes imperative to determine when and how beliefs about human superiority or animal inferiority develop. Children are socialized to endorse perceptions of human superiority over other animals through parental influence, religious teachings, cultural traditions, and/or experiences with industries condoning the exploitation of nonhuman animals. These socialization practices presumably lead children to endorse the cultural 'legitimacy' of dominating, victimizing, or ignoring the plight of nonhuman animals."

The authors write about the importance of "rehumanizing" outgroups. From my perspective, other animals are often thought of as "outgroups" in the same way that immigrants are, and other animals would also benefit from being "rehumanized," or treated as equivalent beings to us. I've written about the foible of human exceptionalism elsewhere (see "Animal Minds and the Foible of Human Exceptionalism," page 42), and their insights are very helpful to me as I ponder how we can and must rewild our hearts and reconnect with other animals and nature as a whole.

I look forward to much more research in this challenging area.

[ORIGINALLY POSTED ON JUNE 17, 2012.]

Animals Can Be Ambassadors for Forgiveness, Generosity, Peace, Trust, and Hope

JASPER IS A MOON BEAR. I try to practice what he teaches and incorporate his lessons about compassion and love into my life. Jasper, Jethro, and many other amazing animal beings teach us numerous lessons about forgiveness, generosity, dignity, peace, trust, and love. We must listen to these lessons carefully and incorporate them into our lives.

Jasper arrived at the Moon Bear Rescue Centre outside of Chengdu, China, in 2000, where he was given the name he proudly carries. Jill Robinson (founder of Animals Asia, www.animalsasia.org) and the wonderful humans who work with her receive bears from bear farms after the bears are no longer useful to the farmers, who extract bile from the bears to treat various ailments in the name of traditional Chinese medicine. Bears usually arrive in horrible condition, suffering from serious physical and psychological trauma. Each bear is given a complete physical and a psychological evaluation. Many need surgery because of their physical condition (such as missing paws, worn-down teeth, or liver cancer). After they've acclimated to the center, some bears have to be kept alone, whereas others can be introduced to other bears (for details about bear farming and bear rescue, see the Endnotes).

Here's why Jasper is such an inspiring bear being. He's a true survivor. I'm sure he and his friends remind of us the dogs, cats, and other animals to whom we give care. For fifteen years Jasper's home was a tiny, filthy "crush cage" in which he couldn't move on a bear farm in China. Jasper was continually squashed to the bottom of his filthy cage to squeeze out his bile. Imagine being pinned in a phone booth for even fifteen minutes and all you could do was turn your head to drink water and eat. As if this wasn't enough, Jasper also had a rusty metal catheter inserted into his gall bladder so that his bile could be collected. Despite it all, Jasper survived and his story must be told and shared widely.

When I first met Jasper he immediately reminded me of my longtime companion dog Jethro — kind and gentle with big brown eyes that stared right into my heart. Each had a tan stripe across his chest; for Jasper the tan crescent is the reason he's called a moon bear. I'm sure it was Jasper's optimistic spirit and trust that's allowed him to thrive. Today, Jasper's spiritual path is as an inspirational lesson for how we can all be healthy, alive, and connected, and recover from untold and unimaginable trauma. He displays unbounded empathy for others.

Jasper's gentle, omniscient eyes say, "All's well, the past is past. Let go and move on." When I met him, Jasper's gait was slow and smooth as he approached me; I fed him peaches out of a bucket. I then gave Jasper peanut butter, and his long and wiry tongue glided out of his mouth and he gently lapped the tasty treat from my fingers. Jill Robinson best describes Jasper's softness, his kind disposition: "Touching the back of his paw one day I saw his head turn toward me, soft brown eyes blinking with trust, and I knew that Jasper was going to be a special friend."

Jasper knew that things were going to get better and that he would recover. Jasper tells people and other bears, "All will be okay, trust me." When Jasper was finally released from his recovery cage at the rescue center, he was delighted to be free. Jill watched him approach a bear on the other side of the bars separating them and reach out as if to shake paws with the stranger, who would become his best friend. The other bear, Delaney, a.k.a. Aussie, sniffed Jasper's paw, and then he put his paws through the bars so that Jasper could return the favor. Jasper and Aussie remain close friends, and I've had the pleasure — I might say a delightful treat and honor — of watching them play, rest together, and perhaps share stories of their horrible pasts and the wonderful humans with whom they're lucky to live with now.

Many of the bears love to play, and this is an indication that they've substantially recovered from their trauma. When I visited the Moon Bear Rescue Centre in October 2008, I saw Aussie and Frank frolicking on a hammock. They were having a great time, and it was incredibly inspiring to see these bears enjoying life. Jill and I shared their joy as we laughed at their silly antics. When Aussie saw Jasper ambling over, he jumped off the hammock, approached Jasper, and they began roughhousing — caressing one another, biting one another's scruff and ears, and falling to the ground embracing and rolling around. After a while Jasper went over to a water hole and invited Aussie in, but Aussie decided to stay on the shore and watch Jasper play in the water. Tears came to my eyes. Not only were these bears telling one another that the day was going just fine but they were also telling Jill and me that all was okay. Much of the deep trauma that they'd experienced was in the past and whatever lingered wasn't stopping them from enjoying themselves and spreading joy to other bears. Traumatized animals don't play and surely aren't as outgoing as these awesome bears.

Jasper remains the peacemaker. He makes other bears feel at ease. Perhaps Jasper knows what the other bears have experienced and wants to reassure them that everything will be okay now that they've been rescued. Jasper truly opens up his heart to everyone he meets. And, I think Jasper knows the effect he has on others. Jill told me that at a social function to celebrate their 2008 book *Freedom Moon*, Jasper stole the show. He always does — and he knows it. But there's no arrogance at all — just trust and confidence that all is well and will continue to be so.

If one didn't know what Jasper had experienced, they'd never guess. Are Jasper and a few others special, and if so, why? Why did they recover and others didn't? Bears, like dogs and other animals, display different personalities. Big Aussie still runs back into his den when he hears a strange noise or even when he sees a caterpillar in the grass. As an ethologist, I always want to learn more about each being as an individual, what they feel, how they travel through life, and how they keep their dreams alive.

I wonder what Jasper, Aussie, and other moon bears carry in their head — what remnants of unspeakable abuse and trauma remain. Perhaps they also talk about how lucky they are to have been rescued and that not all humans are bad, that they can trust some of us. Many of the bears have been able to get over a lot of what they experienced, at least overtly, and depend on the trust, loyalty, and love that they've developed over time with the same mammalian species — human beings — who couldn't care less about their well-being.

Jasper is the spokes-bear for forgiveness, peace, trust, and hope. I can't thank Jasper enough for sharing his journey and his dreams. Jasper, like the dogs, cats, and many other animals who also need us, makes us more humane and thus more human. The true spirit of humans, our inborn nature, is to help rather than to harm.

How Jasper and other moon bears recover from their unspeakable trauma is a lesson to us all for expanding our compassion footprint and for spreading compassion throughout the world. It behooves us to be mindful and to listen to their tales very carefully, for we will learn a lot about them and also a lot about ourselves. The gifts that Jasper and many other animals have shared with me are priceless. I can't put in words how indebted I am. I like to think I'm a better human being for gaining their generosity and trust. I also thank Jill Robinson and all the fine people at Animals Asia for their tireless commitment to rescue and rehabilitate abused moon bears and occasional dogs and cats. Thousands of bears still await rescue.

Another aspect of my last trip to China is worth sharing. I accompanied the moon bear team to the Qiming Animal Rescue Centre outside of Chengdu, China, where I met dogs and cats who were rescued after the terrible earthquake that devastated large parts of the Sichuan Province in May 2008. I had already met two awesome dogs aptly named Richter and Tremor (a.k.a. Rambo, because as a small dog Tremor carried himself with the confidence of Sylvester Stallone) who had somehow survived the earthquake and were living at the rescue center. At Qiming there were many dogs who needed care, and Heather Bacon, the chief veterinarian at the moon bear center, performed some minor surgeries and gave shots and medications when needed.

We brought five dogs back to the bear center for further care, as if the fine people working with the bears needed more work. I was asked to name the dogs, so I did: Henry, Stevie, Lobster, Matilde, and Butch. I was especially attracted to Henry because he reminded me of Jethro, minus about seventy pounds. Henry had been caught stealing meat from a butcher, who had lopped off most of Henry's right front leg. Somehow Henry survived and wound up at Qiming. Stevie was blind and had to have his eyes removed because they were terribly infected. Lobster also had a broken leg that healed and looked like a lobster claw, and Matilde weighed in at about ten pounds and should have weighed around forty. Butch had lost an eye in a fight with another dog and needed to have it removed. When I last inquired, all were doing well, and I was told that Matilde now weighs about forty pounds and that Henry was jumping around like a kangaroo on his remaining legs.

There is no doubt that these dogs and the moon bears are incredibly lucky for having the attention of all the fine people at the rescue center. The animals who I met and the people who help them selflessly are amazing beings. We can all be inspired by them and know that we must always keep our hopes and dreams alive. The good, the bad, the ugly, and our commitment to help those in need make us better humans. Compassion begets compassion. Through pain comes hope.

[Originally posted on July 8, 2009]

Letting a Friend Go:
We Usually Know When It's Time
to Say Good-bye

"COME ON, MARC, it's time for a hike, or dinner, or a belly rub." I was constantly on call for Jethro, my companion dog and my very best friend. Jethro was a large German shepherd/Rottweiler mix with whom I shared my home for twelve years. I rescued Jethro from the Humane Society in Boulder, but in many ways he rescued me. As he got older, it became clear that our lives together soon would be over. The uninhibited and exuberant wagging of his whip-like tail — which fanned me in the summer, occasionally knocked glasses off the table, and told me how happy he was — would soon stop.

What should I do? Let him live in misery or help him die peacefully, with dignity? It was my call and a hard one at that. But just as I was there for him in life, I needed to be there for him as he approached death, to put his interests before mine, to help end his suffering, to help him cross into his mysterious future with grace, dignity, and love. For sure, easier said than done.

Dogs trust us almost unconditionally. It's great to be trusted and loved, and no one does it better than dogs. Jethro was no exception. But along with trust and love come many serious responsibilities and difficult moral choices. I find it easiest to think about dog trust in terms of what they expect from us. They have great faith in us; they expect we'll always have their best interests in mind, that we'll care for them and make them as happy as we can. Indeed, we welcome them into our homes as family members who bring us much joy and deep friendship. Because they're so dependent on us, we're also responsible for making difficult decisions about when to end their lives, to "put them to sleep." I've been faced with this situation many times and have anguished trying to "do what's right" for my buddies. Should I let them live a bit longer, or has the time really come to say good-bye?

When Jethro got old and could hardly walk, eat, or hold his water, the time had come for me to put him out of his misery. He was dying right in front of my eyes, and in my heart, I knew it. Even when eating a bagel, he was miserable. Deciding when to end an animal's life is a real-life moral drama. There aren't any dress rehearsals, and doing it once doesn't make doing it again any easier. Jethro knew I'd do what's best for him, and I really came to feel that often he'd look at me and say, "It's okay, please take me out of my misery and lessen your burden. Let me have a dignified ending to what was a great life. Neither of us feels better letting me go on like this."

Finally, I chose to let Jethro leave Earth in peace. After countless hugs and "I love yous," I took him on his last car ride, something he loved to do, and to this day I swear that Jethro knew what was happening. He accepted his fate with valor, grace, and honor. And I feel he told me that the moral dilemma I faced was no predicament at all, that I had indeed done all I could and that his trust in me was not compromised one bit, but, perhaps, strengthened. I made the right choice, and he openly thanked me for it. And he wished me well, that I could go on with no remorse or apologies.

Let's thank our animal companions for who they are. Let's rejoice and embrace them as the amazing beings they are. If we open our hearts to them, we can learn much from their selfless lessons in compassion, humility, generosity, kindness, devotion, respect, spirituality, and love. By honoring our dogs' trust, we tap into our own spirituality, into our hearts and souls. Sometimes that means not only killing them with love, but also mercifully taking their lives when their own spirit has died and life's flame has been irreversibly extinguished. Our companions are counting on us to be for them in all situations, to let them go and not to let their lives deteriorate into base, undignified humiliation while we ponder our own needs in lieu of theirs. We are obliged to do so. We can do no less.

[ORIGINALLY POSTED ON JUNE 24, 2009]

PART 2

AGAINST SPECIESISM

Why All Individuals
Are Unique and Special

ANIMALS COME IN ALL SHAPES AND SIZES. Biologists try to organize and make sense of this variety by classifying animals as members of different phyla, classes, orders, families, genera, species, and subspecies. In this way, scientists create our "family tree," which shows how the various types of animals are related and where they diverge. Often scientists use words like "simple" and "complex," or "higher" and "lower," to characterize different species based on particular traits, such as the complexity of the nervous system or the size of the brain relative to the size of the body. Within biological classification systems, these words are useful. However, they are also often translated into qualitative judgments: "higher" becomes "better" or "more valuable"; "lower" becomes "lesser" or "easily discarded." In the essays in this part, I argue that this usage is misleading, incorrect, and inappropriate. It is "speciesism," which serves little purpose except to justify the killing or bad treatment of certain classes of animals that humans find either useful or inconvenient. We should not use species membership to make decisions about how an animal can be treated, or more pointedly, what level of mistreatment is permissible. Rather, we should approach each animal as an individual with unique characteristics and an inherent value equal to all other beings. Individual animals do what they need to do to be card-carrying members of their respective species. Within their species, this has the most value, and no individual is "better" or "more valuable" than the rest. Just as all species count, all individuals count, and all beings are unique and special in their own ways.

Individual Animals Count:
Speciesism Doesn't Work

SPARE THE CHIMPS, *boil the shrimps, shock the mice, kill the lice, eat the hogs, pith the frogs, blind the rabbits — what drives these habits?*

One hundred and fifty years ago Charles Darwin published his classic book *On the Origin of Species*. This book is considered by many to be one of the most influential works ever published. There and elsewhere Darwin emphasized that differences among species are differences in *degree* rather than *kind*, and his ideas about evolutionary continuity revolutionized the ways in which we think about who "we humans" are versus who "they," or other animals, are.

Human animals use nonhuman animals in many ways — for food, research, education, entertainment, and testing cosmetics and other products. Animals are also routinely and wantonly killed because humans want to expand their horizons — building more shopping malls, parking lots, subdivisions, or office buildings. This is largely accepted because human benefits are said to outweigh the costs to the animals — their anxiety, pain, and death — and human interests invariably trump those of other animals.

People often use species membership to decide which animals can and cannot be used for various purposes. Using species membership for such decisions rather than an individual's unique characteristics is called "speciesism," a term coined by the psychologist Richard Ryder to indicate prejudice based on physical differences.

The Oxford English Dictionary defines speciesism as "discrimination against or exploitation of certain animal species by human beings, based on an assumption of mankind's superiority." For example, all and only humans might constitute a protected group, regardless of an individual human's unique characteristics. When animals such as great apes are protected from invasive research, this decision is speciesist because all great apes are protected regardless of an individual's unique characteristics. Speciesism results in animals being classified hierarchically as "lower" and "higher," with humans on the top rung of the ladder. This speciesist view is bad biology. Hierarchical speciesism ignores individual variations in behavior within and between species and results in endless harm.

Speciesists often use taxonomic or behavioral (cognitive and emotional) closeness to humans, similar appearance, or the possession of various cognitive capacities displayed by normal adult humans to determine those animals who are more deserving of respect or protection by humans and those who are acceptable to exploit. Cognitive abilities include the capacities for self-consciousness, to engage in purposive behavior, to communicate using a language, to make moral judgments, and to reason.

Using these criteria, many animals cannot qualify for protection. But there also are some humans — for instance, young infants and any adults whose lives are compromised physically or psychologically — who cannot qualify either. This creates a logical problem for speciesists who rely on species-typical cognitive or emotional capacities and ignore individual differences.

Because of individual differences, species-typical distinctions can be difficult to apply consistently. This doesn't stop speciesists, however, who treat "higher" and "lower" biological classifications as value judgments, with humans always at the top. As a result, based solely on species membership, any individual who is thought to be lower — not as smart, emotional, good, or valuable — can be mistreated. But such an "us" versus "them" perspective fails to consider the lives and the worlds of the animals themselves.

While there are obvious species and individual differences in behavior, in and of themselves these mean little for arguments about animal protection. Many animals experience pain, anxiety, and suffering (physically and psychologically) when they are held in captivity or subjected to extreme starvation, social isolation, physical restraint, or any other painful situation from which they cannot escape. And even if what an animal feels is not the same sort of pain, anxiety, or suffering experienced by humans, or even if it doesn't match what's experienced by other members of the same species, their feelings count. As Elizabeth Costello has said (in J. M. Coetzee, *The Lives of Animals*), "Anyone who says that life matters less to animals than it does to us has not held in his hands an animal fighting for its life. The whole of the being of the animal is thrown into that fight, without reserve."

It's *individuals* who count when we consider how we treat other animals. In his book *Created from Animals: The Moral Implications of Darwinism*, philosopher James Rachels presents the important notion of *moral individualism*. This is based on the following argument: "If A is to be treated differently from B, the justification must be in terms of A's individual characteristics and B's individual characteristics. Treating them differently cannot be justified by pointing out that one or the other is a member of some preferred group, not even the 'group' of human beings." According to this view, careful attention must be paid to individual variations in behavior within species. It is individuals who personally feel pain and suffer, not species.

Those people who choose to use animals must show more sensitivity to the animals they use. Animals aren't mere resources or property. We must respect their dignity and their lives. It's a privilege to share their worlds.

In addition, if we consider "higher" species those that are most like us, and thus most deserving of protection, we need to explore and ponder the similarities and differences among animals more closely and how we define ourselves. As philosopher Lynne Sharpe points out in her book *Creatures Like Us?*, "Those who define 'us' by our ability to introspect give a distorted view of what is important to and about human beings and ignore the fact that many creatures are like us in more significant ways in that we all share the vulnerability, the pains, the fears, and the joys that are the life of social animals."

If "them" who are used are so much like "us," much more work needs to be done to justify our choices of how to use animals for human ends. Speciesism fails to provide a strong defense.

[ORIGINALLY POSTED ON AUGUST 24, 2009]

Animal Emotions, Animal Sentience, Animal Welfare, and Animal Rights

MANY OF MY BOOKS and *Psychology Today* blogs deal with animal emotions and animal sentience. Now let's briefly consider the implications that follow from the conclusion that animals can indeed feel pain and experience deep emotions. If animals are able to suffer, then we must be careful not to cause them intentional and unnecessary pain and suffering because it is morally wrong to do so. This is the same moral standard we apply to humans. The starting point for any ethical discussion is that, unless there are compelling reasons to override this principle that are for the benefit of the individual, knowingly and deliberately causing an individual pain and suffering is wrong.

In practice, applying this standard raises numerous complex issues. Human relationships with animals and nature continually confront this ethical dilemma. For instance, should humans never keep other animals in cages, or is this acceptable if the purpose is worthy enough? Is it ever permissible to kill or eradicate animals to benefit human development or welfare? Is it okay to move animals from one habitat where individuals are thriving to another where they may die in order to strengthen the health of the animal's species overall? In the scenarios above, substitute the word "human" for "animal," and the difficulty of deciding becomes clear. Often people wonder why those who have dedicated themselves to animal protection, or those who they perceive to be concerned with the psychological and physical health of animals, can't agree on solutions to existing problems. Often, they don't. To understand why, we need to look at the differences between those who are advocates of "animal welfare" and those who argue for "animal rights."

Advocates of "animal welfare," sometimes called "welfarists," believe that it's permissible, under certain circumstances, to cause animals pain, but not unnecessary pain. They say our main concern is to ensure that, while alive, an animal's welfare or well-being, their quality of life, is acceptable. Welfarists believe that humans should not wantonly exploit or abuse animals, and that we have an obligation to ensure that animals' lives are comfortable, physically and psychologically. Animals have a right to experience life's pleasures, to be happy, and to be free from prolonged or intense pain, fear, hunger, and other unpleasant states. If individuals show normal growth and reproduction, if they are free from disease, injury, malnutrition, and other types of suffering, then they're doing well and we're fulfilling our obligations to them.

That said, welfarists also believe that it is all right to use animals to meet human ends as long as certain safeguards are used. They believe that using animals in scientific experiments and slaughtering animals for food are acceptable as long as these activities are conducted in a humane way. Many also believe keeping animals in zoos and aquariums is permissible, while using them in other forms of human entertainment are not. Thus, while welfarists are united in their desire not to cause animals unnecessary suffering, they often disagree about what this means: what uses are acceptable, what pain is "necessary," and what qualifies as humane care are topics of debate. Different welfarists draw the line, or calculate the equation, differently.

However, at root, all welfarists are utilitarians. They believe that dogs, cats, prairie dogs, or any other animals can be exploited as long as the cost to the animals in pain and suffering is less than the benefits humans receive by using the animals. Animal pain and death can be justified depending on the benefits that humans derive. In other words, the ends justify the means. If there is no way to avoid killing or causing pain to animals in order to achieve certain human gains, so be it. Those who argue for using dogs and other animals to teach medical students often employ the utilitarian argument, as do those who feel comfortable eating formerly "free-range chickens" but not chickens who've been brutally debeaked and imprisoned in inhumane battery cages.

Now what about those who advocate animal rights? Tom Regan, professor emeritus of philosophy at North Carolina State University, is often considered the originator of the modern animal rights movement. His 1983 book *The Case for Animal Rights* attracted much attention to this area.

Advocates who believe that animals have rights stress that all animals are inherently valuable in and of themselves. Some species are not more valuable just because they look or behave more like us, or easier to justify killing just because of what they can do for humans. Animals are not property or "things," but rather living organisms, subjects of a life, who are worthy of our compassion, respect, friendship, and support. Rightists expand the borders of species to whom we grant certain rights. Thus, other animals are not "lesser" or "less valuable" than humans. They are not property that may be abused or dominated at will. Any amount of animal pain and death is unnecessary and unacceptable.

Obviously rightists are also concerned with animals' quality of life. However, they make no utilitarian exceptions. They argue it's wrong to ever abuse or exploit animals or to cause animals any pain and suffering; animals shouldn't be eaten, held captive in zoos, or used in any (or most) educational or research settings. They believe the moral and legal rights of animals includes the right to life and the right not to be harmed. According to Gary Francione, a professor of law at Rutgers University, to say an animal has a "right" to have an interest protected means the animal is entitled to have that interest protected even if it would benefit us to do otherwise. Rightists believe humans have an obligation to honor that claim for animals just as they do for nonconsenting humans (like infants, children, and adults with dementia) who can't protect their own interests. So, for example, a dog who shares your home has a right to be fed, and you have an obligation to feed it, as well as an obligation not to do anything to interfere with feeding the dog. Of course, caring for and preventing harm to an animal isn't always simple. You might prevent your dog from feeding on garbage or something that might harm her, and you might have to give your dog a painful injection to cure a lung infection or to reduce the pain in an arthritic leg. However, in these situations, it's permissible to cause temporary pain if it's necessary for the long-term or overall health of the individual animal.

What about conservation biologists and environmentalists, who are also concerned with animal welfare? Typically, they're welfarists who are willing to trade off individuals' lives for the perceived good of a larger system or population, such as the wider ecosystem or the overall species. Consider the reintroduction of Canadian lynx into Colorado or wolves into Yellowstone National Park. Some conservationists and environmentalists, in contrast to rightists, argue that the death of some individuals — even the agonizingly painful starvation of lynx who are placed in a habitat where it is known that there isn't enough food — is permissible for the perceived good of the species. People who claim it's all right to kill "pests" such as brown rats and other animals because their species is numerous and in no danger of extinction are taking a utilitarian stance. People who allow captive predatory animals to kill and eat other animals (that is, prey who can't get away) to train them so they can be released into the wild also are adopting the utilitarian position.

Labeling an individual a "welfarist" or "rightist" connotes important messages about their views on animal exploitation. One must be careful how these words are tossed around. Welfarists and rightists have radically different perceptions, perspectives, and agendas, and they solve problems differently. They preach very different codes of conduct. Animal welfarism and animal rights are extremely difficult to reconcile. Indeed, many experts think it's an impossible marriage. Nonetheless, it's essential to understand their different perspectives in our efforts to protect animals who can't speak for themselves and whose voices fall on deaf ears. Humans can do anything they want to animals, so animals truly care if they're confronting a welfarist or a rightist, for their very lives are in their hands.

[ORIGINALLY POSTED ON SEPTEMBER 24, 2009]

Animal Minds and the Foible
of Human Exceptionalism

Man in his arrogance thinks himself a great work,
worthy the interposition of a deity.
More humble and, I believe, true to consider him created from animals.

— CHARLES DARWIN, *The Descent of Man*

NONHUMAN ANIMALS are magnificent and amazing beings. They clearly have wide-ranging cognitive, emotional, and moral capacities. We can learn a lot from them if we open or minds and hearts to *who* (not what) they really are. We should be proud of our citizenship in the animal kingdom. Scientific research is changing the way we view other animals. We don't have to go beyond the science or embellish what we know to appreciate how they express their intellectual skills and emotional capacities. Humans are clearly neither the only conscious beings nor the sole occupants of the emotional and moral arenas, which include some surprising residents, like honeybees, fish, and chickens. Surely, we have no right to intrude wantonly into the lives of other animals or to judge them or blame them for our evil ways.

When we say animals are conscious and smart, we mean they know what to do to adapt to ever-changing environments. The versatility and flexibility of their behavior show clearly they are not machinelike automatons, but rather they are actively thinking and feeling beings. Donald Griffin, often called the "father of cognitive ethology" (the study of animal minds), postulated that the ability of animals to adapt to unpredictably changing conditions showed they were conscious and able to assess what needed to be done in a given situation. The real question is not *if* animals are conscious but rather *why* consciousness has evolved.

There are sound biological reasons for recognizing animals as conscious beings. Charles Darwin stressed that variations among species are differences in degree rather than kind. There are shades of gray, not black-and-white differences. So if one species has a trait, other related species have some version of it, too. This is called *evolutionary continuity*. For example, we share with other mammals and vertebrates the same areas of the brain that are important for consciousness and processing emotions. The anthropocentric view that only big-brained mammals — such as ourselves, nonhuman great apes, elephants, and cetaceans, or dolphins and whales — have sufficient mental capacities for complex forms of consciousness is simply bad biology and needs to be abandoned.

The ramifications of this view of other animals in relation to ourselves are wide-ranging. There are social, political, and environmental implications when we deny the capacities of other animals and think of ourselves as above and better than them. A July 2011 essay by philosopher Steven Best provides a penetrating analysis of why human exceptionalism, the belief that human beings have special status based on our unique capacities, is a false view and has serious consequences. It's the idea that humans are "members of a distinct species in relation to other species and Earth as a whole." Best provides a comprehensive review of recent research in cognitive ethology to support his argument that we do indeed share many traits with other animals. The database grows daily, and as I outline in my book *The Animal Manifesto*, science increasingly supports many of our intuitions about the cognitive, emotional, and moral capacities of a wide range of animals.

Clearly, we need to rethink human "uniqueness" and dispense with speciesism. Best notes that humans do indeed display unique capacities, such as writing sonnets, solving algebraic equations, and meditating on the structure of the universe. He also points out that other animals have abilities and traits that we don't have. To assume humanity's traits are superior, or to construct false boundaries between species, as a basis for discriminating against or exploiting certain animals, is merely self-serving. Further, for speciesism to work and confirm human exceptionalism, it must ignore within-species variation, which is often more marked than between-species differences.

What we now know about animal minds — certainly among mammals but also among a wide variety of other species — does not support human exceptionalism. Best concludes, "If humans have for so long failed to understand animal minds it is because their own stupidity, insensitivity, and deep speciesist bias have for so long blinded them."

Indeed, contrary to what speciesism proposes, alienation from other animals, dominating them, and treating them like dispensable objects is not what it means to be human. I often wonder if future humans will sit around and scratch their heads and wonder how we missed what is so obvious about the lives of other animals. Thankfully, as the blinders come off, we're learning a lot about other animals that will make us better people.

We are a significant force in nature. We need to be more compassionate, empathic, and humble and act with greater concern for animals and their homes — or else we will suffer the same indignities to which we expose other animals. In the end we all lose when we ignore nature and act as if we're the only animals who count, that we are exceptional and better and can do whatever we want because we can. Power is license neither to make other animals' lives miserable nor to redecorate their homes with no concern for their well-being.

The time has come to debunk the myth of human exceptionalism once and for all. It's a hollow, shallow, and self-serving perspective on who we are. In their own ways, every species is exceptional and deserving of respect, compassion, and love. Perhaps we should replace the notion of human exceptionalism with *species exceptionalism* or even *individual exceptionalism*. Such a shift might lead us to appreciate other animals for who they are, not who or what we want them to be.

[ORIGINALLY POSTED ON JULY 30, 2011]

Animals Don't Laugh, Think, Get Depressed, or Love, Declares a Psychiatrist

THIS WEEKEND I RECEIVED a few emails about a recent essay written for *Psychology Today* titled "The Seven Things that Only Human Beings Can Do." People were concerned, in some cases deeply troubled, by the erroneous claims of the author. One well-known author wrote, "You would need a front-end loader to dig a path through this." The word "only" in the title of this essay without a modifier such as "supposedly" surely is a warning flag given what we actually know about other animals and given what we're continually discovering about who they are. Indeed, although we've known it for a long time, a group of distinguished scientists felt comfortable enough to recently formally declare that animals are indeed conscious (see "Scientists Finally Conclude Nonhuman Animals Are Conscious Beings," page 116).

So, given my long-standing interests in animal behavior and the cognitive and emotional capacities of other animals, I eagerly searched out this essay expecting to be enlightened. Rather, I was floored by the utter naiveté of the author who clearly felt comfortable making hard-and-fast claims about the lack of cognitive and emotional capacities *that have been well-documented by those scientists who actually study animal behavior.* Since the author of this essay, Neel Burton, had written a book called *Hide & Seek: The Psychology of Self-Deception*, I thought perhaps his essay was a joke and some sort of veiled attempt to show how easy it is to deceive his readers. I was wrong. I wonder why people who don't know much if anything about animals feel free to write about them as if they're experts in the field. (I've also wondered why so many essays posted on *Psychology Today* use animals as the teaser image when the essay itself has nothing to do with animals. Clearly, animals are "in.")

So, getting back to the seven things that *supposedly* only human beings can do, I fully realize we humans are exceptional in various ways, *as are other animals.* I figured I'd read about things such as building computers, driving

45

cars, flying airplanes, cooking food, wantonly waging war, worrying about taxes, and searching for extraterrestrial life, among other behaviors that are distinctly human. However, I read that only humans speak, laugh, cry, think, suffer from mental disorders such as depression and schizophrenia, fall in love, and believe in God.

Here I just want to consider these preposterous and uninformed claims in varying degrees of depth and provide some references for those who would like to see what we actually know. To start, simply scan other *Psychology Today* essays, such as my own and those of John Marzluff and Tony Angell, Lee Dugatkin, Gay Bradshaw, Jessica Pierce, Hal Herzog, Mary Bates, and Agustin Fuentes, among others. You'll quickly see just how misleading the essay "The Seven Things that Only Human Beings Can Do" truly is.

Speaking: Here, the author writes: "Language is not necessary for communication, and many animals communicate effectively by using more primitive forms of communication. However, language is able to give rise to symbolism, and thereby to emotionalism and to creative activity. These *unique* [my emphasis] assets not only make us by far the most adaptable of all animals, but also enable us to engage in pursuits such as art, music, and religion, and so define us as human beings." While there are ongoing debates about whether or not other animals actually have linguistic skills, there's a wealth of data that clearly show that animals have "emotionalism" and are extremely creative. One down, six to go.

Laughing: The author tells us "no one has ever seen a laughing dog." Well, this is simply not so. They've been seen and heard. Consider, for example, the research of the late Patricia Simonet, whose work on dog laughter has been well-accepted (and was discussed by Stanley Coren for *Psychology Today*). Consider also that Charles Darwin, Jane Goodall, and others have described laughter in nonhuman animals. Laughter has also been documented by the renowned neuroscientist Jaak Panksepp, and his research has been published in prestigious journals, including *Science*.

Crying: Here the author contradicts himself. He writes: "All animals shed basal and reflex tears, but only human beings shed emotional tears. There are those who believe that some animals, in particular elephants and chimpanzees, can also shed emotional tears, but this is difficult to verify. On the other hand, we can be pretty sure that crocodiles do not cry." Just because something is "difficult to verify" doesn't mean it doesn't occur, so the claim that only humans shed emotional tears is vacuous.

Thinking: The claim that other animals can't think is so ludicrous it's laughable. Here, the author's text is a simply irrelevant garble in which he cites Aristotle's claim that humans have the unique capacity to reason. Well, Aristotle might have thought this, but clearly he didn't have access to the wealth of information that shows clearly that animals are well able to think and to behave rationally.

Suffering from mental disorders such as depression and schizophrenia: Once again, this claim, in which Aristotle is also cited, is incredibly misleading. Researchers such as physician Hope Ferdowsian and psychologist Gay Bradshaw, for example, have shown that captive animals do indeed suffer a wide range of psychological disorders including PTSD, and I've written about psychological disorders in wild animals (see "Do Wild Animals Suffer From PTSD and Other Psychological Disorders?," page 164). This is one of the hottest areas of research because of the ways in which countless animals are used and abused in a wide range of human venues. And indeed, researchers continue to use animal models of depression and other psychological conditions to try to learn more about similar disorders in humans.

Falling in love: I'm not sure where to begin here because there are so many examples of animals falling in love and remaining in love for long periods of time. Individuals of many different species form long-term and extremely close social bonds characterized by clear affection and attachment, which we call love in human animals. They clearly miss one another when they are separated and suffer from the absence of individuals with whom they're closely bonded. We see love among mated pairs and also between parents and their children and among members of a group. Of course, one can pitch a definition of love so high so as to exclude many humans, but accepted definitions of the word "love" ("strong affection for another arising out of kinship or personal ties; attraction based on sexual desire," per Merriam-Webster's Dictionary) clearly apply to other animals.

Believing in God: I really don't know if animals believe in God, and I expect no one else does either, so perhaps this is something only humans do. However, there is evidence that suggests that animals have spiritual experiences (see "Do Animals Have Spiritual Experiences? Yes, They Do," page 143). Based on her observations of waterfall dances in chimpanzees, Jane Goodall wonders, "If the chimpanzee could share his feelings and questions with others, might these wild elemental displays become ritualized into some form of animistic religion? Would they worship the falls, the deluge from the sky, the thunder and lightning — the gods of the elements? So all-powerful; so incomprehensible."

So, most if not all of the claims in this essay are simply and utterly misleading. The time has come to debunk the myth of human exceptionalism once and for all (for further discussion, see, for example, Lori Gruen's *Ethics and Animals*). It's a hollow, shallow, misleading, and self-serving anthropomorphic perspective on who we are and who other animals are. It egregiously misrepresents other animals, and of course there are severe consequences for these beings who depend on us for their well-being.

[ORIGINALLY POSTED ON SEPTEMBER 3, 2012]

What Makes Us Uniquely Human?

FOR AS LONG AS HUMAN ANIMALS have pondered how we might differ from nonhuman animals, many proposals have come and gone. For example, some religions postulate that humans were created in the image of God, but of course, this isn't a claim that can be proven or disproven. And opinions vary on whether humans are the *only* animals created in the image of God, or even what God looks like. Other claims have been that only humans are rational beings and that only humans manufacture and use tools, have culture, have a sense of self, use complex systems of communication, produce art, have rich and deep emotional lives, and know right from wrong. However, ample research has shown that animals share these traits with us, and so they can't be what make humans unique. I would propose two traits that seem to separate us from other animals: we're the only animals who cook food, and no other species is as destructive of its own and other species.

Now, in his book entitled *The Recursive Mind*, Michael Corballis suggests that recursive thought — such as engaging in mental time travel and having a theory of mind — is a uniquely human trait that separates us from other animals. In an excellent review of Corballis's book, anthropologist Barbara J. King makes many of his arguments palatable to a lay audience while also identifying how they fall short. For example, she writes, recursive thought is when we "communicate by embedding structures within other structures, as when one noun phrase in a sentence is made to contain another. An example of such linguistic recursion is furnished by Corballis. The non-recursive sentences 'Jane loves John' and 'Jane flies aeroplanes' may be combined to produce the recursive sentence 'Jane, who flies aeroplanes, loves John.' Less interested in language than the mind itself, Corballis states flatly that recursion is 'the primary characteristic that distinguishes the human mind from that of other animals.'"

Mental time travel and theory of mind are other recursive ways of thinking. King writes, "During mental time travel, an experience that we've had in the past or that we imagine for ourselves in the future is 'inserted into [our] present consciousness.' Similarly, in theory of mind, we insert what we believe to be someone else's state of mind into our own."

So, how do Corballis's ideas hold up given what we know about the behavior and cognitive capacities of animals? Not that well, according to King, and I agree. King notes that other animals plan for the future and have a theory of mind (which I also note in my previous books, *The Emotional Lives of Animals* and *The Animal Manifesto*). As an example she writes about the hunting behavior of wild chimpanzees described by prominent primatologists Christophe and Hedwige Boesch-Ackerman. In their book *The Chimpanzees of the Taï Forest*, these researchers wrote, a hunting chimpanzee "not only has to anticipate the direction in which the prey will flee..., but also the speed of the prey so as to synchronize his movements to reach the correct height in the tree before the prey enters it.... We also recorded a double anticipation when a hunter not only anticipates the actions of the prey, but also the effect the action of other chimpanzees will have on the future movements of the colobus, that is he does not anticipate what he sees (the escaping colobus), but how a future chimpanzee tactic will further influence the escaping monkeys."

King concludes, "Humanity's recursive ways of thinking are more elaborate than those of other animals, but some other animals do think recursively as well. Can the degree of difference explain the origins of human thought, language, and civilization?" We really don't know. But as more studies are conducted, I'm sure we'll discover other examples showing that recursive ways of thinking are not reliable markers of human exceptionalism and that other animals show highly sophisticated recursive thought.

What's at issue here is not whether humans as a species are distinct from other animals, but whether what makes them different makes them better. This sort of speciesist thinking doesn't have much support. We need to keep an open mind about the cognitive capacities of other animals. Different doesn't mean smarter or better. And really, the most important question is what makes *individuals* unique. There are wide-ranging individual differences within all species, including *Homo sapiens*.

I'm excited to see what future research shows us about the cognitive capacities of other animals. I'm sure other animals are much "smarter" than some give them credit for. Indeed, what we already know shows this to be the case.

[ORIGINALLY POSTED ON NOVEMBER 4, 2011]

PART 3

MEDIA AND THE (MIS)REPRESENTATION OF ANIMALS

IN THIS PART'S FIVE ESSAYS, I look at the ways animals are represented, or more often misrepresented, in the media. While we don't expect cartoon entertainments like *The Lion King* or *Finding Nemo* to represent real animals — and it's alarming and upsetting when movies like *The Grey* (2011) demonize wild animals for profit — we do expect newspapers, magazines, documentaries, and other seemingly objective sources to tell us the truth. Unfortunately, with liberal license and often out of ignorance, the media is notorious for representing other animals in a false and misleading light. As they do with so many topics, the media sensationalizes extremes and reinforces untrue and even harmful stereotypes about animals. It's essential that animals be represented correctly because what people read influences how they perceive and ultimately how they treat other animals. Among the reasons why I write essays for *Psychology Today* about the lives of other animals is to portray them the way they are, not as who we want or imagine them to be.

Animals in Media:
Righting the Wrongs

NONHUMAN ANIMALS are a hot topic these days, but there are still problems with how they are represented in mass media. Ample data, much of it summarized in *New Scientist*, show that animals are smart, emotional, and moral beings and that they care about what happens to them. The language we use to refer to animals informs our thoughts and perceptions of who they are, and our thoughts and perceptions influence our actions. We can do much better. We are the voices for other animals, and it is our ethical responsibility to do so.

In a 2009 *Communication Review* journal article, Carrie Packwood Freeman at Georgia State University shows that when animals appear in the press there are serious concerns about how they are represented. She notes that animals are often objectified by the language used to describe them. In addition to using the inanimate pronoun *it*, we objectify animals when we call them "livestock," "meat," "seafood," and "game" rather than cow, pig, chicken, fish, and elk. She also notes a strong tendency to refer to animals by their utilitarian end, such as beef cattle, dairy cows, laboratory rats, or circus elephants. Indeed, as I wrote about in *The Animal Manifesto*, I'm continually frustrated by computer spell-check programs that automatically change "who" or "whom" into "that," "which," or "it" in reference to animals. This objectifying impulse is so ingrained it's programmed into our computers.

I also heard a recent National Public Radio (NPR) report — which summarized a study showing that ants seem able to count — that provides another example of how language can demean animals even in otherwise positive contexts. In the study, ants were shown to be able to count the steps they take using what are called "pedometer-like" cells in their brain. Part of the experiment demonstrating this ability entailed cutting off parts of the legs of some ants, which the NPR report called a "makeover." This was no doubt meant as a tongue-in-cheek way to make light of the fact that these creatures were actually disfigured in the effort to prove how smart they are.

Would the word "makeover" have been used if the limbs of chimpanzees or dogs were amputated? I doubt it. Such speciesism shows that ants and other "lower" animals aren't thought of in the same light as "higher" animals — who in fact cannot do some of the remarkable things that ants and other insects can do.

Nonetheless, endangered chimpanzees are also misrepresented. They are often depicted as human caricatures, doing silly tricks, wearing clothes, playing musical instruments, driving SUVs or other cars, or reading *Science* magazine, as in a promotional campaign by its publisher, the American Association for the Advancement of Science. Such misrepresentations lead to the perception that chimpanzees are subhuman and not on the brink of extinction, and they can undermine conservation efforts. The author of a 2008 *Connect* magazine report noted, "In addition to media-created misperceptions about chimpanzees' conservation status, media effects can also distort understanding about basic biology."

Also, it's a little-known fact, but animals are misrepresented in still photography and in wildlife films; a good book about this is *Shooting in the Wild* by Chris Palmer. There is little control about letting consumers know they are buying a canned photo or watching a canned wildlife scene. In 2010, a wildlife photographer was stripped of his "photographer of the year" award because he apparently hired a tame Iberian wolf, which is rarely seen in the wild, to stage an image. Animals are also kept on photography game farms, where there are few if any concerns or regulations about the well-being of the animals. These animals are often kept in tiny, filthy cages and euthanized when they're no longer needed.

What can we do about media misrepresentations? Some simple rules of thumb will go a long way to representing animals more accurately. First, we can refrain from using words such as "higher" or "lower" to refer to animals. We should get word processors to stop replacing "who" with "that" when referring to animals. We should stop portraying animals as mock humans. We must pay attention to what we know about the fascinating cognitive, emotional, and moral capacities of animals because misrepresentations underestimate and demean them. We know, for example, that octopuses use tools, mice are empathic rodents, and birds are better at making and using tools than chimpanzees. And while it might be cumbersome, we should use phrases such as "nonhuman animals" or "other animals" because using the word "animals" to identify all creatures who are not "humans" supports a false notion that humans aren't animals. We are part of, and we should be proud of our membership in, the animal kingdom.

Given the enormous amount of press animals are receiving in what might be called the "century of the animal," we should expect that those who write about animals will represent them accurately, as the beings they are, not as who we want them to be or as objects for our use. Nonhuman animals deserve better, and by following a few simple rules of thumb, we can do better for them. No matter in what context we engage with animals or discuss them, we can always strive for more accurate representations. This may make nonhuman animals both less "scary" and less "cute," from our perspective, but it will make their lives better.

[ORIGINALLY POSTED ON JANUARY 25, 2010]

Are Great Apes "Ultraviolent"?

IN A 2011 REVIEW of a new and extremely interesting book on African apes (*Among African Apes* by Martha Robbins and Christophe Boesch), writer Rowan Hooper uses a catchy title to get our attention: "Going Ape: Ultraviolence and Our Primate Cousins." Are great apes "ultraviolent"? No. This isn't who they really are. This sensationalist term misrepresents these amazing beings, probably because the writer knows humans would feel better if we could justify our own "ultraviolence." Sure, great apes and other animals fight, and on occasion they harm and kill one another, but this is *extremely* rare. Even the authors of *Among African Apes* agree the incidences of "extreme violence" they describe in their book are rare.

Available data show animals are far more cooperative than we've previously thought. Jane Goodall noted in her book *The Chimpanzees of Gombe*, "It is easy to get the impression that chimpanzees are more aggressive than they really are. In actuality, peaceful interactions are far more frequent than aggressive ones; mild threatening gestures are more common than vigorous ones; threats per se occur much more often than fights; and serious, wounding fights are very rare compared to brief, relatively mild ones." In *Scientific American* in 2010, John Horgan noted the evidence for hardwired warfare in animals is very weak, and those who claim that great apes and other animals are inherently demonic aren't paying attention to what we really know. He summarizes current data as follows: "All told, since Jane Goodall began observing chimpanzees in Tanzania's Gombe National Park in 1960, researchers have directly observed 31 intergroup killings, of which 17 were infants....Researchers at a typical site directly observe one killing every seven years."

Similarly, Robert Sussman, an anthropologist at Washington University in St. Louis, and his colleagues Paul A. Garber and Jim Cheverud, reported in *The American Journal of Physical Anthropology* (2005) that for many non-human primates, more than 90 percent of their social interactions are affiliative rather than competitive or divisive. *Origins of Altruism and Cooperation*, a 2011 book edited by Sussman and C. Robert Cloninger, also shows clearly that cooperation is far more typical of other animals than is divisive competition and aggression.

Humans, too, are highly cooperative and egalitarian, even among strangers. It's been suggested that large-scale cooperation may have set humans on the path to success. Meanwhile, the 2011 book *Super Cooperators*, by Martin Nowak and Roger Highfield, reviews what we know about the importance of human cooperation in the evolution of human social behavior. The main point is that cooperation is not merely a by-product that evolved because of our aggressive tendencies. Rather, cooperation is an important contributor to the evolution of social behavior and sociality.

Let's stop falsely representing our animal kin as inherently violent and destructive. Violence exists within and among all species, but there's extremely little evidence that suggests any other animal species but our own has "ultraviolent" (some might say evil) tendencies.

Instead, we should be proud of our animal heritage. Calling someone an "animal" is really a compliment.

[ORIGINALLY POSTED ON JUNE 20, 2011]

Chimpanzees and Meerkats:
The Importance of Accurate Media

ANIMALS ARE "IN." It's difficult to pick up a newspaper or magazine (for those who still pick them up) and not see something about the amazing animals with whom we share our one and only precious planet. Two 2011 studies of how endangered chimpanzees are portrayed show clearly that media can influence how animals are perceived. The first, by Stephen Ross and his colleagues, shows "the public is less likely to think that chimpanzees are endangered compared to other great apes, and that this is likely the result of media misportrayals in movies, television, and advertisements." Their detailed study demonstrated "that those viewing a photograph of a chimpanzee with a human standing nearby were 35.5 percent more likely to consider wild populations to be stable/healthy compared to those seeing the exact same picture without a human. Likewise, the presence of a human in the photograph increases the likelihood that they consider chimpanzees as appealing as a pet. We also found that respondents seeing images in which chimpanzees are shown in typically human settings (such as an office space) were more likely to perceive wild populations as being stable and healthy compared to those seeing chimpanzees in other contexts. These findings shed light on the way that media portrayals of chimpanzees influence public attitudes about this important and endangered species."

Another study, conducted by Kara Schroepfer and her colleagues, also discovered that the use of chimpanzees in commercials negatively distorts the public perception of chimpanzees regarding their conservation status and that this distortion can hinder conservation efforts. These two studies should serve as a warning that responsible media is essential for communicating *who* other animals really are and how their lives are in peril. I feel confident that when other studies are done for animals who aren't as charismatic or as closely related to us, the same sort of discoveries will be made. These two studies can serve as models for what needs to be done on a wider scale especially because most people don't have the opportunity to see wild animals firsthand. Many really don't understand how close they are to disappearing forever.

Chimpanzees and other great apes are very smart and emotional beings. That's a no-brainer for most people, although chimpanzees are still used in horrific invasive research, but more and more support is forthcoming to stop it once and for all. However, as we study other animals, we see they too are smart and emotional. Their cognitive capacities rival those of our closest relatives. For example, a very interesting study shows just how clever meerkats can be, for those who don't already know them from the British television show *Meerkat Manor*. Simon Townsend and his colleagues have recently demonstrated, per a story in *Wired*, that wild meerkats recognize other meerkats by their voices. The ability to recognize individual voices is essential for complex social interactions, and it would seem to require rather sophisticated cognitive facilities, but till now it had been confirmed in few other mammals except us and our nonhuman primate cousins. So, just when we think that we are cognitively gifted and separate from other animals, we see we're really not. This story about meerkats is an example of how media should report on the behavior of other animals, accurately and to the point.

I concluded in a recent essay, "The time has come to debunk the myth of human exceptionalism once and for all." Media plays an essential role in doing just this.

[Originally posted on October 24, 2011]

The National Museum
of Animals & Society

[A]nimals are always the observed.
The fact that they can observe us has lost all significance.

— JOHN BERGER, *About Looking*, 1980

OUR RELATIONSHIPS WITH NONHUMAN ANIMALS move us all over the place. We love some animals, hate others, and are indifferent to a wide range of fascinating species. Animals intrigue and inspire us, and as we inquire about who they are, we learn much about who we are.

John Berger, a famous art critic, painter, and author, spent a good deal of time in his seminal work *About Looking* analyzing what it means to gaze at animals. We stare at them for hours in a nature documentary, take a trip to a sanctuary in order to feel connected with them, and marvel at their amazing cognitive, emotional, and moral capacities. An important question on which many people often reflect is, "Why do we engage with other animals in such a myriad of often highly contradictory and inconsistent ways?"

We also need to ask, "What about the animals who are staring back at us?" What is taking place behind the eyes and between the ears of a chimpanzee or a mouse in a laboratory, a deer darting through rush-hour traffic, a wolf running from those who want to kill him, or two dogs romping with their human companion at a dog park? What is happening in their hearts? How do we give animals their due and recognize that they, too, observe and hear and smell us? That they, too, are sentient, thoughtful, and emotional beings who share and engage in this world with us?

There are many books, documentaries, and other venues that can help us answer these and many other questions that center on our relationships with other animals. The relatively new field of anthrozoology (www.isaz .net), which is concerned with research on the nature of human-animal interactions, is gaining a good deal of momentum from researchers representing many different disciplines.

What has been missing, but no longer is, is a museum that can also help us learn more about human-animal interactions. For the past year I've had the pleasure and honor of serving as an advisor to the National Museum of Animals & Society (NMAS), based in Southern California. This museum is dedicated to enriching the lives of people and animals through the exploration of our shared experience when we and other animals encounter one another. In their collections, exhibitions, programs, and educational efforts, the museum centers on the full spectrum of human-animal studies, the history of protecting animals by organizations as well as by everyday people, and the importance of humane education.

NMAS is the first museum to take on this subject matter from a perspective that respects the lives of individual animals, no matter the species. Its subject matter is near and dear to the hearts of millions of people. Among all beings, fascination with "other animals" most likely dates back to the earliest days of the evolutionary journey.

Since the advent of human society, humans have long grappled with the moral, emotional, and spiritual dimensions of our interactions with, and representations of, nonhuman animals. Today, this includes numerous debates about our responsibilities to companion animals as well to wildlife in crisis; the awe and revulsion experienced when witnessing animals in zoos and circuses; our complex feelings about how nonhuman animals are represented in literature, art, and film; and the inspiration that artists, writers, photographers, and others awaken in us as they present the lives of the many animals with whom we share this planet. All this is what NMAS calls "our shared experience."

At different points in history, such moving experiences of connection have motivated people to protect animals from cruelty and to challenge the ways in which we habitually think about and relate to other animals in the grand scheme of things. While sages such as Socrates and his contemporaries gave thought and energy to questions about the welfare of animals, it wasn't until the mid-1700s that the movement to protect animals gathered momentum. In fact, around this same time period, there was much overlap among several social justice causes, such as those to abolish slavery, fight for women's suffrage, and advocate for the interests of children and laborers. Interestingly, all these areas of social justice have been widely represented and discussed in museums except for animals — until now.

NMAS is the brainchild of museum professional and animal advocate Carolyn Merino Mullin, who has long been interested in how we can preserve, interpret, and present our rich and inspiring history of caring for animals. Now in its third year, the museum is fundraising to open exhibition space in Los Angeles, California. Led by an exemplary group of directors, advisors, and academics, NMAS has already produced a number of bicoastal traveling and online exhibitions, ranging from animal welfare in colonial America to a children's exhibit on mythical beings to an innovative and interactive Facebook exhibit called "Souls Awakened: The Animals Who Have Shaped Us" that exposed thousands of children to humane education programs at schools and festivals. NMAS also is acquiring a remarkable collection of historical artifacts (which currently includes about five hundred items).

You can follow NMAS on their website (www.museumofanimals .org), and on Facebook (www.facebook.com/TheNMAS) and Twitter (www.twitter.com/animalmuseum). Support this inspirational, model, and seminal organization and enrich your own life and relationships with other animals in the process. Those people living or vacationing in Southern California also can take advantage of their fall lecture series, guest speakers, events, and much more.

As time goes on, nonhuman animals are enjoying much more positive publicity as we learn that our own health and well-being are tightly associated with how we treat these remarkable beings. NMAS will surely enrich these varied and shared experiences, help us appreciate just how amazing other animals truly are, and foster coexistence with all animals, including humans.

[ORIGINALLY POSTED ON APRIL 7, 2012]

Animals in Art: Nonhumans Benefit from Responsible Representation

LAST WEEK I went to a wonderful and wide-ranging meeting at Intersections Digital Studios (IDS) at Emily Carr University of Art + Design in Vancouver, British Columbia. The meeting was called Interactive Futures (http://interactivefutures.ca), and it was organized by Carol Gigliotti (editor of the 2010 book *Leonardo's Choice: Genetic Technologies and Animals*), Julie Andreyev, and Maria Lantin, director of IDS. Speakers from all over the world attended and spoke about the general theme of "Animal Influence." They spotlighted media artists whose work has been "influenced by the growing wealth of knowledge on animal behavior, cognition, creativity, and consciousness emerging from such fields as ecology, cognitive ethology, psychology, neuroscience, cognitive science, philosophy, zoology, and others. These research areas have focused on new understandings of animal life and are helping to shift assumed conventions concerning animal cognition, consciousness, and agency. While the change in human attitudes toward animals has been documented in news media as well as in more academic venues, the idea that animals might possess emotional, moral, cognitive lives is an idea that has been, in the past, either dismissed or associated with metaphorical or symbolic approaches."

My role was to talk about the emotional and moral lives of animals and why they matter. I also was there to ensure that animals were represented as who they really are. I was so pleased to find that this was the case in just about all the lectures, discussions, and exhibits. Sometimes artists and writers take (a bit too much) liberty with how animals are represented, but this wasn't the case at this inspirational meeting. Nonhumans are amazing individuals, and there isn't any reason to embellish or misrepresent them to make them more appealing than they are. Indeed, it is everyone's responsibility to be as accurate as they can be when doing their work.

To achieve the goals of this unique and inspirational gathering, there were lectures and various exhibits, including hands-on projects. Two in particular caught my attention, though there were many more wonderful projects on display. The first was the rocking robot, a robotic dog who looked and acted like a cow, created by the eminent French artist France Cadet. Her work makes "a critical social comment about ethical questions and possible consequences of a technologically driven future, through ironical caricaturization but which is based on very-real facts." While I watched the robot rock back and forth, I constantly found myself thinking about the many challenging relationships among art, ethics, and technology, topics that are given a lot of attention in Professor Gigliotti's book *Leonardo's Choice*.

The other project that caught my eye involved the way in which various animals see the world by Lisa Jevbratt. Called Zoomorph, this project basically involved first looking at a colored drawing on a board and then on an iPad selecting an animal to see how the colored image would look to them. What a wonderful educational tool for getting people to see how animals see the world. It would be great to have a similar project dealing with the ways in which various animals hear and smell the world, although the latter might be difficult to pull off, given where the noses of various animals wind up. Still, it would be highly educational.

I also met some very talented students. One was Sam Boschmann, who has a well-developed talent for drawing animals. With talent like hers on the horizon, we can look forward to a future in which other animals are well-represented in popular and scientific media and in various types of art.

All of the lectures and exhibits really forced me and everyone to think deeply about how animals are represented in art and about who we are and who "they" are. For many artists in attendance, whether as presenters or audience members, the goal was to find new ways not only to represent animals but to live with them. I really was pleased to see this practical side of what could have been a more "academic" endeavor with little relevance to the real world.

More and more artists are focusing their attention on nonhuman animals, and we need to be sure that they are represented in responsible ways and pay close attention to the ethical questions that are raised. The use of animals in art truly sparks wide-ranging discussions that center on human psychology and our often complex and challenging relationships with non-human beings in our overpopulated and human-dominated world.

[ORIGINALLY POSTED ON NOVEMBER 21, 2011]

PART 4

WHY DOGS HUMP

Or, What We Can Learn
from Our Special Friends

DOGS OCCUPY A VERY SPECIAL PLACE in the lives of millions upon millions of people around the world, and these fourteen essays show why they are considered to be close friends and family members. While the topics are wide-ranging, they center around our canine buddies and their cognitive and emotional lives; hopefully, they illustrate what we mean to them and they mean to us. By the end, you'll also learn why dogs hump. The answer might not be what you think.

Dog Trust:
Some Lessons from Our Companions

WE OFTEN HEAR that the companion animals with whom we share our lives have unqualified trust in us, that they believe we will always have their best interests in mind, and that they love us unconditionally and would do anything for us. And, indeed, they often do take care of us in a seemingly selfless manner.

But dogs and other animals don't love everyone unconditionally. They can be very selective. From time to time it's a good idea to revisit, if only briefly, some common beliefs we have about relationships between ourselves and other animals. I've been asked on many occasions about trust among animals, and this essay puts some of my thoughts on the table for discussion.

What does it mean to say our companions trust us? The notion of trust is difficult to discuss because it's very broad and has many different sides. Trusting another is related to intention. What did a person (or other animal) intend to do, and were their actions in the best interest of another being? It's possible to have the best of intentions and to do something that harms another being. This doesn't mean that the individual who erred shouldn't ever be trusted again.

Now, what about the trust that our companion animals have in us? Their wide eyes can pierce our souls and tell us clearly that they know we'll always do the best we can for them. I find it easiest to think about dog trust in terms of what they expect from us, their innate, ancestral, and deep faith in us, and their unwavering belief that we will take our responsibilities to them as seriously as we assume responsibility for other humans. Basically, they expect that we always will have their best interests in mind, that we will care for them and be concerned with maximizing their well-being.

I believe this inherent trust dogs have in us inspires our devotion to them, not the other way around. So, we feed and exercise our companions regularly, we scratch them behind their ears, we rub their bellies and watch them succumb to our touch, melting like hot butter as our fingers massage them into deep relaxation. We hug them, love them, and welcome them into our homes as family members (which pleases them immensely because they're such social beings). We take them to a veterinarian when they need medical care. They feel better because of our devotion to them, and we feel better, too.

We are our companions' trusted guardians, not their owners. We don't own our companions like we own property, such as our bicycles and backpacks. A number of cities have agreed that dogs are not owned commodities. Having said this, on occasion we may intentionally expose our companions to painful situations, such as allowing them to receive vaccinations or to undergo surgery, when we believe that it's in their best interests. We haven't betrayed our trust by causing them intentional pain if our intention is to help them.

My ever-trusting companion dog, Jethro, on occasion needed acupuncture for bad arthritis in his left elbow, and he clearly didn't like it the first two times he was stuck with the needles. But afterward he settled in and went through the treatments with no hesitancy, even dragging me into the veterinarian's office! After eight treatments he went from a dog who struggled to walk for ten minutes to a frisky romping canine!

The pain to which I exposed Jethro was caused intentionally by me and the veterinarian. But we did not betray his trust in us. However, if we beat our companion animals or otherwise abuse them, leave them in a hot car, starve them, neglect their need for love, or allow them to be abused in horrible experiments, we betray them. We let them down. But regardless, amazingly, in most instances our companion dogs will still trust us in the future. It's just who they are, or who they have become via the evolutionary process of domestication.

Dogs are so attached to humans that, even after being abused in experiments and in other situations, they will only look up at the human and wag their tails as if to say, "This hurts me, but you must mean well. How could you possibly mean otherwise?" Their "dog talk" says it all. It breaks my heart to know that some people can be so evil. Betraying the trust of our companions is simply unacceptable behavior that must never be tolerated.

Dogs and other animals tell us they trust us by their actions, by their willingness to allow us to do just about anything to them. Remember this when you interact with our animal companions. They trust us unconditionally to have their best interests in mind, and it's a malicious double-cross to betray that trust. Nevertheless, in most cases dogs will joyfully prance back for more of whatever we dish out. They're that trusting and confident.

However, it's indisputable that we severely psychologically and physically harm our companions when we let them down, when we neglect them or dominate them selfishly, not caring about the deep hurt for which we're responsible. When we betray our companion's innocence and trust, our actions are ethically indefensible. We become less than human; it's simply wrong, so let's not do it — ever.

The hearts of our companion animals, like our own hearts, are fragile, so we must be gentle with them. You can never be too nice or too generous with your love for our dear and trusting companions, who are so deeply pure of heart. Indeed, by honoring our companion's trust in us, we tap into our own spirituality. These wonderful beings make us more human.

Let's openly and graciously thank them for who they are, for their unfiltered love, and embrace their lessons in passion, compassion, devotion, respect, spirituality, and love. Surely, we will never have any regrets by doing so. Much pure joy will come our way if we clear the path for deep and rich, trusting, interdependent relationships with our canine companions and, indeed, all other beings.

[ORIGINALLY POSTED ON JUNE 29, 2009]

My Dog Always Eats First:
Homeless People and Their Animals

MOST OF US HAVE SEEN HOMELESS PEOPLE on the streets, many accompanied by their nonhuman animal companions, especially dogs. On any given night there are about 640,000 homeless people in the United States; however, estimates vary quite a lot. It's also been estimated that 5 to 10 percent of homeless people have dogs or cats as their companions, but the numbers vary geographically and it's difficult to come up with highly accurate statistics. Nonetheless, a large number of animals live with homeless humans, and in many cases the animals are the lifeline and reason for living for these people without a home and surviving in a stigmatized and marginalized environment in which few if any would choose to live.

Homeless people have told me on more than one occasion that their animal companion is their best friend, the oxygen without whom life wouldn't be worth living. For many, their animal friend is their only family. For instance, last year while I was eating lunch in my hometown of Boulder, Colorado, I started talking with a homeless man named Joe. He told me that when he lost his job and became homeless, he sold most of his very few possessions so that he could keep his dog, Clive, without whom Joe wouldn't be able or want to live. I've heard similar stories in cities around the world.

Homeless people are often viewed with suspicion or fear. When people see the homeless and their animals, they do a number of things. Some give them money or food and some look away. Others judge them unworthy of animal companionship. Whatever the reaction, most of us would have no idea how to survive on the street with (or without) an animal.

A new book by University of Colorado sociology professor Leslie Irvine is the first to explore what it takes to live on the streets with an animal. Using interviews with more than seventy homeless people in four cities, *My Dog Always Eats First: Homeless People and Their Animals* reveals what animals mean for homeless people and how they care for their four-legged friends. Dr. Irvine's book provides rich descriptions of how animals have provided social and emotional support and protection from harm and, in some cases, even helped turn around the lives of people who had few other reasons to live.

Dr. Irvine initially found this research to be very challenging. Because homeless shelters do not typically allow animals, homeless pet owners usually stay on the street and "under the radar." She made connections with veterinarians who hold street clinics for the pets of the homeless, such as VET SOS (www.vetsos.org) in San Francisco and the Mercer Veterinary Clinic for the Homeless (www.vetmed.ucdavis.edu/clubs/mercer) in Sacramento, California. She interviewed people at the clinics and even went on veterinary "house calls" into homeless camps, where she would not have ventured on her own.

Building on the work she began in her book *If You Tame Me: Understanding Our Connections with Animals*, Dr. Irvine continues to explore how animals serve as "significant others" for their human companions. Homeless people told her how their dogs encouraged interaction with others and kept them from becoming isolated. Former addicts and alcoholics described how their animals inspired them to get clean and sober. People who had spent years on the streets explained how they responded to the insults they heard from strangers who thought they should not have a pet. And they praised those who provided pet food and a kind word.

My Dog Always Eats First is full of compelling stories and solid research. It is an inspirational must-read for anyone who cares about animals and about the people who care for them. I learned a lot from this first-of-a-kind book, and I encourage anyone interested in the nature of human-animal relationships to read and share it widely.

[ORIGINALLY POSTED ON JANUARY 22, 2013]

Chancer and Iyal:
A Dog, His Boy, and His Dog

WHEN I CHECKED MY EMAIL THIS MORNING, there were a few requests for me to alert readers to a heartwarming story in the *New York Times* about Chancer, a handsome golden retriever, and a young boy, Iyal, to whom he provides much-needed care and love. I encourage you to read the entire story, titled "Wonder Dog" by Melissa Fay Greene, when you have time, as it is a wonderful and inspiring tale of devotion and love. For now, here are a few brief passages from the story to whet your appetite and help you appreciate just how important dogs can be for us and how good we are for them.

The morning after Chancer's first night in the house outside Atlanta, the Winokurs woke up after a full night's sleep for almost the first time since 1999. They looked at each other in semihorror: was Iyal still alive? They found him snoozing beside the big yellow dog, the latter hogging the mattress. Since Chancer's arrival in the house, they've rarely been disturbed in the night. Iyal may still wake up, but he's evidently reassured by the dog's presence and returns to sleep.

"The moment he walked in the house with Chancer, I knew something had changed," Harvey says. "I could feel it instantly, the magnetism between Iyal and the dog....Chancer was an emotional and physical anchor for a kid who was pretty lost in the world."

When Iyal is distressed, Chancer is distressed. Unlike Iyal, Chancer knows what to do about it. Iyal rages by crossing his arms, sitting down hard on the floor and screaming and kicking. Chancer unknots the crossed arms by inserting his wide muzzle through the locked arms from below, opening them up and nuzzling toward Iyal's face, licking and slobbering, until the boy's screams turn to tears of remorse or to laughter.

Chancer sometimes heads off tantrums before they start. If a tutor or a therapist has worked with Iyal in the dining room a bit too long, Chancer moves between the visitor and the boy, clearly relaying: We're done for today. From two floors away, he will alert, flicking his ears, tuning in. Sensing that Iyal is nearing a breaking point, he gallops up or down the stairs to find him, playfully head-butts and pushes him down to the floor, gets on top of him, stretches out and relaxes with a satisfied groan. Helplessly pinned under Chancer, Iyal resists, squawks and then relaxes, too. The big dog lies on top of the boy he loves, and seals him off from the dizzying and incomprehensible world for a while....

Chancer doesn't know that Iyal is cognitively impaired. What he knows is that Iyal is his boy. Chancer loves Iyal in a perfect way, with an unconditional love beyond what even the family can offer him. Chancer never feels disappointed in Iyal or embarrassed by Iyal. Beyond cognitive ability or disability, beyond predictions of a bright future or a dismal one, on a field of grass and hard-packed dirt, between the playground and the baseball diamond, you can see them sometimes, the two of them, running, laughing their heads off, sharing a moment of enormous happiness, just a boy and his dog.

Chancer was trained as a service dog, and every time I meet these amazing dog beings and their human companions I'm moved beyond belief, often to tears, at the close relationship that develops and how reciprocal it can be.

I've also worked with the Psychiatric Service Dog Society (PSDS), founded by Joan Esnayra. A few summers ago I gave my lecture on the emotional lives of animals and met a group of wonderful veterans of the wars in Iraq and Afghanistan and their dog buddies. The bond between them was incredibly strong, and each human, most of whom were suffering from PTSD and a wide variety of physical injuries, wanted to know how they could make the life of their dog better to pay them back for their unyielding care, devotion, and love. Driving home that afternoon, I couldn't wait to share my experience with as many people as possible.

Dogs are amazing beings who deserve our unyielding care, devotion, and love. The examples above in which dogs are the lifeline, the oxygen, for people in need are but a very few in which the tight and enduring bond is good for all involved. It's truly a win-win situation, and bless all the dog beings and human beings who work in these wonderful programs.

[ORIGINALLY POSTED ON FEBRUARY 3, 2012]

Going to the Dogs Is a Good Idea:
It's Not a Dog-Eat-Dog World

IN THE UNITED STATES, about 40 percent of households have one or more companion dogs (of which there are 75 million in total) and about 34 percent of US households have one or more companion cats (of which there are 88 million). Dogs are like family to most people, and more than 75 percent of US children live with companion animals and are more likely to grow up with a nonhuman companion than with both parents. American boys are more likely to care for their companion animals than for older relatives or younger siblings. In a September 1, 2009, *Psychology Today* blog, Alexandra Horowitz, author of *Inside of a Dog*, explains why we treat dogs better than we treat their wild relatives, wolves, from whom they evolved.

Here I just want to alert readers to some current ideas about the use of dogs in cognitive research and some recent discoveries based on an August 2009 essay titled "Going to the Dogs" by Virginia Morell in the prestigious professional journal *Science*. Dogs have had a rocky reputation in research, depending on the nature of the study. Over the years, millions of dogs have been used and severely abused in a wide variety of invasive biomedical and psychological experiments, but when it comes to behavioral research scientists have had varied opinions about whether or not dogs are good subjects. I was told years ago that studying social play behavior in dogs was a waste of time, not only because we could never get a handle on what play is and why animals love to do it, but also because play in dogs isn't like play in other animals because dogs aren't "real" animals, since they have been radically changed by humans during domestication. I decided these skeptics were totally wrong, and after about thirty-five years of research, I have clearly shown that this was a ridiculous worry, as have many of my colleagues (for instance, see *The Genesis of Animal Play* by Gordon M. Burghardt and *The Playful Brain* by Sergio and Vivien Pellis).

Today, the tide is changing, and most scientists see the value in studying our best friends with whom we've been associated ever since we domesticated them to be who we want them to be. The summary from "Going to the Dogs" reads as follows:

> Dogs are fast becoming the *it* animal for evolutionary cognition research. Our canine pals, researchers say, are excellent subjects for studying the building blocks underlying mental abilities, particularly those involving social cognition. Their special relationship with humans is also seen as worthy of study in its own right; some researchers see *Canis familiaris* as a case of convergent evolution with humans because we share some similar behavioral traits. And because all dogs are descended from gray wolves (*C. lupus*), they can reveal how domestication has altered a species' mental processes, enabling the dog to survive in its new habitat, the human home. Some researchers even think that dogs may teach us more about the evolution of some aspects of our social mind than can our closest kin, the chimpanzee, because Fido is so adept at reading and responding to human communication cues. But not everyone agrees, arguing that the skills dogs share with humans are a matter of learning rather than evolutionary change.

The essay in *Science* also shows that there's a lot of interest in how the mind of dogs developed similarly to the mind of humans, but I don't find the arguments as yet all that compelling. We should appreciate dogs for who they are, whether or not they're like us.

It's also really interesting that dogs do things that wolves can't, even wolves who are raised with humans. Research in Adam Miklósi's laboratory in Budapest, Hungary, has shown that four-month-old puppies in a choice test always preferred a human companion to a dog, whereas young wolves showed no preference. Much of what is currently known about the cognitive abilities of dogs and wolves and why they differ is reviewed in a 2009 article in the peer-reviewed online journal PLOS ONE:

> In sum, in dogs the necessary social skills for utilizing human pointing signals or the preparedness for their rapid development

have been selected for in the domestication process. For wolves, a compensating developmental route might enable the establishment of the behavioural basis of successful communication and cooperation with humans in some tasks. Wolves, however, react to a lesser degree to socialisation in contrast to dogs, which are able to display control of agonistic behaviours and inhibition of actions in a food related task early in development. The synergistic hypothesis suggests that the dog-wolf difference in the sensitivity for human gestural cues emerges both at the evolutionary and developmental level. Further studies are needed to investigate whether this can be interpreted in the phenotype as a developmental change in the timing (heterochrony) of some social skills in dogs.

Regarding these conclusions, it's worth pointing out that wolves are *not* domesticated animals, even those with whom we share our homes or can interact. From time to time people tell me that they live with or know a domesticated wolf because the wolf is friendly and gets along well with people. These are socialized individuals, but wolves have not undergone domestication. Domestication is an evolutionary process, one in which humans decide what traits they want and then selectively breed individuals to achieve their desires. Charles Darwin called this *artificial selection* to contrast it with natural selection. Indeed, one of the best examples of artificial selection is the numerous breeds of domesticated dogs who roam the planet. So, when someone says they live with a domesticated wolf, what they really mean is that they're living with a *socialized* wolf. *A domesticated wolf is a dog!*

I talked about the *Science* essay and dogs in general with my colleague and dog expert Mark Derr, author of three wonderful books on dogs (*A Dog's History of America*, *Dog's Best Friend*, and *How the Dog Became the Dog*), and he agrees that we also need to be careful about comparing dogs to young children because each occupies a different perceptual world from our own, which is one reason they are so helpful to us.

What's so exciting is that there is so much to learn about our companion dogs, and it can be done in noninvasive experiments as well as while they're having fun on the run with their friends. Research data and good anecdotes are all needed to increase our knowledge about what dogs and other animals are able to do and what they know and feel. We need to keep the door open on how smart and adaptable they are and also on how domestication has played a role in defining who they are and who we are.

[ORIGINALLY POSTED ON SEPTEMBER 3, 2009]

Wild Dogs in Captivity Are Still Wild Dogs

A NUMBER OF PEOPLE have asked me to write something about the absolutely horrific tragedy that occurred at the Pittsburgh Zoo when a two-year-old boy, Maddox Derkosh, fell into an exhibit and was killed by a pack of African wild dogs (also called painted dogs) on Sunday, November 4, 2012. I was going to write something the day it happened, but after reading the account through teary eyes, I simply couldn't sit down and write anything at all.

Now, a few days later, with a clearer perspective, I'm glad to respond to these requests with a short piece about this tragedy in particular and about zoos in general. A number of people have blamed the mother for apparently holding up her son so that he could get a better view of the dogs. I honestly don't see any reason to blame Maddox Derkosh's mother. She did what countless parents and adults do when they go to a zoo. It's easily understandable that they want their children to have the best experience they can have.

An interesting essay I just read about this incident titled " 'Well-Mannered Predators' and Other Speciesist Notions about Animal Captivity" by Kathleen Stachowski raises a number of questions about zoos, people's attitudes toward animals in zoos, and what people think about whether or not the wild dogs should be killed for what they did. She points out that these tragedies are "human tragedies — and needless ones but for our speciesist insistence on keeping wild beings for our own pleasure and profit." She goes on to write:

> It's almost impossible to contemplate the two-year-old child who fell into the African wild dog exhibit at the Pittsburgh zoo. This horrendous incident has prompted all sorts of online chatter — everything from mommy/baby forums ('Poll question: Do you think the African painted dogs should be put down?') to gun owner forums ('If you're carrying, open carry or concealed carry, in a zoo…and you see something like this happening…do you

draw and fire at the animals to stop the attack?'). *Argh*. One article alone generated 660+ comments. There's compassion for the
mother as well as condemnation that goes beyond cruel. There's
bravado, there's anguish. Would-be wildlife experts abound. The
dogs have many defenders, as does the zoo. 'Sue the zoo,' others
advise. And so it goes.

While there is much about this incident to discuss, I feel there is *nothing* to be gained by killing the dogs. What's interesting is that the poll question asks if the dogs should be euthanized, but this is *not* euthanasia because
euthanasia is mercy killing, or a "good death," when individuals need to
be relieved of interminable pain. This killing would actually be an example
of what I call "zoothanasia" (See "'Zoothanasia' Is Not Euthanasia: Words
Matter," page 218), *and it must not be confused with euthanasia.*

Nothing is to be gained by blaming and killing the dogs, who are condemned to captivity. This zoo and other zoos have to take more precau-
tions if they choose to house natural-born predators. One can easily argue
that these and other animals simply do not belong in zoos.

Christine Dell'Amore, writing for *National Geographic News*, wonders why the African wild dogs attacked the boy. The answer really is
pretty simple. The dogs were doing what they've evolved to do, and once
Maddox Derkosh fell into their home, they reacted instinctively. These
captive dogs are still wild animals, and "you can't take the wild out of
the animal," as Stachowski writes. (The same is true for exotic pets; see
"Buddy the Chimpanzee Killed in Nevada Because He Wasn't Really a
Pet," page 233.) What's interesting in this regard is that experts do not
think this was a predatory attack. The wild dogs simply responded to an
unexpected event.

The real question at hand — once again — is why zoos exist and what
they do, if anything, for the animals who find themselves living in totally
unnatural spaces. While people take sides on the value of zoos, it remains a
fact that in the long term, they do little, if anything, for educating the public about their residents or for the conservation of the residents' wild relatives (see "Zoos and Aquariums Do Not Accomplish What They Claim

They Do," page 213, and "Rewilding Animals: Going Home at Last," page 227). The animals in zoos are what could be called "faux animals," or fabricated animals, and they are not at all representative of their wild relatives. Sure, we hear stories from people about how going to the zoo changed their opinion about animals, but very few go on to have careers in related fields or make meaningful financial contributions to conservation efforts. If zoos are to have a meaningful or significant impact, numerous more people have to "walk their talk."

Going to zoos is not part of the process of rewilding our hearts. Be that as it may, zoos are here to stay, at least for a while, and all of their residents must be given the very best lives possible. If that means removing animals from public display and placing them in sanctuaries where they can live out their lives safely and in peace and dignity, so be it.

[ORIGINALLY POSTED ON NOVEMBER 11, 2012]

Can Dogs Experience Guilt, Pride, and Shame: Why Not?

DOGS ARE AMAZING nonhuman animals, and anyone who's known a dog knows this. Just today Dr. Stanley Coren published a very interesting essay on the *Psychology Today* website called "Which Emotions Do Dogs Actually Experience?" He concluded, among other things: "However, we know that the assortment of emotions available to the dog will not exceed that which is available to a human who is two to two-and-a-half years old. This means that a dog will have all of the basic emotions: joy, fear, anger, disgust, and even love. However, a dog will not have those more complex emotions like guilt, pride, and shame."

After an email exchange with Dr. Coren about my response to his essay, he modified his conclusion to read, "However, based on current research it seems likely that your dog will not have those more complex emotions like guilt, pride, and shame."

While this conclusion is extremely interesting, it remains a hypothesis in that the necessary research has not really been done. So, until the detailed research is conducted, we don't really know "that the assortment of emotions available to the dog will not exceed that which is available to a human who is two to two-and-a-half years old."

We also don't know if dogs experience guilt, pride, and shame. However, because it's been claimed that other mammals with whom dogs share the same neural bases for emotions do experience guilt, pride, shame, and other complex emotions (see Endnotes, page 333), there's no reason why dogs cannot. And there's solid biological and evolutionary reasons to assume dogs can and do. Recall Charles Darwin's ideas about evolutionary continuity (see "Animal Minds and the Foible of Human Exceptionalism," page 42), in which the differences among species are seen to be variations in degree rather than kind — if some mammals experience something, most or all mammals probably do, too.

One more point needs to be made concerning doggy guilt. Consider the research conducted by Alexandra Horowitz, author of *Inside of a Dog* and a *Psychology Today* writer (see the "Minds of Animals" column, www.psychologytoday.com/blog/minds-animals). As I noted in a February 4, 2013, essay called "The Genius of Dogs and the Hidden Life of Wolves," Dr. Horowitz's research is often misinterpreted. For example, in the book titled *The Genius of Dogs: How Dogs Are Smarter than You Think*, Brian Hare and Vanessa Woods consider Dr. Horowitz's research on doggy guilt. They write that Horowitz "conducted an experiment to see whether dogs can feel guilty," but this misinterpreted what Dr. Horowitz was actually trying to do. Her research showed that people were not all that good at reading guilt in their dog; however, her data do *not* show that dogs cannot feel guilt. I frequently hear people say that Dr. Horowitz's project showed dogs *cannot* feel guilt, and this is not so (see the Endnotes, page 333, for more on this).

Let's keep the door open about the emotional lives of dogs and other animals and also extend a hearty thanks to Dr. Coren for once again writing a very interesting and stimulating essay.

Finally, one can also question the value of comparing young humans with other animals. I don't find these comparisons to be especially compelling, and other researchers have agreed that they are fraught with difficulties, as are many cross-species comparisons concerning the cognitive and emotional capacities of individuals of different species. As I like to say, animals do what they need to do to be card-carrying members of their species. This means each species is different and often exceptional in ways that other species are not. We should replace the notion of human exceptionalism with species or individual exceptionalism in order to appreciate other animals for who they are.

[ORIGINALLY POSTED ON MARCH 14, 2013]

Hidden Tales of Yellow Snow: What a Dog's Nose Knows – Making Sense of Scents

DOGS SPEND LOTS OF TIME with their well-endowed nostrils stubbornly vacuuming the ground or pinned blissfully to the hind end of other dogs. They have about twenty-five times the area of nasal olfactory epithelium (which carry receptor cells) and have many thousands more cells in the large olfactory region of their brain (mean area of 7,000 mm2, or square millimeters) than humans (500 mm2). Dogs can differentiate dilutions of one part per billion, can distinguish T-shirts worn by identical twins, can follow odor trails, and are ten thousand times more sensitive than humans to certain odors.

When dogs wiggle their noses and inhale (suction) and exhale (snort), they concentrate odors, pool them into mixtures, and expel others. Like wild relatives (wolves, coyotes) dogs gather much information from the symphony of odors left behind. Urine provides critical information about who was around, their reproductive condition, and perhaps their mood. Dogs expel millions of gallons of urine wherever they please (more than 1.5 million gallons, along with more than twenty-five tons of feces, per year in New York City alone), and they use it well.

Odors are powerful stimulants. It's said that Sigmund Freud used soup smells to stimulate clients to recall past traumas. Although my late companion dog Jethro (a.k.a. Hoover), enjoyed visiting his veterinarian, he showed fear if he went into an examination room where the previous canine client was afraid. Fear is conveyed via a pungent odor released by the previous dog's anal glands.

Now, what about sniffing other dogs' urine? At one point, while taking Jethro on his daily walk, I conducted a study of his sniffing and urination patterns. To learn about the role of urine in eliciting sniffing and urinating, I moved urine-saturated snow ("yellow snow") from place-to-place during five winters to compare Jethro's responses to his own and other dog's urine. Immediately after Jethro or other known males or females urinated on snow, I scooped up a small clump of the yellow snow in gloves and moved it to different locations. For some reason, passersby thought I was strange and generally left me alone.

Moving yellow snow was a useful and novel noninvasive method for discovering whether Jethro spent less time sniffing his own urine than that of other males or females. Other researchers have also noted that male dogs (and coyotes and wolves) spend more time sniffing the urine from other males compared to their own urine. Also, dogs usually spend more time sniffing urine from females in heat compared to urine from males or reproductively inactive females.

The differences in Jethro's response to the displaced urine from other males or from females are worth noting, especially when considering "scent-marking" behavior. "Scent-marking" is differentiated from "merely urinating" by a number of criteria, which include sniffing before urinating and following this by directing the stream of urine at the urine known to be present or at another target.

When Jethro arrived at displaced urine that was his own urine, he sniffed it and then only infrequently immediately urinated over it (or "scent-marked" it). But if the displaced urine was from other dogs, especially males, he sniffed and then immediately scent-marked the urine significantly more often.

While domestic dogs are usually not very territorial (despite myths to the contrary), their wild relatives are, and they show similar patterns of scent-marking behavior in territorial defense. I hope this brief foray into the olfactory world of dogs removes the mystery of dog sniffing and gives some idea of what the dog's nose tells the dog's brain. You can easily repeat this simple experiment (and risk being called weird). The hidden tales of yellow snow are quite revealing about the artistry of how dogs make sense of scents.

[ORIGINALLY POSTED ON JUNE 29, 2009]

I'll Have What She's Having:
Dogs Do It, Too

ONE OF THE MOST WELL-KNOWN LINES from a movie comes from *When Harry Met Sally*. After watching Meg Ryan's character do a great job at faking an orgasm in Katz's Delicatessen (my father's favorite), a middle-aged woman says to her waitress, "I'll have what she's having."

Humans are not the only animals who make choices based on what others are having. We now know that dogs will base their decision on what food is the most desirable by watching what humans eat. According to a *Scientific American* report on a 2012 study, dogs "recognize human signals about what's good."

In the study, researchers let dogs choose between two plates, one with a single piece of food and one with six pieces. It wasn't much of a surprise that the dogs preferred the larger amount of food. However, "when a human being showed a clear liking for the smaller plate, the canines likewise went for the skimpier choice. The dogs apparently recognized and responded to the humans' social cues." However: "When the human approached but did not touch the smaller portion, dogs ignored the attention-drawing gesture. For a social signal to influence behavior, it had to demonstrate intention" and the "most effective cues also involved communication, such as looking from the food to the dog and back while talking encouragingly."

This research adds to what we know about the behavior of dogs and how it has been influenced by their close relationship with us humans. (For an extensive discussion of how dogs became dogs, see Mark Derr's 2011 book *How the Dog Became the Dog*.)

Dogs are really interesting animals, and by studying their behavior we've learned much about them and about us. Unsurprisingly, our long-term and close relationship with our best friends has changed both of us.

[ORIGINALLY POSTED ON MAY 3, 2012]

Dogs Know What Others Know:
Some New and Exciting Findings
about Our Best Friends

DOMESTIC DOGS ARE BEING STUDIED more and more because we can learn so much not only about our best friends but also about how they compare to their wild relatives — wolves and coyotes, for example — and other animals such as nonhuman primates.

In one 2010 study, we learn that when young dogs are exposed to videos during early life, this experience can help them to overcome fear and enhance coping strategies. This information could be used to help individuals who, for a variety of reasons, have had restricted upbringings, though how to do so awaits further study and application.

Meanwhile, another 2010 study shows that dogs know what others can and cannot hear. We already know that rhesus monkeys and other nonhuman primates also have this ability. Here is an abbreviated abstract from the study done on dogs.

Recent research suggests some nonhuman primates (e.g., chimpanzees, rhesus macaques) consider what others hear when acting in competitive situations. We explored whether dogs living in private homes or sourced from an animal shelter would show this same predilection. Following an inhibition task where dogs (*Canis familiaris*) were commanded not to take a treat left on a plate by a human, we presented subjects with the opportunity to take food from one of two containers. These containers were located within the proximity of a human gatekeeper who was either looking straight ahead or not looking at the time of choice. One container was silent when food was inserted or removed while the other was noisy.... [D]ogs preferentially attempted to retrieve food silently only when silence was germane to obtaining food unobserved by the human gatekeeper.

Thus, dogs selectively steal food quietly if humans are listening to what they do (for more on this, see "Stealth Dogs Steal Food in the Dark and Snatch It Quietly," page 93). It also turned out that shelter dogs didn't differ from companion dogs who lived at home with humans. Previous work had demonstrated differences between shelter and house dogs in various cognitive abilities. The researchers wrote: "Shelter dogs, like pet dogs, preferentially tried to retrieve food silently only if silence was relevant to obtaining food unobserved by a human gatekeeper. This result conflicts with other recent data suggesting that shelter dogs perform more poorly than pet dogs in tasks involving human social cues."

These data suggest that dogs have a theory of mind, and like other animals, especially great apes, can attribute beliefs and knowledge to others. As we learn more about domestic dogs, we come to realize they are very intelligent and that domestication — our interfering in their lives by selectively breeding for a variety of traits — hasn't made them "dumbed-down wolves."

[ORIGINALLY POSTED ON JULY 19, 2010]

Stealth Dogs Steal Food
in the Dark and Snatch It Quietly

JUST ABOUT EVERYONE WHO LIVES WITH A DOG has a story, or perhaps many tales, about how their companion is an Einsteinian genius with an incredibly rich and deep emotional life who even knows right from wrong. What's very interesting is that scientific research is supporting these stories coming from nonscientists who take the time to watch how their dogs behave in various situations, some of whom even perform citizen-scientist research projects.

Two recent studies published in the May 2013 issue of *Animal Cognition* show just how stealthy dogs can be when stealing food. In the first project, aptly titled "Dogs Steal in the Dark" — conducted by researchers from the University of Portsmouth in the United Kingdom and the Max Planck Institute for Evolutionary Anthropology in Leipzig, Germany — dogs were found to steal significantly more food in the dark compared to when it was light. Before testing, a human forbade the dogs from taking a piece of food, so the dogs knew they were doing something they weren't supposed to do. The researchers also discovered that the dog's behavior while stealing food depended on the type of illumination in the room. If the human was illuminated but not the food, the dogs stole significantly more food. When the food was illuminated, but not the human, the dogs didn't try to steal the food. The results of this research suggest that dogs take into account the human's visual access to the food, their visual perspective, and not necessarily their presence, while making their decision whether to steal it or not.

In the second study, titled "Domestic Dogs Conceal Auditory But Not Visual Information from Others," some of the same researchers discovered that when given a choice of approaching forbidden food through a silent or a noisy tunnel, dogs preferred to silently approach the food. However, when dogs couldn't see a human present, they didn't try to hide their approach. The researchers concluded that "dogs probably rely on what they themselves can perceive when they assess what the human can see and hear." In other words, the dogs figured that if they couldn't see or hear the human, the human couldn't see or hear them.

Stay tuned for more on the fascinating behavior of our crafty companions. You might be able to do some of these sorts of noninvasive experiments with your own companion dogs. In addition to having fun and enriching their lives, you can also enrich your own and learn more about their well-developed cognitive and reasoning skills.

[ORIGINALLY POSTED ON NOVEMBER 29, 2012]

Dogs: Looking at the Way We Look at Our Best Friends

DOGS COMPRISE one of the most physically diverse species on the planet. But without humans, would dogs naturally range in appearance from pug and poodle to Great Dane and Weimaraner? Probably not. Have humans selected dogs for particular physical appearances?

The conventional wisdom is that dogs have been selected to look cute. Nobel laureate ethologist Konrad Lorenz proposed that human and nonhuman animals have particular physical features that encourage humans to nurture and attend to them (see also "Animals in Our Brain: Mickey Mouse, Teddy Bears, and 'Cuteness,'" page 7). These features correspond with neoteny, or juvenilization, and could include, Lorenz wrote, a "relatively large head, predominance of the brain capsule, large and low-lying eyes, bulging cheek region, short and thick extremities, a springy elastic consistency, and clumsy movements." The preference for baby-like features is called *kindchenschema*, or baby-schema. Pugs, shar-peis, and many others exemplify dogs who retain "cute," juvenilized appearances into adulthood.

But could there be more to the story than simply preferring juvenilized features? For example, humans also ascribe *meaning* to the way dogs look, as shown by, among other things, American Kennel Club breed standards. The expression of the Great Pyrenees is described as "elegant, intelligent, and contemplative," and the Chihuahua is said to have a "saucy" expression. The *meanings* we ascribe to dogs are very much intertwined with the way dogs look. And of course, this phenomenon can be explored in fun studies.

Researchers in Alexandra Horowitz's Dog Cognition Lab (www .columbia.edu/~ah2240/) at Barnard College in New York City investigate the general topic of anthropomorphic attributions to dogs. For example, does the so-called "guilty look" map to a dog's knowledge of disobedience or is it related to owner behavior? (See Alexandra Horowitz's 2009 study "Disambiguating the 'Guilty Look.'")

I had the pleasure of hearing Julie Hecht recently present her and Alexandra Horowitz's research at the Third Canine Science Forum in Barcelona, Spain. In their study, participants viewed two nearly identical images of mixed-breed, adult dogs and implicitly selected which image in each pair they liked best. Unbeknownst to the participants, one image in each pair had been slightly altered to explore a particular physical feature. Some features related to neoteny, while others related to human-like traits. Peoples' choices indicated their preferences, or lack of preferences, for particular physical features.

They found that the story does not begin and end with neoteny. Participants preferred some but not all characteristics of neoteny. For example, larger eyes were preferred over smaller, but an enlarged cranium was not. Participants also preferred human-like traits such as distinct smiles or colored irises.

They dug deeper and found that preferences differed based on preconceptions about animals. In contrast to self-ascribed "animal people," those who self-characterized as "nonanimal people" did not have a preference either way for eye size or a distinct smile.

The physical features of dogs to which humans are attracted aren't trivial matters. These findings can have important welfare implications. Do our preferences for particular physical features always benefit our canine companions? While "animal people" seem drawn to dogs with larger eyes, big eyes can be associated with health issues like brachycephalic ocular syndrome and exposure keratitis. In other words, pugs are bred for their particular look, but the shape of their features can create breathing problems. Maybe humans don't prefer larger nostrils on dogs, but what if that physical attribute enhanced their ability to breathe?

Clearly, humans have implicit preferences about the physical features of dogs and these preferences can be systematically investigated. I look forward to more research on this fascinating topic.

I thank Julie Hecht, Alexandra Horowitz, and Paul McGreevy for their input on this essay.

[ORIGINALLY POSTED ON AUGUST 21, 2012]

Why Dogs Hump

"ON A BEAUTIFUL, WARM AFTERNOON, I watched a group of dogs frolic in a dog park. Suddenly, I heard a woman's high-pitched yelp, followed by the pounding of human feet. There was no need to look; it was obviously about humping, which we can also refer to as mounting." So wrote Julie Hecht in her excellent review in August 2012 of humping by dogs. Indeed, because humping often offends some people, Julie titled her essay "H*mping."

Mounting and humping by dogs are among those behavior patterns about which humans make lots of assumptions, but we really don't know much about them. From a wide variety of positions, dogs will mount and hump other dogs, other (nonhuman) animals, human legs, and inanimate objects such as beach balls, water buckets, food bowls, pillows, and garbage pails without a care in the world. If you want to watch, please do, but an audience isn't necessary. Sometimes they hold on for upwards of twenty to thirty seconds, and sometimes they just jump on and slide off and saunter away. And size doesn't matter.

While many humans feel embarrassed when they see a beloved four-legged friend mount and hump in public places, this behavior is a normal part of a dog's behavioral repertoire. Both males and females mount and hump, and these behaviors first appear early in a dog's life, particularly during play. Mounting and humping should not be considered abnormal behavior patterns.

While mounting is best known for its role in reproduction, it also occurs in many other contexts and emotional states. Dogs mount when they're excited and aroused and even when they're stressed and anxious. Take out the leash to go for a walk, and Lassie starts humping Toto. You come home after a long day's work, and Spot goes for your leg.

Mounting could also be what ethologists call a displacement behavior, meaning that it's a by-product of conflicted emotions. For some dogs, a new visitor to the house could elicit a mixture of excitement and stress that could make for a humping dog. And as we might flip on the TV when we're bored, some dogs develop the habit of mounting during downtime, getting better acquainted with a pillow. Mounting is also very common during play, sometimes as an attention-getter, an affiliative behavior, or when a dog is overexcited. I've seen dogs going "berserk," enjoying that "doggy fit" — running here and there and mounting and humping a friend and then a ball.

What about dominance and mounting? In "H*mping," Hecht quotes a recent article on mounting by Peter Borchelt, a certified applied animal behaviorist (CAAB) in New York City, who noted, "Mounting could be part of a suite of behaviors associated with aggression, such as high posture, resource guarding, direct stares, and threats and standing over. But mounting, in and of itself, doesn't indicate a status issue. By itself, mounting might not mean a lot."

In my own studies of the development of social behavior in young dogs, coyotes, and wolves, mounting, clasping, and humping were not directly related to dominance, nor were they associated with dominance for the wild coyotes my students and I studied in the Grand Teton National Park outside of Jackson, Wyoming.

I wonder if in some situations dogs mount and perhaps hump others when there are dogs around who can see them doing it. Years ago in a detailed study of urination patterns in dogs I could easily follow, I discovered they often engaged in what I called "dry marking"; they'd lift a leg but wouldn't urinate. When I looked at the social situations in which this happened, it turned out that dry marking occurred more when other dogs were around than when the dog was alone. I concluded that leg lifting might be a visual signal in and of itself telling other individuals something like "I just peed." It would be interesting to know if dogs mount and hump more when other dogs can see them, and if so, perhaps in some situations mounting and humping may have something to do with telling others about relative dominance.

However, are mounting and humping problems about which we should be concerned? Mounting, including humping and masturbation, are normal behaviors according to the ASPCA (and others), although for some dogs, they could become a compulsive habit, such as excessive tail chasing.

The bigger question is, "What do mounting and humping mean to your dog?" In truth, we really don't know all that much about these behavior patterns, such as how often they're linked together and in what circumstances, so generalizations about what they mean to all dogs need to be put on hold until further research is done.

You can, however, attempt to answer this question for your own dog by considering the behaviors in the contexts when one or the other occur. For example, what happens before mounting, and how often and how long does it occur? If mounting suggests a dog is understimulated, perhaps the dog could be provided with additional mental or physical activities. If mounting suggests anxiety, it would be good to increase a dog's comfort level in a particular situation. Or if a dog gets overstimulated and goes bonkers or gets rude or impolite during social interactions with other dogs or people, it would be good to encourage mutually-beneficial interactions. Guardians (a.k.a. owners) can intervene in mounting and humping by getting the dog's attention or by teaching an alternate behavior to assist the dog in their interactions with others.

Or perhaps your dog mounts and/or humps only occasionally because they like to do it. If the behavior isn't causing any problems except embarrassment for their human companion, perhaps you can let them have at it. Julie Hecht concludes her article "H*mping" as follows: "When trying to get behind any behavior (pun intended), [Marc] Bekoff recommends becoming an at-home ethologist. 'Get a paper and pencil, and watch and record what happens before and after the behavior of interest. This can tell you more about the behavior itself.' This technique can help you determine when a behavior needs to be managed and when it's just fine.

"If dogs could talk — and they actually are with their behavior — they'd ask us not to clump mounting into one universal meaning. So what's your dog's mounting behavior telling you?"

Clearly, there isn't a single explanation for mounting or humping.

Mounting and humping are normal behavior patterns, so let's not allow our own discomfort to get in the way of dogs doing what comes naturally. You can turn away, pretend it isn't happening, or giggle nervously and, simply put, let them be dogs. One thing's for sure, dogs hump because they can.

[ORIGINALLY POSTED ON SEPTEMBER 1, 2012]

Social Dominance Is Not a Myth:
Wolves, Dogs, and Other Animals

THE CONCEPT OF SOCIAL DOMINANCE is not a myth. A myth is an invented story. The concept of dominance has been, and remains, a very important one that has been misunderstood and misused, often by those who haven't spent much time conducting detailed studies of other animals, including those living in the wild.

Dominance is a fact. All animals engage in dominance, including human animals, in a number of ways. For instance, individuals may dominate (1) to control access to various resources, including food, potential and actual mates, territory, resting and sleeping areas, and the location in a group that's most protected from predators; (2) to influence the movements of others; or (3) to get the attention of others, an idea put forth by Michael Chance and Ray Larsen in *Social Structure of Attention*. Even if dominance interactions are rare, they do occur, and that is why it's important to log many hours observing known individuals. As one gets to know individuals in a group, he or she also learns more and more about the subtle ways in which a wide variety of social messages are communicated, including those used in interactions in which one individual controls another.

Complicating the picture is the phenomenon of situational dominance. For example, a low-ranking individual may be able to keep possession of food even when challenged by another individual who actively dominates him or her in other contexts. I've seen this in wild coyotes, dogs, other mammals, and various birds. In these cases, possession is what counts. I've studied social relationships in a wide variety of species, and any introductory textbook on animal behavior (for example Lee Dugatkin's *Principles of Animal Behavior*, third edition) contains various definitions of dominance and many examples. Another complicating factor is that there's a lot of variation in the way in which dominance is expressed both within and between species.

What has happened over the past thirty or so years based on extensive comparative behavioral research is the discovery that dominance is not a simple or ubiquitous explanatory concept, as some once took it to be. For example, for many years it was assumed that dominant animals mated the most and controlled access to various resources. Now we know this isn't necessarily so in all species or even within different groups of the same species. Often, less-dominant or subordinate animals are able to mate and can control others in different contexts.

So, is there much new under the umbrella of dominance? Yes and no. In 1981 renowned primatologist Irwin Bernstein published a most important essay on dominance, in which he discussed all of the above and more. Bernstein and others since have convincingly argued that the concept of dominance is useful despite newly discovered complexities and subtleties, so we need to be very cautious about throwing out the baby with the bathwater.

To be sure, ethologists have not called dominance a myth. Rather, they've noted that a univocal explanation of dominance, one relying on a single unambiguous meaning of what dominance is, is misleading and simplistic.

Dominance surely is a slippery concept with respect to how it's expressed and how individual variations in social dominance influence behavior. A narrow definition doesn't necessarily hold across species, within species, or across different contexts. Many discussions in which the broad concept of social dominance is criticized are very informative, but to claim that dominance is a myth flies in the face of what we know about the subtle, fleeting, and complex social relationships and ongoing social dynamics of many group-living species.

In particular, some of the critics of social dominance include those who study and/or train dogs, and it was Lee Charles Kelley's *Psychology Today* blog, "Deconstructing the Dominance Myth (Again...)" that got me revisiting the notion of dominance. In this essay the author writes, "Dr. David Mech, the world's leading expert on wolves, says that in thirteen years of studying the wolves on Isle Royale in Michigan he *never* [my emphasis] saw any displays of dominance." When I read this I was (and remain) incredulous. In the limited time I watched wild wolves in

Yellowstone National Park, I saw dominance displays on a number of occasions, and other researchers also report these sorts of interactions.

Some of the critics' concerns are legitimate because we need to be very careful about generalizing from the behavior of wild and captive wolves (from whom dogs emerged) to the behavior of domestic dogs. It's also important to realize that the misuse of the concept of dominance that results, for example, in a person violently dominating a dog (see "Did Cesar Millan Have to Hang the Husky?," page 104), is not a valid, respectful, or humane way to treat or to train our best friends.

It's essential that people working with dogs know what ethologists mean when they use the word "dominance" or the term "dominance hierarchy." It's clear from research on dogs, wolves, and many other animals that dominance hierarchies exist, and what we know can be applied to training methodologies and used in positive ways. Dominance does not necessarily mean that one animal "beats up" another individual. Rather, it refers to an animal's ability to control the behavior of another, frequently in nonaggressive ways, for example, using body movements, gestures, odors, vocalizations, eye contact, or a combination of signals.

[Note: This essay was originally written as a critical response to a February 2012 blog by another *Psychology Today* writer, dog trainer Lee Charles Kelley, called, "Deconstructing the Dominance Myth (Again...)." I took issue with Kelley's characterization of dominance as a "myth," and I questioned some misrepresentations of current research, particularly by Dr. David Mech (for more on Dr. Mech, see the Endnotes). To his credit, Kelley agreed with my criticisms and apologized, to myself and Dr. Mech, in a following essay a week later ("A Mea Culpa to Mech, an Apology to Bekoff"). I've included my original essay because confusions about dominance remain, particularly as it relates to dog training.]

[ORIGINALLY POSTED ON FEBRUARY 15, 2012]

Did Cesar Millan
Have to Hang the Husky?

BECAUSE OF WHAT I DO, I'm always getting emails about the latest information on animal cognition and animal emotions and also on animal abuse. I usually receive reports or videos of abuse in research laboratories, zoos, circuses, and rodeos or on factory farms, but from time to time people ask me questions about dog training. Last year I received a video showing Cesar Millan (a.k.a. the "dog whisperer") hanging a husky who was ill-behaved on his TV show. This treatment of a sentient being named Shadow sickened me, and I soon discovered that many others also were horrified by this so-called "training" session. (For further discussion of Millan's methods, please see Mark Derr's *New York Times* editorial "Pack of Lies.")

When I speak with dog trainers, I mention this video, and by and large most people agree that putting a noose around a dog's neck, yanking them off the ground, and suspending them in the air is unnecessarily cruel and abusive. They all say they would be really upset if this were done to their dog. So would I. However, recently, I was told by a few people that it was just fine to string up a dog who needed to be disciplined. I then asked them if they would do this to a child or another human being. They emphatically said, "No, of course not." Well, then, why allow it to be done to a dog? When considering how to treat dogs during training, it's also useful to ask if we would let someone do the same thing to ourselves. If not, why not?

This is what dog expert Mark Derr wrote to me about the stringing up of Shadow: "First, it looks to me like Millan provokes and prolongs the attacks in order to string the dog up in such a way that he puts pressure on the carotid artery. Second, when he pins it with his hand, he definitely seems to put pressure on the carotid artery as well. If these observations are true, it's no wonder the dog is subdued. Makes me wonder whether that knuckle pinch also is aimed at the carotid?" If you have the courage to watch the video (see the first endnote for page 104 on page 335), you'll see that Shadow wasn't "merely" lifted off the ground.

Indeed, Shadow was put in his place, and this degree of trauma likely will have a long-term effect, as does any abuse to which an individual is exposed, intentional (as in this case) or unintentional. We know that dogs and other animals suffer from long-term depression and PTSD after being traumatized, and training techniques that cause trauma shouldn't be sanctioned and should be strongly opposed (see "Do Wild Animals Suffer from PTSD and Other Psychological Disorders?," page 164).

I'm writing about Shadow because there simply has to be a limit to what is permissible when trying to get dogs to behave in acceptable ways. Stringing up dogs or other animals goes well beyond what I would accept, and if I saw someone doing this, I'd call the police immediately. I imagine most people would do the same. If one thinks a dog deserves this sort of treatment, then it would be useful to know why this is so and discuss how nonabusive techniques can be used instead of those that harm and intimidate. Many people who work with domestic and wild animals are using and continually developing training techniques based on positive reinforcement, and so too should everyone who works with our best friends. Training must factor in the capacity for any individual being to suffer and experience deep and enduring pain.

As Mark Derr notes, "Properly treating aggression, phobias, anxiety, and fears from the start can literally save time and money. Mr. Millan's quick fix might make for good television and might even produce lasting results in some cases. But it flies in the face of what professional animal behaviorists — either trained and certified veterinarians or ethologists — have learned about normal and abnormal behavior in dogs."

Quick-fix training techniques based on severe intimidation and various forms of psychological and physical abuse need to be removed from training protocols, and our objections to these methods need to be louder than mere whispers behind closed doors. Shadow's saga, his very sad story, forces us to think about who we are, who other animals are, and how we must treat them.

Dogs expect us to treat them with dignity and respect, and when they become challenging and try our patience, we must never, ever forget that they are sentient beings who thoroughly depend on our goodwill. It's a dirty double-cross to intentionally abuse them and commit them to a life of fear. It's a betrayal of their trust that we will always have their best interests in mind. It also demeans us.

The hearts of our companion animals, like our own hearts, are fragile, so we must be gentle with them. Let's openly and graciously thank them for who they are, for their unfiltered love, and embrace their lessons in passion, compassion, empathy, devotion, respect, spirituality, and love. Surely, we will never have any regrets by doing so, and much pure joy will come our way as we clear the path for deep and rich reciprocal relationships based on immutable trust with our companions and all other beings. Elliot Katz, founder of In Defense of Animals (www.idausa.org), suggests we drop the word "training" and start using the word "teaching." Training often becomes synonymous with "breaking." Training should not mean breaking their fragile hearts.

[ORIGINALLY POSTED ON APRIL 21, 2012]

PART 5

CONSCIOUSNESS, SENTIENCE, AND COGNITION

A Potpourri
of Current Research on
Flies, Fish,
and Other Animals

THIS IS AN INCREDIBLY EXCITING TIME to study the behavior of other animals. It seems like every day we're learning more and more about the fascinating lives of other animals — how smart and clever they are and how they're able to solve problems we never imagined they could. Here I consider a wide range of research on animals that shows clearly just how well-developed and amazing are their cognitive skills. A very few people continue to ignore what we really know about other animals, but they are in the vast minority. Here you can read about flies, bees, lizards, fish, a back-scratching dog, how climate change is influencing behavior, and why respected scientists are pondering the spiritual lives of animals.

However, before getting into this wonderful research on animal minds and consciousness, I start this part with an essay that tackles one of the main and enduring criticisms of such research and of my work in particular: anthropomorphism, or the attribution of human characteristics to non-human animals, objects, or events (such as when people talk about "nasty thunderstorms." The charge of anthropomorphism is often used to bash ideas that other animals are emotional beings. Skeptics claim that dogs, for example, are merely acting "as if" they're happy or sad, but they really aren't; they might be feeling something we don't know or feeling nothing at all. Skeptics propose, because we can't know with absolute certainty the thoughts of another being, we should take the stance that we can't know anything or even that consciousness in other animals doesn't exist. For *Psychology Today* and elsewhere, I have written extensively about the "problem" of "being anthropomorphic." For instance, see "Anthropomorphic Double-Talk" in my book *The Emotional Lives of Animals* (see Endnotes, page 335). In my opinion, there's no way to avoid anthropomorphism. Even those who eschew anthropomorphism must make their arguments using anthropomorphic terms, and they often do so in self-serving ways. If a scientist says an animal is "happy," no one questions it, but if the animal is described as sad or suffering, then charges of anthropomorphism are leveled. Scientists can accept and treat their own companion animals as if they feel love, affection, gratitude, and pain, and then deny these very emotions in the animals they use, and abuse, while conducting experiments in the lab.

Instead of being a "problem," it is possible that our ability to anthropomorphize is an adaptive skill, closely related to empathy, that helps us understand and relate to other animals. We might ask, when animals seem to respond independently to our own human versions of pain or happiness, are they "anthropomorphizing" us, that is, translating what they see in us into their own terms? How do they seem to know with such confidence how we feel? Following up on Charles Darwin's ideas about evolutionary continuity, we see that it's bad biology to rob other animals of their emotional lives, and this may include the ability to anthropomorphize. In the end, as I hope the first essay makes clear, anthropomorphism isn't really much of a problem at all. We simply need to be careful when making claims about what other animals are thinking and feeling. We need to make sure we don't go overboard and that we use solid science and an ever-growing database to confirm what seems to be true. As the other essays in this part clearly show, our "anthropomorphic instincts" are usually right on the mark when we theorize about what other animals are feeling. And finally, just because we can be wrong on occasion doesn't mean we're wrong all of the time. Good science is all about proposing theories based on evidence, gathering more evidence, and refining our theories accordingly. Anthropomorphism isn't really a problem, only bad science, so let's get over it.

Animal Consciousness
and Science Matter

IN 2007 I PUBLISHED A BOOK called *Animals Matter*, and at about the same time Erin Williams and Margo DeMello published a wonderful book called *Why Animals Matter*. And in 2012 another book called *Why Animals Matter* was published, this one by Oxford University's Marian Dawkins. Though all three books argue for the importance of animal welfare, Dawkins takes a very different approach. She encourages skepticism regarding animal consciousness and mistakenly claims that anthropomorphism is antiscience. I think of this as "Dawkins's Dangerous Idea."

Early in Dawkins's book, she specifically singles me out for criticism. On pages 21 and 22, I learned that "others, most notably Marc Bekoff, go in for full-blooded, genuine anthropomorphism." Dawkins goes on to write that my and other scientists' brand of anthropomorphism "may well be right," and then she misleadingly claims, "Bekoff is essentially saying that there are no limits to how we interpret animal behaviour." Nothing could be further from the truth. While I maintain we should consider all sorts of data, I've also written on many occasions that solid and noninvasive science are needed as well to assess their reliability.

Dawkins then goes on to cite something I wrote and still stand by: "To live with a dog is to know firsthand that animals have feelings. It's a no-brainer." Dawkins follows, "It began to look as though no further thought or investigation were going to be necessary. Even worse, this new wave of anthropomorphism threatened the very scientific basis of the study of animal behaviour itself, particularly that branch of it known as cognitive ethology." This is really overdramatic and plain wrong, as many researchers see the heuristic value of "being anthropomorphic" and then determining how correct or incorrect these sorts of explanations may be.

I was even more shocked to read this because I have never set up an "anthropomorphism versus science" dichotomy. While on occasion I can be critical of science, I also am proud to be a scientist and to do science.

Indeed, in 2000, following the publication of *The Smile of a Dolphin*, in which numerous distinguished scientists wrote essays about the emotional and conscious lives of the animals they studied, I published an essay in *BioScience* about what I called *biocentric anthropomorphism*. This followed up on Gordon Burghardt's notion of *critical anthropomorphism* and how we can use science to access the minds of other animals. Here is an excerpt from what I wrote:

> The way human beings describe and explain the behavior of other animals is limited by the language they use to talk about things in general. By engaging in anthropomorphism — using human terms to explain animals' emotions or feelings — humans make other animals' worlds accessible to themselves (Allen and Bekoff 1997, Bekoff and Allen 1997, Crist 1999). But this is not to say that other animals are happy or sad in the same ways in which humans (or even other conspecifics) are happy or sad. Of course, I cannot be absolutely certain that Jethro, my companion dog, is happy, sad, angry, upset, or in love, but these words serve to explain what he might be feeling. However, merely referring acontextually to the firing of different neurons or to the activity of different muscles in the absence of behavioral information and context is insufficiently informative. Using anthropomorphic language does not have to discount the animal's point of view. Anthropomorphism allows other animals' behavior and emotions to be accessible to us. *Thus, I maintain that we can be biocentrically anthropomorphic and do rigorous science.*

Dawkins also writes, "Rampant anthropomorphism threatens the very basis of ethology by substituting anecdotes, loose analogies, and an 'I just know that the animal is thinking so don't bother me with science' attitude to animal behaviour." I've argued elsewhere that what I call the "A" words, namely anthropomorphism and anecdote, play a large role in helping us to understand animal behavior and consciousness, but they are *not* substitutes for solid science.

So, what's science got to do with it? A lot. Frankly, I find Dawkins's misrepresentation of my and others' view to be off-putting, serving no purpose other than to set up sides on the important issues at hand. We may indeed disagree on some matters, but being anthropomorphic and paying attention to anecdotes is *not* to be against the need for good science.

Later in her book Dawkins notes, "Animal welfare needs new arguments.... [I]t needs the best scientific evidence available, not wishful thinking or anthropomorphism." This not-so-subtle implication that other researchers and I are antiscience is truly insulting.

Dawkins goes on to discuss different areas of animal consciousness, remaining skeptical throughout because the scientific evidence is "indirect" and that "there is no proof either way about animal consciousness and that it does not serve animals well to claim that there is." She goes on to write, "The mystery of consciousness remains. The explanatory gap is as wide as ever and all the wanting in the world will not take us across it."

I firmly disagree with this assertion, and I know I'm not alone. While the mystery of consciousness, nonhuman and human, remains, we have made great advances in reducing the explanatory gap. There is ample, solid, and direct scientific evidence that shows that many other animals are conscious beings (for instance, see "Crabs and Fish Feel Pain: Expanding the Circle-of-Sentience Club," page 156). We know enough right now to use this information for interpreting and explaining the behavior of a wide range of species and for developing and implementing strict guidelines for animal protection.

Charles Darwin's ideas about evolutionary continuity also strongly argue in favor of other animals being sentient and conscious beings. That said, it's important to stress that their sentience and consciousness does not have to be just like ours to make them members of the sentience-and-consciousness club. Dawkins seems to be taking more of a dualistic approach that, in my opinion, is rather weak not only because it questions continuity but also because it ignores much of what we already know about other animals. Along these lines it's important to note that the Lisbon Treaty, passed on December 1, 2009, recognizes animals as sentient beings, meaning "they can feel pain and suffer; learn from experience; make choices; feel joy, fear, or misery; and enjoy the company of others."

Dawkins claims that to make animal welfare more of interest to the masses we need to appeal to human self-interest and not rely on anthropomorphism or flimsy science. While there is something to the argument that we can achieve animal welfare without recognizing animal consciousness (the topic of her chapter 7), there is ample evidence that many other animals are conscious and care about what happens to them. It is also true that innumerable people come to care because of what science tells us about the intellectual capacities of animals.

So, do I recommend this book? Well, yes and no. Surely, it's essential for students and others to know more about existing data and alternative views that are based on solid science. When I put Dawkins's combative style aside, I can see her skepticism as her way of keeping the discussion going. But it shouldn't be at the expense of the professional reputations of myself and others (including renowned scientists Donald Griffin, Michel Cabanac, Jaak Panksepp, and Joseph LeDoux; however, she is a fan of Temple Grandin) by offering misleading views on our attitudes toward science, and surely not by ignoring solid research.

There's really not that much new that Dawkins hasn't written or spoken about elsewhere. This is mostly a more-strident effort to set up false and misleading divisions and offer the same old skepticism that surprisingly dismisses much solid scientific research. She claims, "[I]t is much, much better *for animals* if we remain skeptical and agnostic [about consciousness]....Militantly agnostic if necessary, because this keeps alive the possibility that a large number of species have some sort of conscious experiences....For all we know, many animals, not just the clever ones and not just the overtly emotional ones, also have conscious experiences." I disagree, and frankly I don't see how anyone who works closely with any of a wide array of animals could remain skeptical and agnostic about whether they are conscious. I really don't know anyone who does. I and many others see such a wealth of scientific data on this that it makes skepticism, and agnosticism, antiscience and harmful to animals.

I am not a science-basher, nor do I ridicule scientists for "pointing out how hard it is to study consciousness." I believe Professor Dawkins has done a disservice to the many researchers with whom she takes issue and whose hard work she easily discounts. One of my colleagues who read this piece thought I was being "too nice and forgiving" given Dawkins's rather harsh words about what she takes to be my views on the matters at hand. My colleague felt there was something "disturbingly unprofessional" about Dawkins's strident and dismissive prose. Be that as it may. On the one hand, Dawkins could also be considered antiscience, or more specifically "anti the science with which she disagrees," just as much as the research she questions (or ignores), all of which has been published in highly prestigious peer-reviewed professional journals and books. On the other hand, I thank her for making me think about these issues and for helping me articulate a firmer basis for rejecting much of what she writes.

While Dawkins feels that loose science and anthropomorphism will harm efforts to protect animals, I argue that her skepticism — the naysaying, doubt, and denial that flies in the face of available data — and the failure to heed what we know are more harmful. Additional noninvasive research, such as that done recently on empathy in rats (see "Empathic Rats and Ravishing Ravens," page 180) is what is sorely needed. Much research can be enriching to the animals who are studied, and it does not have to be nor should it be harmful. We also need to factor in what we know about free-ranging animals who are able to perform the full array of species-typical behavior patterns. Although we can always welcome more data, we know enough now about a wide array of animals to use this information to work hard to protect them.

So, why do animals matter? Animals matter because they exist, not because of what they can do for us, although they surely do a lot. By paying attention to what we know about their fascinating lives and who (not what) they are, we can and must all work together, in harmony, to make their lives better. As I travel all over the world, I see that we are making much progress because so many people really do care about the well-being of other animals. We can rewild our hearts by respecting who other animals are and by working on their behalf. And we can rest assured that solid science firmly supports our efforts to offer more protection to the billions of animals who are abused in myriad ways.

[ORIGINALLY POSTED ON MAY 7, 2012]

Scientists Finally Conclude
Nonhuman Animals Are Conscious Beings

EVERY NOW AND AGAIN I receive an email message I ignore after reading the subject line. I know I'm not alone in following this rule of thumb, but today I broke down and opened a message whose subject line read: "Scientists Declare: Nonhuman Animals Are Conscious." I honestly thought it was a joke, likely from one of my favorite newspapers, *The Onion* (www.theonion.com). However, it wasn't.

The email was about a story published by my colleague Michael Mountain about a recent meeting held in Cambridge, England, at which, he wrote, "Science leaders have reached a critical consensus: Humans are not the only conscious beings; other animals, specifically mammals and birds, are indeed conscious, too." At this gathering, called the Francis Crick Memorial Conference (http://fcmconference.org), a number of scientists presented evidence that led to this self-obvious conclusion. It's difficult to believe that those who have shared their homes with companion animals didn't already know this. Of course, many renowned and award-winning field researchers reached the same conclusion years ago.

It's interesting to note that of the fifteen notables who spoke at this conference, only one has actually done studies of wild animals. It would have been nice to hear from researchers who have conducted long-term studies of wild animals, including great apes, other nonhuman primates, social carnivores, cetaceans, rodents, and birds, for example, to add to the database. Be that as it may, I applaud their not-so-surprising conclusion, and now I hope it will be used to protect animals from being treated abusively and inhumanely.

Some might say we didn't *really* know that other animals were conscious before, but this is an incredibly naive view given what we already know about the neurobiology, cognition, and emotional lives of other animals. *Indeed, it was appeals to these very data that led to the conclusions of this group of scientists.* Did we really need a group of internationally recognized scientists to tell us that the data are really okay? Yes and no.

I agree with Michael Mountain that, "It's a really important statement that will be used as evidence by those who are pushing for scientists to develop a more humane relationship with animals. It's harder, for example, to justify experiments on nonhumans when you know that they are conscious beings and not just biological machines. Some of the conclusions reached in this declaration are the product of scientists who, to this day, still conduct experiments on animals in captivity, including dolphins, who are among the most intelligent species on Earth. Their own declaration will now be used as evidence that it's time to stop using these animals in captivity and start finding new ways of making a living."

The scientists went so far as to write up what's called "The Cambridge Declaration on Consciousness." This declares that this prominent group of scientists agrees that: "Convergent evidence indicates that nonhuman animals have the neuroanatomical, neurochemical, and neurophysiological substrates of conscious states along with the capacity to exhibit intentional behaviors. Consequently, the weight of evidence indicates that humans are not unique in possessing the neurological substrates that generate consciousness. Non-human animals, including all mammals and birds, and many other creatures, including octopuses, also possess these neurological substrates."

It's fair to ask what these scientists and others are going to do now that they agree that consciousness is widespread in the animal kingdom. We know, for example, that mice, rats, and chickens display empathy (see "Empathic Rats and Ravishing Ravens," page 180), and the scientists could also have included fish, for whom the evidence supporting sentience and consciousness is also compelling (see "Crabs and Fish Feel Pain: Expanding the Circle-of-Sentience Club," page 156). Will this knowledge finally become factored into the Federal Animal Welfare Act in the United States?

I'm frankly astounded that these data and many other findings about animal cognition and animal emotions have been ignored by those who decide on regulations about the use and abuse of other animals. However, the Treaty of Lisbon, passed by member states of the European Union on December 1, 2009, recognizes that, "In formulating and implementing the Union's agriculture, fisheries, transport, internal market, research and technological development and space policies, the Union and the Member States shall, since animals are sentient beings, pay full regard to the welfare requirements of animals, while respecting the legislative or administrative provisions and customs of the Member States relating in particular to religious rites, cultural traditions and regional heritage."

Let's applaud the Cambridge Declaration on Consciousness and the Treaty of Lisbon and work hard to get animals the protection they deserve from invasive research and other forms of abuse, in many cases horrifically inhumane.

Also, perhaps what I call "Dawkins's Dangerous Idea" will now finally be shelved given the conclusions of the Cambridge gathering (see "Animal Consciousness and Science Matter," page 111). I frankly don't see how anyone can remain "skeptical" or "agnostic" about animal consciousness anymore. Now, at last, the prestigious Cambridge group shows that such a position is indeed "antiscience." Bravo for them! So, let's all work together to use this information to stop the abuse of millions upon millions of conscious animals in the name of science, education, food, amusement and entertainment, and clothing. We really owe it to them to use what we know on their behalf and to factor compassion and empathy into our treatment of these amazing beings.

[ORIGINALLY POSTED ON AUGUST 10, 2012]

Do Animals Know Who They Are?

DID DAVID GRAYBEARD, the chimpanzee who was first observed to use a tool by Jane Goodall, have any idea of who he was? Do elephants, dolphins, cats, magpies, mice, salmon, ants, or bees know who they are? Was Jethro, my late companion dog, a self-conscious being? Do any of these animals have a sense of self? What do these animals make of themselves when they look in a mirror, see their reflection in water, hear their own or another's song or howl, or smell themselves and others? Is it possible that self-awareness — "Wow, that's me!" — is a uniquely human trait?

Because there's much interest and much exciting work to be done concerning what animals know about themselves, it's worth reflecting on what we do and don't know about animal selves. There are academic and practical reasons to do so.

In his book, *The Descent of Man and Selection in Relation to Sex*, Charles Darwin pondered what animals might know about themselves. He wrote: "It may be freely admitted that no animal is self-conscious, if by this term it is implied that he reflects on such points, as whence he comes or whither he will go, or what is life and death, and so forth."

Darwin also championed the notion of evolutionary continuity and believed that animals had some sense of self. In the same book, he wrote, "Nevertheless, the difference in mind between man and the higher animals, great as it is, certainly is one of degree and not of kind." Thus, there are shades of gray and not black-and-white differences between humans and other animals in cognitive abilities. So, while animals might not ponder life and death the way humans do, they still may have some sense of self.

After decades of studying animals ranging from coyotes, gray wolves, domestic dogs, and Adelie penguins and other birds, I've come to the conclusion that not only are some animals self-aware but that there are degrees of self-awareness. Combined with studies by my colleagues, it's wholly plausible to suggest that many animals have a sense of "mine-ness" or "body-ness." So, for example, when an experimental treatment, an object, or another individual affects an individual, he or she experiences that "something is happening to this body." Many primates relax when being groomed and individuals of many species actively seek pleasure and avoid pain. There's no need to associate "this body" with "my body" or with "me" (or "I"). Many animals also know the placement in space of parts of their body as they run, jump, perform acrobatics, or move as a coordinated hunting unit or flock without running into one another. They know their body isn't someone else's body.

In my book *Minding Animals: Awareness, Emotions, and Heart* and elsewhere, I argued that a sense of body-ness is necessary and sufficient for most animals to engage in social activities that are needed in the social milieus in which they live. But while a sense of body-ness is necessary for humans to get along in many of the situations they encounter, it's often not sufficient for them to function as they need to. A human typically knows who he or she is, say by name, and knows that "this body" is "Marc's," or if I'm being self-reflective, "Marc." There's a sense of "I-ness" that's an extension of "body-ness" or "mine-ness."

So, my take on animal selves means that David Graybeard and Jethro knew they weren't one of their buddies. Many animals know such facts as "this is my tail," "this is my territory," "this is my bone or my piece of elk," "this is my mate," and "this is my urine." Their sense of "mine-ness" or "body-ness" is their sense of "self."

How do animals differentiate themselves from others? Many studies of self-awareness have used mirrors to assess how visual cues are used. They've been effective for captive primates, dolphins, and elephants. Although mirror-like visual images are absent in most field situations, it's possible that individuals learn something about themselves from their reflections in water. But we also need to know more about the role of senses other than vision in studies of self-awareness because some animals, for example rodents, who can distinguish among individuals don't seem to respond to visual images. Odors and sounds are very important in the worlds of many animals. Many mammals differentiate between their own and others' urine and glandular secretions, and many birds know their own and others' songs. Moving Jethro's "yellow snow" from place to place allowed me to learn that Jethro made fine discriminations between his own and others' urine (see "Hidden Tales of Yellow Snow: What a Dog's Nose Knows — Making Sense of Scents," page 88). Perhaps a sense of self relies on a composite signal that results from integrating information from different senses.

While there are "academic" questions about animal self-awareness, there also are some very important practical reasons to learn about animal selves. Achieving reliable answers to questions about animal selves is very important because they're often used to defend the sorts of treatment to which individuals can be ethically subjected. However, even if an animal doesn't know "who" she is, this doesn't mean she can't feel that something painful is happening to her body. Self-awareness may not be a reliable test for an objective assessment of well-being.

So, do any animals, when looking at themselves, hearing themselves, or smelling themselves, exclaim, "Wow, that's me"? Do they have a sense of "I-ness"? We really don't know, especially for wild animals. It's time to get out of the armchair and into the field. Speculation doesn't substitute for careful studies of behavior.

Some people don't want to acknowledge the possibility of self-awareness in animals because, if they did, the borders between humans and other animals would become blurred, and their narrow, hierarchical, anthropocentric view of the world would be toppled. But Darwin's ideas about continuity, along with empirical data and common sense, caution against the unyielding claim that humans and perhaps a few other animals, such as other great apes and cetaceans, are the only species in which some sense of self has evolved.

[ORIGINALLY POSTED ON JULY 6, 2009]

Do Dogs Really Feel Pain and Are They Really Conscious?

THE ANSWERS TO THE QUESTIONS "Do dogs *really* feel pain and are they *really* conscious?" — yes and yes — are so obvious it seems ridiculous even to ask them given what we know about animal cognition and sentience. Nonetheless, they do arise, and not only in philosophical circles where wide-ranging discussions often take place but also among a very few skeptical researchers. New York University philosopher Dale Jamieson and I wrote about the idea of nonconscious pain twenty years ago and refuted Peter Carruthers's assumption that "in the case of brutes: since their pains are nonconscious (as are all their mental states), they ought not to be allowed to get in the way of any morally-serious objective." Just a few weeks ago I was told that these sorts of discussions are still going on.

Empirical researchers also get into the fray. Following up on what I call "Dawkins's Dangerous Idea" (see "Animal Consciousness and Science Matter," page 111), Marian Dawkins wrote, "from a scientific view, we understand so little about animal consciousness (and indeed our own consciousness) that to make the claim that we do understand it, and that we now know which animals experience emotions, may not be the best way to make the case for animal welfare." Indeed, it's a small leap to claim that we also should question whether human animals experience emotions.

That dogs and other animals *really* do feel pain and *really* are conscious beings is assumed in veterinary medicine; in human-oriented biomedical research; in the establishment of guidelines for such research; in research on animal cognition, emotions, and moral sentiments; and in animal training. It's not a matter of *if* these traits have evolved and are shared by other animals, but *why*.

Two quotations from a 2012 essay by Jeff Warren about personhood in whales support what I just wrote above and what the majority of researchers believe based on available empirical evidence:

Despite not being able to locate the seat of consciousness in the animal brain — something true for humans as well — most scientists no longer ask whether animals have inner experiences. Some degree of sentience is considered self-evident. For neuroscientist Jaak Panksepp, one of the world's leading experts on the neural origins of mind and emotion, "the denial of consciousness in animals is as improbable as the pre-scientific anthropocentric view that the sun revolves around the Earth."

In a sense the human-to-animal mind question may simply be an exaggerated version of the human-to-human mind question: We can never entirely know another person's experience — all the more so if that person was raised in a different culture — but there are vast areas of overlap that can, with science and empathy and imagination, be expanded.

At a few recent meetings after I spoke about animal consciousness, self-awareness, and emotions, we had wide-ranging discussions about whether animals know who they are and if their level of self-awareness is the same as ours. I've discussed these topics elsewhere (see "Do Animals Know Who They Are?," page 119), and I suggested that it really doesn't matter if their consciousness is like ours. While other animals may or may not know who they are and may or may not have a sense of what I call "I-ness," they do have a sense of "body-ness" and "mine-ness." Much more research on the question of "I-ness" is needed because we really don't know much, especially for wild animals.

At many gatherings, discussions of animal pain and animal emotions often follow talk about animal consciousness. When I ask if people believe that dogs, for example, feel pain, as far as I can see every hand goes up. But then someone often asks, "Do they know they are in pain?"

Once again, I'm happy to have my philosopher colleagues debate the notion of nonconscious pain (and other experiences) and whether an animal *knows* that she or he is in pain, but from a practical point of view that underlies so much of what we do to make sure animals don't suffer, we all assume that they feel pain. So, for example, when my companion dog Jethro limped over to me after tripping on a rock, squealing and holding his left front leg in the air, and presenting himself to me to take care of him, it really didn't matter to what degree he was self-aware of these actions. He felt pain, and I'd venture to say he knew it was his pain, and when I took him to the veterinarian, she confirmed that he had a badly torn muscle and was indeed in pain. Some painkillers and rest really did the trick, the same as they would for a human animal.

Whether or not the experience of pain and consciousness in nonhuman animals are just like ours isn't the important issue. Speciesists like to draw distinctions to justify human exceptionalism (see "Individual Animals Count: Speciesism Doesn't Work," page 35), but these distract from all that we as animals share.

In Bruce Friedrich's review of the 2012 documentary *Speciesism: The Movie* by Mark Devries, Friedrich offers two powerful quotations that are worth noting. They come from women who have had vastly different experiences with other animals. In the first, renowned primatologist and conservationist Jane Goodall notes, "Farm animals feel pleasure and sadness, excitement and resentment, depression, fear, and pain. They are far more aware and intelligent than we ever imagined.... [T]hey are individuals in their own right."

The second quotation comes from Temple Grandin's book *Animals in Translation.* Grandin, who works to improve animal welfare at slaughterhouses, writes, "When it comes to the basics of life... [other] animals feel the same way we do." Friedrich, who works for Farm Sanctuary (www.farmsanctuary.org), notes that Grandin "goes on to explain that both humans and other animals share the exact same core emotions ('rage, prey chase drive, fear, and curiosity/interest/anticipation') and the same 'four basic social emotions: sexual attraction and lust, separation distress, social attachment, and the happy emotions of play and roughhousing.'" While Dr. Grandin and I do have our differences (see "My Beef with Temple Grandin: Seemingly Humane Isn't Enough," page 248), I'm so pleased to see these words from her. Of course, she does what she does because of what we know from solid scientific research about animal pain, consciousness, and emotions.

Continued discussions about the degree to which nonhuman animals are conscious about what they experience may be interesting to pursue in the ivory tower, but we know enough right now to claim they do indeed really feel pain and really are conscious and really do experience a wide range of emotions. From a practical point of view, these questions are central to some of my own interests, including ways to rewild our hearts and to stop the process of dehumanization. It's also bad biology. It goes against the basic tenets of Darwinian ideas about evolutionary continuity to rob animals of these traits and to claim human exceptionalism. As I wrote above, it's not a matter of *if* these traits have evolved and are shared by other animals, but *why*.

Clearly, there's a lot at stake for other animals and *we should never let them suffer because of our failure to appreciate who they are based on solid scientific evidence*. It's really a no-brainer.

[ORIGINALLY POSTED ON JUNE 21, 2012]

Age Before Beauty:
Older Elephant Matriarchs Know What's Best

WHEN I WAS FORTUNATE ENOUGH to spend some time in the field in northern Kenya with elephant expert Iain Douglas-Hamilton, founder of Save the Elephants (www.savetheelephants.org), I noticed that individuals in one herd of elephants seemed to be less socially bonded with one another. They were walking with their heads and trunks down and seemed to be lost, aimlessly wandering here and there. I asked Iain why this was happening, and he explained that the matriarch of the group, the oldest female and most important individual, had recently died. Other elephants just down the road in an intact herd with the matriarch present were walking around, heads and trunks up, and playing. They also were clearly closely bonded with one another.

It's long been known that matriarchs are the "social glue" who hold elephant groups together. They have a wealth of knowledge about social relationships and travel routes, for example. Now we've just learned that matriarchs over sixty years of age assess threats from lions more accurately than do younger matriarchs. In response to lion roars that were broadcasted over a loudspeaker, groups with matriarchs over sixty more easily determined if a lion's roar was from a male or female and also organized themselves more quickly as a response to the roar. Age trumps beauty for the survival of elephants.

Researchers know that the death of a matriarch can be devastating to a group. According to elephant expert Karen McComb, "If you remove these older individuals, you're going to have a much bigger impact than you realize because they're repositories of ecological knowledge and also of social knowledge....Poachers, targeting the big old elephants, pose a particular menace to the species." She also noted, according to a *New York Times* story, that "matriarchs remain group leaders until they die, seemingly never losing their cognitive abilities....Most live well into their sixties, and suffer no hearing loss, the key ability to identify lion roars."

[ORIGINALLY POSTED ON APRIL 11, 2011]

What Do We Learn
from a Tool-Making Genius Bonobo
and Copy-Cat Orcas?

EARLIER TODAY I WROTE ABOUT NATASHA, the valedictorian of captive chimpanzees, who participated in a study of their cognitive abilities. The researchers used the word "genius" to refer to Natasha, but it's pretty rare to see this word used to describe nonhuman animals. Just this evening I came across the report of another study of an amazing great ape, in this case a bonobo named Kanzi, who was studied for many years by Dr. Sue Savage-Rumbaugh and her colleagues and who is famous for his linguistic abilities, including making up words.

An essay in *New Scientist* titled "Bonobo Genius Makes Stone Tools Like Early Humans Did" caught my eye not only because I had the pleasure of meeting Kanzi a few years ago and because of his celebrity status but also because he is called a genius. Kanzi and another bonobo named Pan-Banisha made and used stone tools, but Kanzi did it better. The abstract of the original research paper reads as follows:

Using direct percussion, [the] language-competent bonobo-chimpanzees Kanzi and Pan-Banisha produced a significantly wider variety of flint tool types than hitherto reported, and used them task-specifically to break wooden logs or to dig underground for food retrieval. For log breaking, small flakes were rotated drill-like or used as scrapers, whereas thick cortical flakes were used as axes or wedges, leaving consistent wear patterns along the glued slits, the weakest areas of the log. For digging underground, a variety of modified stone tools, as well as unmodified flint nodules, were used as shovels. Such tool production and utilization competencies reported here in *Pan* indicate that present-day *Pan* exhibits *Homo*-like technological competencies.

Kanzi's behavior closely reflects that of early humans of the genus *Homo*. But what does the behavior of Kanzi and other captive, pampered, and highly trained bonobos who had a lot of interactions with humans tell us about the behavior of their wild relatives? Researchers agree that it's unclear if bonobos would make these sorts of tools on their own, but it's surely worth heading out into the field to see if they do. And of course, whether they do or don't, it doesn't take anything away from Kanzi's so-called genius. The article about Kanzi also mentions Irene Pepperberg's research on Alex the parrot "who could purportedly [*sic*] count to six" and Betty, a smart New Caledonian crow, who crafted a hook out of wire and used it as a tool.

Another study reported in another issue of *New Scientist* also is concerned with the cognitive abilities of captive animals, in this case killer whales, also called orcas. This essay, titled "Cultured Killer Whales Learn by Copying," deals with imitation by three captive orcas living in an aquarium in Antibes, France, who also had a lot of contact with humans. In a nutshell, these captive killer whales learned to imitate an action that another whale was performing by learning the meaning of the command "do that."

Wild killer whales might also display imitation. It's known that orcas show variations in behavior depending on where they live. Thus, killer whales living in Patagonia learn to climb onto beaches to catch sea lions, whereas their relatives living around the Antarctic Peninsula create waves to knock seals off of ice floes. Whales living around Norway herd herring into densely-packed balls and then slap the balls with their tails to stun the fish. These variations in predatory behavior might be culturally learned behaviors that are shared by discrete populations of killer whales, and imitation may be important in their spread through a local group of animals.

However, one very difficult question to answer is, what can we learn about wild animals from studies of captive animals? It's worth pondering because so much research on animal cognition is performed on captive animals. These three studies and many others raise questions about the importance and relevance of studies of captive animals. Surely we can learn quite a lot about behavior from studying captive animals, but I want to stress that this alone does not justify keeping them in captivity nor breeding more animals to take their place as they age or are no longer useful for various sorts of studies. Indeed, one can question the use and reuse of the same individuals in various studies. A respected colleague told me that he believes that some individuals don't do what they really are able to do because they're simply bored.

It's possible that captive studies exaggerate the cognitive skills of animals because of intensive training and contact with humans, but it's also possible that studies of captive animals depress their behavior — individuals aren't able to express their full behavioral repertoire because they're kept in unnatural groups living in deprived social and/or nonsocial environments. There might also be within-species individual variations in behavior that need to be taken into account. Kanzi and Natasha show this to be the case, as do many studies of a wide variety of animals.

I raise the question about the relevance of captive studies because in some research programs individuals are asked to perform unnatural acts in which humans partake, and the animals don't do what they need to do to support the claim that they have certain cognitive skills. For example, this is true of studies asking if animals have a theory of mind, which, to quote the definition on Wikipedia, is "the ability to attribute mental states — beliefs, intents, desires, pretending, knowledge, etc. — to oneself and others and to understand that others have beliefs, desires, and intentions that are different from one's own."

Researchers disagree, and the results on captive animals are equivocal. Nonetheless, those working with Kanzi argue that he does indeed have a theory of mind. My own research on social play behavior in dogs, coyotes, and wolves, including field work on coyotes, has also led me to conclude that they have a theory of mind. This is because of their ability to negotiate and coordinate their behavior in highly variable circumstances that would be very difficult or impossible to do without their being able to attribute mental states to themselves and to others. Much more research has to be done, and slowly but surely researchers are asking these questions for wild animals.

It's fair to ask what Kanzi, Alex, Betty, and other animals tell us about the behavior of their wild relatives. Right now we need to be very cautious about generalizations until the necessary research is conducted. Nonetheless, it's very clear that individuals representing diverse species are capable of learning rather sophisticated cognitive skills — they're really smart — and of course what we know about their intelligence and emotional lives means we must treat them with care and make sure that they are not abused in the name of research as we try to learn more about them.

Along these lines, the long overdue Cambridge Declaration on Consciousness (see "Scientists Finally Conclude Nonhuman Animals Are Conscious Beings," page 116) shows that we need to expand our circle of concern, compassion, and empathy for the nonhuman beings with whom we interact in myriad ways. We must use what we know to act on their behalf.

[ORIGINALLY POSTED ON AUGUST 29, 2012]

Spider Builds Complex Lifelike Replica
Decoys Outside Web

SPIDERS ARE AMAZING ANIMALS. Recently I wrote about a rare and endangered spider called the Braken Bat Cave meshweaver whose presence stopped the construction of a highway underpass project in San Antonio, Texas. In this essay I noted that researchers have described play in spiders and how it is influenced by the personality of the individual and about spiders who belong to the genus of jumping spiders called *Portia* who change their behavior depending on the behavior of their prey. These spiders show complex predatory strategies that involve problem solving and future planning despite having a small brain.

Now we've learned there is a spider who is a member of the genus *Cyclosa* (and perhaps even a new species) living in the Peruvian Amazon who builds complex lifelike decoys of itself, apparently to confuse or to distract potential predators. While trekking through the Amazon Basin, scientist and educator Phil Torres spotted this spider, according to one report, "perched above an intricate, lifelike replica of itself constructed from leaves, dead bug parts, and other scraps.... The spiders arrange debris among specialized silk strands called stabilimenta in a symmetrical form that makes it look almost like a larger spider hanging in the web."

It turns out that some members of this genus who build deceptive little balls in their web, which look like tasty egg sacs, have a higher survival rate than other spiders who don't against predators such as paper wasps because the wasps wind up attacking the false egg sacs. However, no one has ever observed debris that includes legs and a torso, and we still don't know if this perhaps new species of *Cyclosa* benefits from having evolved such an artistic talent. It's difficult to imagine there aren't any survival benefits.

People also wonder if this spider has to have some degree of self-awareness to be able to create an image of itself. We don't know yet, but let's keep the door open and hope that scientists can come up with tests similar to those that are used on other animals to study self-awareness.

[ORIGINALLY POSTED ON DECEMBER 20, 2012]

Flies on Booze and Apes on Apps

JUST WHEN YOU THINK YOU'VE HEARD IT ALL, we know now that flies will self-medicate by drinking alcohol to kill a parasitic wasp who lays its eggs in their brood. This fascinating behavior is not known to be widespread in insects. A PBS story about this phenomenon reports, "A new study published last week in the journal *Current Biology* takes the insect's attraction to alcohol a step farther, showing that fruit flies infected by parasitic wasps are more likely to seek out higher concentrations of alcohol to kill off these parasites. This study adds to a growing body of literature showing that animals ranging from caterpillars to chimpanzees will seek out toxic plants and other materials in their environment to fight infections." And, infected larvae who drank the booze were more likely to survive than nondrinkers. What this all means for humans remains unclear, but I and many others find that alcohol in moderation seems to ward off all sorts of maladies.

Apes and apps are also in the news. While many people, including myself, are against keeping apes and other animals in captivity, many animals still remain behind bars in cages of various sizes. Now, in order to make their lives better by making them more enriched, orangutans are being trained to use iPads to paint and to video chat with other orangutans. And, according to some people, it's working. Zookeepers see the benefits of enrichment, and once a number of zoos have their orangutans acclimated to using the iPads, according to one news story, "they will be able to use Skype or the iPad's FaceTime feature to communicate remotely with orangutans at other zoos during 'play dates,' according to Orangutan Outreach founder Richard Zimmerman." We know how smart orangutans are, and Mr. Zimmerman, the story continues, "recently visited Jahe, an orangutan at the Memphis Zoo who used to live at the Toronto Zoo.... When Zimmerman showed Jahe a photo on his iPhone of some of her relatives still living in Toronto, she appeared to recognize them."

No one is saying that enriching the lives of captive animals is a reason to keep them in captivity. However, as long as these amazing beings are kept behind bars, it is our obligation to provide them with the very best life possible until they no longer are forced to reside in these places. Thus, all sorts of enrichment needs to be used, and by doing this we'll surely discover more about just how smart they are. This information can be added to the wealth of data we already have that show that our closest relatives and many other diverse animals are far smarter than we ever gave them credit for.

[ORIGINALLY POSTED ON MARCH 2, 2012]

Bold Fish and Brilliant Lizards

FISH ARE AMAZING BEINGS, and as we learn more about them, we see that they're hardly just streams of protein to serve as food for nonhuman and human animals. We know they're conscious and sentient (see "Crabs and Fish Feel Pain: Expanding the Circle-of-Sentience Club," page 156), and they even punish others who steal food. Now, we've just learned that they, like other animals, show changes in behavior due to rising carbon dioxide concentrations (or climate change). It turns out that ocean acidification can reverse the response of nerve cells so that the scary and aversive scent of predators suddenly becomes alluring, and fish become increasingly bold. What this behavioral change means — approaching rather than avoiding dangerous predators in the real world — awaits further study, but the changes in behavior are real, and there surely can be negative consequences for entering into perilous situations.

Lizards are also affected by climate change. They become super-intelligent when they develop in warmer temperatures because of changes in how the brain develops. Here are a few snippets from a report on this fascinating discovery for tiny lizards known as three-lined skinks:

When the skinks were a few weeks old and smaller than your pinkie finger, [researcher Joshua] Amiel gave them a simple learning test. Each lizard was placed in a 24°C cage with two hiding places — overturned plastic flower-pot trays with entry holes cut in the sides. But one was a decoy, its opening blocked with Plexiglas. Clever lizards, after bumping the window a few times, should give up on the fake hiding place and go to only the good one, Amiel reasoned.

He tested each lizard 16 times over 4 days, touching its tail with a paintbrush to spook it into hiding. Amiel logged an "error" every time a lizard bumped its nose on the Plexiglas window and logged a successful "escape" if it found the real hiding place in

30 seconds. Lizards from warm nests and cool nests started out making a "relatively equal" number of errors, Amiel says. But the warm-incubated lizards improved, making on average one or two more escapes during the second 2 days than they had during the first 2 days. Cool-incubated lizards showed no such gains.

Yes, despite the skinks' natural preference for colder temperatures, heat actually unlocks learning centers of their brain that they never knew they had. And this cognitive advantage would likely prove successful in nature as well — after all, this sort of problem solving could prove extremely useful when cornered by predators, a situation that would end with the cooler, dumber skinks being eaten.

There can be no doubt that many different animals will show changes in behavior as a result of climate change, and detailed comparative studies are needed to learn more about these phenomena and what they mean for the future of a given species.

[ORIGINALLY POSTED ON FEBRUARY 23, 2012,
as "Bold Fish, Brilliant Lizards, and Heartbeat Detecting Snakes"]

Tool Use by a Dingo and a Dog

IT'S WELL KNOWN THAT CHIMPANZEES, birds, and many other "smart" animals make and use tools. What we currently know about this behavior has recently been reviewed in a wonderful book by Robert Shumaker and his colleagues, *Animal Tool Behavior* (2011), and the examples they show from a wide range of animals will surely surprise you. Now, we can add another animal to the long list of tool makers and users.

Bradley Smith of the University of South Australia and his colleagues working at Melbourne's Dingo Discovery and Research Centre have just published a paper showing tool use by Sterling, an eighteen-month-old male dingo. The video included with the AnimalWise report (see Endnotes, page 338) is well worth watching.

As described in their 2011 paper, "After several unsuccessful attempts at jumping for the envelope, Sterling 'solved' the task by first moving and then jumping up onto a trestle table,...which allowed him to gain the additional height necessary to reach the food item. To move the table, Sterling clamped his mouth onto the strut between the legs of the table. He then walked backwards, dragging the table approximately 2 m, until it appeared that either his back leg or tail touched the enclosure mesh. He then jumped onto the table, but as he was still at least a body-length away from the envelope, he had to span the gap between the table and the enclosure mesh by propping his front paws onto the mesh, gradually moving them towards the envelope. At full stretch, he reached the envelope on his second attempt."

Shumaker and his colleagues have a few stories about tool use by dogs, including a springer spaniel who used a Frisbee to carry a hockey puck. The dingo study reminded me of a story I was told in 2002 about a dog named Grendel who fashioned a marrow bone as a back scratcher. Grendel's human friend, Lenny Frieling, told me the following story.

It would have been about 1973 that Grendel made her first tool. Because of her short legs and long torso, she could not reach the

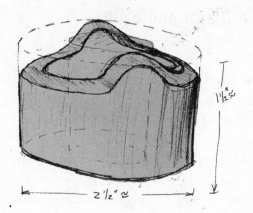

GRENDEL'S BACK
SCRATCHER

center of her back to scratch. One day we gave her a bone which was likely sawn from a large leg bone, perhaps lamb, because it was quite hard. It was cylindrical, with parallel flat sides. About a week (at most) after we gave her the bone, we noticed that she had chewed it so that one side was still flat, and the other side had two raised ridges (shaped like a sine wave going around the outer rim of the bone). She would place the bone, flat side down, on the floor, and roll over onto the two raised ridges using the protrusions to scratch the center of her back. I was convinced that she had made a tool, but in my mind I thought that behavior had to be repeated to be scientifically significant. She had that first bone, as I recall it, for quite a while, maybe a year. It disappeared. We gave her another bone, and within days, or a week, she had carved the second bone into a very similar shape and used it for the same purpose. She had repeated the making of the tool.

I find these observations to be fascinating, and as time goes on I'm sure we will continually add many animals to the already long list of tool makers and users.

[ORIGINALLY POSTED ON DECEMBER 8, 2011]

Chimpanzees in the Crossfire:
Are They Cleverer Than Us?

THERE'S MUCH CONTINUED DEBATE about how clever we are and how clever other animals are. This was among the wide variety of topics discussed at a 2011 meeting I attended about the similarities and differences between us and other animals, mainly the great apes. It was hosted by the Arcus Foundation and called "Humans and Other Apes: Rethinking the Species Interface." While we certainly are exceptional in many arenas, so too are other animals, so the question of who's cleverer loses a good deal of force when we try to compare one species to another.

We shouldn't be asking who's cleverer than whom, but rather try to understand what individuals of different species need to do to be card-carrying members of their species. This information will help us learn more about who we are and who "they" are. And we shouldn't be the standard against which other species are compared. What usually happens is that when we outperform other animals on some task, we claim we are cleverer or smarter than them, but if they outperform us, we rarely claim that they are smarter. Then, the conclusion that we're smarter often becomes a way to say we're more important or more valuable, which leads us down the road to animal abuse.

A newspaper article reporting on comparisons in performance between five-year-old chimpanzees and adult humans in a test of mental agility and memory asks, "Are chimps cleverer than us?" It turns out the chimpanzees won. So what does that mean? The author, Michael Hanlon, asks, "Are chimps really brighter than us, even in this sort of memory test? And if so, what does this mean for the way that we treat them? After all, how could it be right to lock up creatures more intelligent than ourselves in zoos or laboratories?" He goes to write, "In fact, the more science discovers about the animal mind, the less comfortable, philosophically, the findings become. And this has led to a small but growing movement that says we have to rethink our relationship with the animal world." This was precisely some of what was covered in the Arcus Foundation meeting.

Mr. Hanlon covers many of the important questions and concerns that center on comparative measures of intelligence and animal ethics. He asks, "So what does this mean? Should the fact that we now know that some animals have hitherto-unsuspected mental skills change our attitude to them? ... If we accept that other animals are far more sophisticated, intelligent, and sentient creatures than we thought, it would seem to be illogical not to grant them some rights, too." And perhaps in the future after this is accomplished, all other animals will also be granted rights. This is a huge and complex project on which the lawyer Steven Wise has been tirelessly working for decades. For instance, see his books *Drawing the Line: Science and the Case for Animal Rights* and *Rattling the Cage*.

Finally Mr. Hanlon notes, "What the Japanese research does prove is that once again, a new and hitherto unsuspected ability has been unearthed in animals. And as science uncovers more and more about the animal mind, it seems as though the voices of those clamouring for a change in the way we treat these creatures will become louder and more plausible."

I couldn't agree more. The scientific literature concerning the cognitive skills and emotional lives of a wide variety of nonhuman animals is growing almost daily, and right now we know enough to change the ways in which we treat other animals. We don't have to make up stories about who they are — intelligent and emotional beings — and what they want and need from us when held in captivity and living in the wild — to be treated with respect and dignity and to be able to live safely and in peace. They want to be treated better or left alone. That's not really asking too much, is it? We really do decide who lives and who dies and why, and we must be very careful not to abuse this power. Power does not give us license to do whatever we want because we can.

[ORIGINALLY POSTED ON AUGUST 19, 2011]

Apes Say "No" with a Head Shake, Animals Are Lefties and Righties, and Getting Out in Nature Is Good. Duh!

WE OFTEN THINK WE'RE ALONE in the cognitive and emotional arena, but as data accumulate we learn how wrong we can be. Recently, bonobos, also known as a pygmy chimpanzees, were filmed saying "no" by shaking their heads. These preventive head shakes were used in a number of situations in which an individual wanted to prevent another bonobo from doing something they didn't want them to do. Perhaps they are important in negotiating social conflict. Further research is needed to see if bonobo "no" head shaking is a precursor of human "no" head shaking.

Another very interesting finding is that animals show a preference for using one "hand" rather than the other, even individuals of the same species. This is called lateralization. Some examples from a *New Scientist* article include:

> Dogs: See if Fido wags his tail to his left or right. If he's like most dogs, furious wagging to the right means he is relaxed and ready to approach whatever he sees; if he wags to the left, he might prefer to withdraw.
>
> Cats and rodents: Give your cat, rat, or hamster a jar with a tasty treat and see which paw they use to try and extract it. If your pet is a cat, expect toms to use their left paws and the females to use their right.
>
> Fish: Place an unfamiliar object in the centre of your fish tank and record if your fish go around it clockwise or anticlockwise, indicating their eye preference.
>
> Reptiles and amphibians: Move a food morsel into your pet's field of view from either the left or right side and watch which direction elicits more or quicker catches. For most species tested so far, the right side appears to be the favourite.

In humans it's been discovered that "left-handers have an advantage in many sports involving a direct opponent, such as tennis or boxing, and the advantages may run to more serious encounters."

Finally, something we "know" has been verified: "Just five minutes of exercise in a 'green space' such as a park can boost mental health." The strongest impact is on young people. While this report doesn't mention the importance of seeing or simply sensing the presence of animals while "out in nature," there are data that show the presence of animals also boosts our morale even in the workplace. (See Allen Schoen's *Kindred Spirits* and Meg Olmert's *Made for Each Other*.)

While we are different from other animals, we are also rather similar. We must recognize and honor the differences and similarities as we negotiate our interactions with our animal kin. How lucky we are to share the world with fascinating animals and that there is ongoing research to learn more about who we are and who "they" are.

[ORIGINALLY POSTED ON MAY 7, 2010]

Do Animals Have Spiritual Experiences?
Yes, They Do

IN CONJUNCTION with *Psychology Today* blogger Steven Kotler, I've been pondering whether nonhuman animals have spiritual experiences and if they are religious. Here, Steven and I want to offer some ideas and hope readers will weigh in.

As I've discussed in many of my *Psychology Today* blogs, ample evidence shows that animals are extremely smart and that they demonstrate emotional and moral intelligences. But what about their spiritual lives? Do animals marvel at their surroundings, have a sense of awe when they see a rainbow, find themselves by a waterfall and ponder their environs? Do they ask where does lightning come from? Do they go into a "zone" when they play with others, forgetting about everything else save for the joy of playing? What are they feeling when they perform funeral rituals?

We can also ask if animals experience the joy of simply being alive. And if so, how would they express it so that we would know they do? Wild animals spend upwards of 90 percent of their time resting: What are they thinking and feeling as they gaze about? It would be nice to know. Again, science may never be able to measure such emotions with any precision, but anecdotal evidence and careful observation indicate such feelings may exist.

So too does evolutionary theory. Recall Charles Darwin's ideas about evolutionary continuity in which differences among species are differences in *degree* rather than differences in *kind*. The bottom line is that if we have something, other animals do, too, and it would behoove us to study the questions at hand rather than dismiss them because other animals can't possibly do or experience something that we think is uniquely human. For years it was thought that only humans were rational, self-conscious, linguistic, or moral beings, but we now know this isn't so. Darwin also commented that we really can't be sure that animals don't reflect on past pleasures and pains, for they have "excellent memories and some power of imagination."

So, what can we say about animal spirituality? Of course, much turns on how the word "spiritual" is defined, but for the moment let's simply consider nonmaterial, intangible, and introspective experiences as spiritual, of the sort that humans have.

Consider waterfall dances, which are a delight to witness. Sometimes a chimpanzee, usually an adult male, will dance at a waterfall with total abandon. Why? The actions are deliberate but obscure. Could it be they are a joyous response to being alive, or even an expression of the chimp's awe of nature? Where, after all, might human spiritual impulses originate?

Jane Goodall wonders whether these dances are indicative of religious behavior, precursors of religious ritual. She describes a chimpanzee approaching one of these falls with slightly bristled hair, a sign of heightened arousal. "As he gets closer, and the roar of the falling water gets louder, his pace quickens, his hair becomes fully erect, and upon reaching the stream he may perform a magnificent display close to the foot of the falls. Standing upright, he sways rhythmically from foot to foot, stamping in the shallow, rushing water, picking up and hurling great rocks. Sometimes he climbs up the slender vines that hang down from the trees high above and swings out into the spray of the falling water. This 'waterfall dance' may last ten or fifteen minutes." Chimpanzees also dance at the onset of heavy rains and during violent gusts of wind. Goodall asks, "Is it not possible that these performances are stimulated by feelings akin to wonder and awe? After a waterfall display the performer may sit on a rock, his eyes following the falling water. What is it, this water?"

Goodall wonders, "If the chimpanzee could share his feelings and questions with others, might these wild elemental displays become ritualized into some form of animistic religion? Would they worship the falls, the deluge from the sky, the thunder and lightning — the gods of the elements? So all-powerful; so incomprehensible."

Goodall admits that she'd love to get into their minds even for a few moments. It would be worth years of research to discover what animals see and feel when they look at the stars. In June 2006, Jane and I visited the Mona Foundation's chimpanzee sanctuary near Girona, Spain (www.mona-uk.org). We were told that Marco, one of the rescued chimpanzees, does a dance during thunderstorms during which he looks like he is in a trance. Perhaps numerous animals engage in these rituals, but we haven't been lucky enough to see them. Even if they are rare, they are important to note and to study.

Like Jane, I too would love to get into the mind and heart of a dog or a wolf even if I couldn't tell anyone about it afterward — what an amazing experience it would be.

For now, let's keep the door open to the idea that animals can be spiritual beings, and let's consider the evidence for such a claim. Meager as it is, available evidence says that yes, animals can have spiritual experiences. We need to conduct further research and engage in interdisciplinary discussions before we say that animals cannot and do not experience spirituality.

[Originally posted on November 30, 2009]

PART 6

THE EMOTIONAL LIVES OF ANIMALS

The Ever-Expanding
Circle of Sentience Includes
Depressed Bees
and Empathic Chickens

ANIMALS HAVE rich and deep emotional lives. We've known this for a long time, and solid scientific research is supporting our intuitions. The different species of animals that fall into the emotional area, the circle of sentience, is constantly expanding, and we're learning more and more about the incredible diversity of emotions they experience, ranging from joy and happiness to empathy and compassion to grief and despair. Emotions serve as social glue and are the reasons we're so attracted to other animals. It's also why they are drawn to us. Our own emotions are the gifts of our ancestors. How lucky we are to have inherited our own passionate lives from these awe-inspiring beings.

One surprising member of the expanding circle of sentience is the honeybee, who, it turns out, isn't always a happy worker, collecting pollen and making honey with legendary industriousness. Bees can become just as depressed on the job as people. Bees also use their right antenna to tell friend from foe. Please read on.

Emotional Honeybees and Brainy Jellyfish

JUST WHEN YOU THINK YOU'VE HEARD IT ALL, two recent research projects have discovered that honeybees have emotional lives and the nervous system of jellyfish and their behavior is far more complex than previously thought.

In the first study, Melissa Bateson and her colleagues at Newcastle University in the United Kingdom have shown that when honeybees are stressed, such as when their hive is shaken to simulate a predatory attack, the agitated bees display an increased expectation of bad outcomes. In other words, they become pessimists and show some of the same behavioral and physiological responses that humans show when they are anxious or depressed. When similar behavior is observed in vertebrates, it is explained as having an emotional basis.

In their research project, Professor Bateson and her coworkers first trained bees to associate different tastes, a sugar solution and a bitter solution of quinine, with different odors. After some of the bees were subjected to the simulated predatory attack, they were much less likely to stick out their tongues to new odors that were associated with quinine than were those bees who were not agitated. According to one report, "Bateson says the results can be interpreted to mean that the 'anxious' bees had a greater expectation of being 'punished' with the bitter quinine." In other words, they expected a bad outcome, as do depressed humans. The agitated bees avoided other bees and also showed altered levels of neurochemicals (dopamine, serotonin, and octopamine) that are associated with depression. This fascinating study shows that we need to be very careful making claims that invertebrates do not have emotional lives or feelings. In fact, there are marked similarities with vertebrates. Another study showed that bees also outperform computers in solving what is called "the traveling salesman problem," which for humans involves the following question: "Given a list of cities and the distances between each pair of cities, what is the shortest possible route that visits each city exactly once and returns to the origin city?" After exploring the location of flowers, bees learn to fly the most efficient and shortest route for saving time and energy.

Jellyfish also have been in the news. They're much more than plasma and poison. These ancient multiorgan carnivorous animals are much more than mindless protoplasm. They possess a complex visual system that allows them to navigate the swamps in which they live and have what can be called a central nervous system and a brain. They're not merely passive floaters, and the behavior patterns they exhibit are not simple reflexes but rather well-organized. For example, when they're staring into the heavens, they're actually seeking navigational guidance.

The more we study other animals, the more we learn about their fascinating lives. How exciting it is to learn more about animals who we typically write off as being "lower" and not especially intelligent or emotional. Fish also are far more complex than previously thought (see "Crabs and Fish Feel Pain: Expanding the Circle-of-Sentience Club," page 156) and are now considered to be very intelligent and sentient beings. Indeed, drawing lines between "higher" and "lower" species, a practice called speciesism, is fraught with errors and shouldn't be done. We need to remember that numerous nonhuman animals outperform us in many different ways.

[ORIGINALLY POSTED ON JUNE 18, 2011]

The Birds and the Bees and Their Brains: Size Doesn't Matter

MANY CURRENT THEORIES relating neuroanatomy and neurophysiology to cognition and behavior were developed a generation or more ago, while much significant research has been done in the past several years. It's clear that many assumptions made about animals and humans are no longer valid. For example, functional magnetic resonance imaging (fMRI) gives results in seconds, whereas brain phenomena occur in milliseconds. Thus, attempts to precisely correlate regional brain events with cognitive events are imperfect and "the gap between circuits and behavior is too wide."

In addition, hypotheses about the relationship of brain size and structure to stages of evolution, behavior, and cognitive capacities need to be reevaluated in light of new data and new theories. It should also be noted that, because absolute brain size can be a misleading measure, researchers often rely on the encephalization quotient (EQ) when making comparisons of brain size among different species. The EQ is, according to the Wikipedia definition, "a measure of relative brain size defined as the ratio between actual brain mass and predicted brain mass for an animal of a given size." (See the Wikipedia entry for "encephalization quotient" for a chart with estimates for the EQs for different species and discussions of what they mean about intelligence and various behavior patterns.)

Sophisticated cognitive abilities have been observed in a wide variety of species and include very unlikely candidates. This general discussion will focus on birds, reptiles, and bees, all of whom display more intelligence than would be explained by a simple comparison of their brains with human brains. Birds perform complex behavior using a very small brain without a neocortex. Songbirds learn songs from mentors and make adjustments through practice and feedback. Finches use strict rules of syntax. New Caledonian crows show the advanced capability of metacognition, as well as counting and making and using tools as well or better than many nonhuman primates; they also display remarkable memory. Crows remember specific people, cars, and urban situations, and they can hold grudges with specific people and cars for several years. Some birds show advanced planning and art. Alex, the world-renowned African gray parrot, did arithmetic, mastered same-different relationships, invented words, and the night before he died told his doctor friend that he loved his friend and researcher, Dr. Irene Pepperberg.

Most remarkably, bees with tiny brains use abstract thought and symbolic language. Each day they solve an advanced mathematical problem of how to most efficiently travel between multiple sites. They know when to mix medications for the hive and distinguish complex landscape scenes, including types of flowers, shapes, and patterns. Bees also learn categories and sequences and adjust them for future rewards. They consider social conditions, locations, time of day, and multiple senses. They are masters of mazes and show short-term and long-term memory, ranging from days to entire life spans.

How can these unexpected observations of complex behavior patterns be explained in terms of brain-size structure? Recently, it's been discovered that the brains of all of these animals have unusually complex neurons, neurons that are similar to the types that exist in the human brain, but in different brain structures. In birds a brain center that is correlated with some of their advanced abilities is in a so-called primitive region in the striatum, not the neocortex. When songbirds learn their songs from mentors, specific neurons in the brain stem signal for the singing tutor's sound and the young bird's sound.

Recently, regions have been found in the brains of birds and turtles that are similar in some ways to the human neocortex levels 4 and 5, but in very different structures (for more on reptiles, see "The Emotional Lives of Reptiles: Stress and Welfare," page 158). In turtles the brain region with these specialized neurons are distributed in one layer. In birds a region called the dorsal ventricular ridge has cells that input data like the human layer 4, and cells that output data like the human layer 5, functioning like the human neocortex. In some ways, the bird's arrangement is superior for language and cognitive tasks. An example is a specialized region for vocalization that doesn't exist in the complex multisensory and multimodal human brain.

The tiny honeybee brain has only around one million neurons, and according to one report, bees "contradict the notion that insect behaviour tends to be relatively inflexible and stereotypical. Indeed, they live in colonies and exhibit complex social, navigational and communication behaviours, as well as a relatively rich cognitive repertoire." As Marc Bekoff has noted earlier (see "Emotional Honeybees and Brainy Jellyfish," page 149), Melissa Bateson and her colleagues have shown when honeybees are stressed, they display behavior (and altered levels of neurochemicals) that in humans would be interpreted as "pessimistic," or showing signs of emotional depression.

Now we've learned that thrill-seeking individuals, known as scouts — who, according to a *New York Times* article, "fearlessly leave their hives and search for new sources of food and new hive locations for the rest of the colony" — have unique genetic brain patterns that are different from other bees. And, there are marked similarities with humans. "Just as human novelty seekers run the gamut from bold leaders to drug takers to enthusiasts for extreme sports like bungee jumping, the new research indicates that scouting bees also have a range of brain variations.... The chemicals that seem to be connected to scouting activity include catecholamine, glutamate, and gamma-aminobutyric acid — all chemicals that are also involved in regulating thrill-seeking behavior in humans and other vertebrates." These and other fascinating studies show that we need to be very careful making claims that invertebrates do not have emotional lives or feelings. In fact, there are marked similarities with vertebrates.

Honeybees have forty different kinds of neurons, several comparable to humans'. The mushroom body, with 20 percent of the bee's brain volume, is a unique integrator of multiple senses, relaying sensory information into value-based information. It functions as a combination of the human hippocampus and cortex. One advanced neuron in the mushroom body has been shown to influence cognitive functions mediating reward-based learning. This neuron is similar to the human dopamine neuron, but is in a totally different place and structure. Bees' brains also show multiple different places for memories working together. The bee brain also uses the advanced feature of inhibitory neurons much the same way as inhibitory interneurons in humans.

Current research shows that human-like neurons can occur in many other formats than the one for mammals, allowing for cognitive abilities that are very surprising. Higher-level capacities clearly can occur in animals with totally different brain structures than humans. It is certainly possible that, the more we study animal brains, additional unusual structures will be found.

Based upon what we're learning about small-brained animals, Marc Bekoff has been developing what he calls "the cognitive maximization hypothesis" that suggests that perhaps animals with relatively small brains maximize the use of what they have — their neural endowment — and perhaps they use the relatively little they have more efficiently than do big-brained animals. Big brains in and of themselves don't really matter to the animals themselves, and they do just fine with what they have. Future research will be needed to determine if this is so. The claim that humans use about 10 percent of their brain is a myth, so perhaps the efficiency of processing information is a factor to consider. Regardless, small-brained animals do just fine in their own worlds.

So, where to from here? What's so good about big brains? In an essay titled "Are Bigger Brains Better?" researchers Lars Chittka and Jeremy Niven conclude:

> Attempts to relate brain size to behaviour and cognition have rarely integrated information from insects with that from vertebrates. Many insects, however, demonstrate that highly differentiated motor repertoires, extensive social structures and cognition are possible with very small brains, emphasising that we need to understand the neural circuits, not just the size of brain regions, which underlie these feats. Neural network analyses show that cognitive features found in insects, such as numerosity, attention and categorisation-like processes, may require only very limited neuron numbers. Thus, brain size may have less of a relationship

with behavioural repertoire and cognitive capacity than generally assumed, prompting the question of what large brains are for. Larger brains are, at least partly, a consequence of larger neurons that are necessary in large animals due to basic biophysical constraints. They also contain greater replication of neuronal circuits, adding precision to sensory processes, detail to perception, more parallel processing and enlarged storage capacity. Yet, these advantages are unlikely to produce the qualitative shifts in behaviour that are often assumed to accompany increased brain size. Instead, modularity and interconnectivity may be more important.

Big brains and high encephalization quotients (EQs) may be useful for those animals who need them to be card-carrying members of their species, but small-brained animals do very well as long as they can do what they need to do to survive and thrive in their own worlds. The notion that small-brained animals are "less intelligent" than big-brained animals and "suffer less" also needs to be revisited, as it's surely a myth.

The rapidly growing fields of comparative cognitive neuroscience and cognitive ethology (the comparative study of animal minds) continue to provide exciting information about the brains and incredibly active minds of the fascinating animals with whom we share our planet. What an exciting future lies ahead.

[Note: This essay was cowritten with Jon Lieff, MD, a neuropsychiatrist specializing in the interface of medicine, neurology, and psychiatry.]

[ORIGINALLY POSTED ON APRIL 5, 2013]

Crabs and Fish Feel Pain:
Expanding the Circle-of-Sentience Club

OVER THE YEARS scientists have discovered that many animals feel pain, including some "surprises." I put the word "surprises" in quotes because solid evolutionary theory and "good biology" strongly support the notion that a large number of animals should in fact feel pain.

Now we know that crabs also feel pain. In a 2013 study by Barry Magee and Robert W. Elwood published in the prestigious peer-reviewed journal *The Journal of Experimental Biology*, these researchers, according to one article, "allowed shore crabs...to choose between one of two dark shelters in a brightly lit tank. One shelter came with a mild shock. After just two trials, crabs that initially chose the shocking shelter began opting for the zapless shelter, suggesting they learned to discriminate between the two options and headed for the less painful one." Previous research had shown that "prawns whose antennae were doused with caustic soda vigorously groomed their antennae, as if trying to ameliorate pain. Importantly, this behavior *didn't* occur if Elwood treated the antennae with an anesthetic first" [my emphasis].

Thus, crabs now join fish in the "pain club." In fact, it is still often assumed that fish are not sentient beings and not all that intelligent, but in her 2010 book, *Do Fish Feel Pain?*, the renowned scientist Victoria Braithwaite presents an incredible amount of recent scientific data that supports the contention that fish are indeed sentient. Professor Braithwaite makes a strong case for protecting fish and other aquatic animals from harm. At the beginning of her chapter titled "Looking to the Future," she writes: "I have argued that there is as much evidence that fish feel pain and suffer as there is for birds and mammals — and more than there is for human neonates and preterm babies."

Professor Braithwaite then goes on to note that these data will require us to change the ways in which we interact with fish because we now know that they suffer and feel pain. Catch-and-release programs surely need to be curtailed because, even if fish survive their encounter with a hook, they do suffer and die from the stress of being caught, fighting to get the hook out of their mouth or other body areas, and the wounds they endure (see the Endnotes for a study on mortality and catch-and-release methods). Torturing a fish at the end of a hook is just wrong.

We are continually expanding the circle of sentience and consciousness (see "Scientists Finally Conclude Nonhuman Animals Are Conscious Beings," page 116). Crabs, many other invertebrates, and fish who supposedly don't feel pain are served up as food in the countless billions. It's time to reconsider how these animals are treated in the food industry and in our everyday lives. It would be singularly unethical not to increase protection for fish and other animals who we previously thought weren't sentient. One place to start would be teaching our children that ever-popular catch-and-release programs are inhumane. This would make the lives of fish and other aquatic animals a lot more pleasant.

[THIS ESSAY ORIGINALLY APPEARED AS TWO ESSAYS:
"Crabs Feel Pain: Expanding the Circle of Sentience Club,"
POSTED ON JANUARY 17, 2013, and
"Fish Do Feel Pain: Yes They Do, Science Tells Us,"
POSTED ON APRIL 23, 2010]

The Emotional Lives of Reptiles: Stress and Welfare

REPTILES ARE AN EVOLUTIONARILY OLD and diverse class of vertebrates who are used in different sorts of research, some of which can be harmful to their psychological well-being. Various reptiles show complex parental behavior and also have been observed to play. Gordon Burghardt, who works out of the University of Tennessee, and his colleagues have been among the leaders in research on the behavior and welfare of reptiles, and his published papers and the references contained therein provide an ample database for those who want to know more about these intriguing and underrated animals.

In 2013, a fascinating essay was published by the British Veterinary Association (http://inpractice.bmj.com). Written by Clifford Warwick and his colleagues, it offers many useful tips for caring for reptiles that will be of interest to many readers, professionals and nonprofessionals alike. They note, for example, that, "unlike dogs and cats, reptiles will almost universally be 'life-restricted' in small, arbitrarily and poorly conceived vivariums maintained by non-professionals.... Contrary to common perceptions, reptiles manifest an array of abnormal behaviours that indicate stress."

The authors' summary table of behavioral signs of captivity-stress is an invaluable resource. For example, in response to stress, reptiles display hyperactivity, hypoactivity, anorexia, head-hiding, inflation of the body, hissing, panting, pigment change, and other abnormal patterns of behavior and physiological responses. They also provide a very useful self-assessment test for assessing reptile welfare using behavioral criteria.

The authors note that while there are stressors in nature, "captive conditions typically replace many features of the natural world with artificial and frequently poorly matched alternatives that deprive animals of known normal behaviour and associated biological needs, such as hunting, spatial range, and macro-habitat investigation." Even field research can alter the behavior of reptiles. For example, eye contact between researchers and free-living iguanas can change patterns of hierarchical perching.

I highly recommend this informative and timely essay not only for those people who are interested in reptiles but also for those who are interested in broader discussions of the emotional lives of animals. It's well known that many different animals suffer in captivity, and this excellent essay opens the door for further comparative research that will result in better care for the animals who find themselves living in a wide variety of nonnatural conditions.

Note: In a very interesting essay in *New Scientist* magazine called "Tender Turtles: Their Mums Do Care After All," author and tropical biologist Adrian Barnett writes about the fascinating parental behavior of Amazon river turtles and other reptiles and how what we're learning needs to be factored into conservation efforts. He ends his essay as follows: "if many turtles do care for their young, some of the strategies intended to save them could be casting them alone and adrift from an early age. And what would a mother turtle have to say about that?"

[ORIGINALLY POSTED ON MARCH 26, 2013]

Gorilla Joy and Chimpanzee Grief
Without a Doubt

HERE'S A WONDERFUL STORY that'll make your day. After three years apart, two gorilla brothers, Kesho and Alf, were reunited at Longleat Safari Park in the United Kingdom. They were separated when Kesho was sent to London Zoo to breed. Their reunion has hit the press because it's so clear what Kesho and Alf are feeling — deep and uninhibited joy. As someone who's studied nonhuman animal behavior and animal emotions for decades, I'm thrilled to see the press feature these sorts of events showing just how emotional other animals truly are.

In her wonderful story about Kesho and Alf, accompanied by photographs and a video, biologist and gorilla researcher Dr. Charlotte Uhlenbroek nicely sums up this wonderful reunion: "The photographs in yesterday's *Mail* of two gorilla brothers hugging each other in delight at being reunited after three years apart are deeply moving. The affection is unmistakable. They react just as human brothers might. It's heartwarming but not at all surprising to me. Many years spent working in the wild with these beautiful animals and their close cousins the chimpanzees have convinced me that the great apes have a range of powerful emotions identical to our own." This is joy with a capital J.

Dr. Uhlenbroek's concluding sentence says it all: "Deep emotion is invisible, intangible...but whatever it is, our cousins have got it too."

In another example of nonhuman animals experiencing deep emotions, this time in response to an infant's death, researchers at the Max Planck Institute for Psycholinguistics have observed a chimpanzee mother showing "behaviours not typically seen directed toward live infants, such as placing her fingers against the neck and laying the infant's body on the ground to watch it from a distance. The observations of Katherine Cronin and Edwin van Leeuwen provide unique insights into how chimpanzees, one of humans' closest primate relatives, learn about death."

How like us are they? In the story about the research, researcher Mark

Bodamer of Gonzaga University notes: "It was only a matter of time, and the right conditions, that chimpanzees' response to death would be recorded and subjected to analysis that would reveal remarkable similarities to humans."

I like to say that emotions are gifts of our ancestors. Critics often say something like, "Oh, you're just being anthropomorphic," when we speak about animal emotions. However, it's *not* being anthropomorphic to say we know other animals have deep and rich emotional lives because we're not inserting something human into animals. Rather, we're identifying commonalities and then using human language to communicate what we observe. It's simply bad biology to rob other animals of their emotional lives. Anthropomorphism is not antiscience.

[THIS ESSAY ORIGINALLY APPEARED AS TWO ESSAYS:
"Gorilla Joy Without a Doubt," POSTED ON AUGUST 17, 2012, and
"Whipping Horses Doesn't Work and New Observations of Grief
in Chimpanzees," POSTED ON FEBRUARY 2, 2011]

Gorillas Dismantle Poachers' Traps: Compassionate Conservation of the Gorilla-Kind

GORILLAS ARE AMAZING APE BEINGS. They're very smart and emotional (witness two brothers gleefully reuniting after three years; see "Gorilla Joy and Chimpanzee Grief Without a Doubt," page 160), and now there are some solid observations that they know what a trap means and are able to dismantle them and cover up what they've done.

According to *ABC News*:

> Staff at the Dian Fossey Gorilla Fund's Karisoke Research Center in Rwanda recently witnessed two 4-year-olds and a teenage mountain gorilla work together to destroy the types of snares that have killed at least two young gorillas this year. It was also the first time staff members have been able to see up close exactly how gorillas dismantle the snares.... One of the staff members reported he moved to dismantle the snare when a silverback (adult male) in the group grunted at him, warning him to stay back. Then two youngsters named Dukore and Rwema and a blackback (teen male) named Tetero ran toward the snare. Together they jumped on the taut branch attached to a rope noose and removed the rope. They then ran over to another nearby snare and destroyed it the same way. Pictures the staff members took show the young gorillas then examining broken sticks used to camouflage the noose on the ground.

Gorillas are clearly doing their part to protect themselves and others, and these fascinating observations add another dimension to the compassionate conservation movement (see "Ignoring Nature No More: Compassionate

Conservation at Work," page 303). While there is an amazing amount of work that still needs to be done to protect gorillas and many other animals, it's surely good to get help from the animals themselves.

[Originally posted on August 18, 2012]

Do Wild Animals Suffer from PTSD and Other Psychological Disorders?

ABOUT FIFTEEN YEARS AGO a woman in my advanced animal behavior course asked me if wild nonhuman animals suffer from post-traumatic stress disorder (PTSD) or other psychological disorders. And just yesterday a therapist who works on human animals asked me if it's possible that wild animals don't naturally suffer from PTSD but only when they're mistreated by humans or experience family and friends tortured by humans. These are great questions to which there seem to be no good answers. Here's what I wrote in 2007 in my book *The Emotional Lives of Animals* about the possibility of wild animals suffering from various psychological disorders.

Because it's usually ignored, I want to pose a final question in this chapter: if animals feel many, if not most, of the emotions humans feel, can they also become mentally ill? While we see emotions being freely and openly expressed in a wide variety of species, often there are individuals who seem be "out of it." For example, on occasion I've seen a young animal who just doesn't seem to get it, an individual who just doesn't know how to play. I remember a coyote pup named Harry who didn't respond to play signals by playing, as did most of his littermates. Harry also didn't use play bows very often and just didn't seem to have a clue about how to initiate play, or even how to play if he got to do it at all. For a long time I simply chalked it up to individual variation, figuring that since behavior among members of the same species can vary, Harry wasn't all that surprising.

But I was recently asked if there were autistic animals, and I thought about Harry and realized I wasn't sure. Because there are autistic humans, there likely are nonhuman animals who suffer from what might be called autism. Perhaps Harry suffered from coyote autism. Simon Baron-Cohen has made great strides in learning about human autism using ethological studies, and ethologist Niko Tinbergen eventually turned his attention to the study of autism, so there may indeed be a useful connection.

I remember other animals. There was another coyote, a large male named Joe, who seemed to go all over the place. He'd often seem to be sulking and moping around for no obvious reason and then instantaneously run around as if he were happy, seemingly without a care in the world. Then there was Lucy, a young wolf who behaved similarly to Joe. Some days Lucy behaved "normally," like a typical wolf, whereas on others she was either really wired or really down. Other colleagues have also remarked that on occasion one of the animals they're watching seems to be very unusual. But we never thought to call the out-of-the-ordinary individuals autistic or bipolar.

Currently, we're really not much closer to knowing much about wild animals, but it's clear captive animals do indeed suffer a wide range of psychological disorders including PTSD. Research by Dr. Hope Ferdowsian and her colleagues has clearly shown that captive chimpanzees display behavior patterns similar to post-traumatic stress disorder and depression. The same goes for elephants abused in circuses, where they are treated incredibly harshly (egregiously and inhumanely "broken") so they will perform unnatural tricks, and for other animals kept in tiny cages in zoos absent social companions and a physical environment where they can do the things their wild relatives routinely do. It's also been suggested that captivity drives killer whales crazy. I'm sure when similar research is conducted on other animals we'll discover the same trends. It's not all that surprising that captive animals show severe signs of stress and depression given how their lives are reprehensibly and severely compromised.

Nor is it surprising that dogs used in war, like humans who survive violent combat, return home suffering from PTSD. A 2011 article in the *New York Times* notes, "If anyone needed evidence of the frontline role played by dogs in war these days, here is the latest: the four-legged, wet-nosed troops used to sniff out mines, track down enemy fighters and clear build-ings are struggling with the mental strains of combat nearly as much as their human counterparts." Further, it's estimated that "more than 5 per-cent of the approximately 650 military dogs deployed by American combat forces are developing canine PTSD. Of those, about half are likely to be retired from service." Various treatments are used, including drugs that work on humans and also a process called desensitization. It's too early to know about the fate of these dogs who selflessly serve. I'm thrilled these amazing dogs are finally getting the treatment they fully deserve, whether they can go back to combat or not.

Scanty but compelling observations show exploited wild elephants also display signs of trauma and depression (see Gay Bradshaw, *Elephants on the Edge*). I remember meeting a highly traumatized orphaned young elephant at the David Sheldrick Wildlife Trust (www.sheldrickwildlifetrust.org), outside of Nairobi, Kenya, who was being treated after seeing, hearing, and smelling her family and friends being killed by humans. At this won-derful rehabilitation center, incredibly dedicated caregivers remain with these individuals, sometimes for years on end, to help them get through their severe trauma. Some do, and very sadly some don't. When I put my hand in this youngster's mouth, her entire body went limp with relaxation. As we locked eyes, tears came to mine.

Perhaps wild animals who deeply grieve the loss of family and friends from natural conditions also suffer severe and prolonged psychological problems. I once saw individuals in a pack of wild coyotes deeply grieve the loss of their mother. We (and most likely they) never knew if she went off and died or simply disappeared, but their demeanor showed clearly they missed her and were depressed. But after a few weeks, life went on as usual because it had to. There was no one who could or would take care of them. Traumatized wild animals seem to recuperate rapidly because they must. In his book *Waking the Tiger*, renowned psychologist Peter Levine considers the ways in which wild animals overcome trauma and applies this to his work on humans.

I don't know of any data that show that wild animals torment one another to the extent of causing severe psychological trauma that even marginally resembles how humans routinely harm other humans or members of other species. I've seen a very few scapegoats in wild packs of coyotes who were unrelentingly threatened and occasionally dominated by other pack members. After a while the scapegoats just avoided the more dominant individuals and were left alone. Did these scapegoats suffer long and enduring depression? It didn't seem so, and on two occasions a male and female subsequently became fully functioning members of their pack.

Because wild animals don't get the medical care to which our companion animals are privy, those who suffer from extreme and debilitating psychological disorders simply die, as do those who suffer serious physical injuries and illness.

So, my guess is yes, wild animals do indeed suffer from PTSD and other psychological disorders under natural conditions. As time goes on we will learn more about the extent of these maladies. I encourage field workers to look for this and to report instances of psychological trauma. Even in the absence of a sufficient database, I can't imagine that the extent of psychopathologies among wild animals comes close to how rampant PTSD and other disorders are among captive animals. Their lives have been highly compromised by humans by their being forced to live in highly unnatural conditions in unnatural social groups.

What allows us to continue to abuse and torment other animals as well as other humans needs more study because this is another example of human exceptionalism, one about which we should not be proud. We suffer the indignities to which we subject others, and we need to change our ways. We can learn a lot from other animals.

[ORIGINALLY POSTED ON NOVEMBER 29, 2011]

Did a Female Burro
Commit Suicide?

EVERY NOW AND AGAIN someone asks me if nonhuman animals commit suicide. This past weekend I gave two lectures as part of the Collegiate Peaks Forum Series in Buena Vista, Colorado. After I talked about grief and mourning in a wide variety of species, someone in the audience asked me this question. My answer was that there are some good observations of animals seemingly taking their own lives in situations when one might expect a human to take his or her own life. For example, it's been suggested that whales intentionally beach themselves to end their lives, highly stressed elephants step on their trunks or jump over a cliff to end prolonged pain, and cats stressed out by earthquakes kill themselves.

After one of my talks in Buena Vista, one woman in the audience, Cathy Manning, told me a very simple but compelling story about a burro who seemed to kill herself. Cathy knew a female burro who gave birth to a baby with a harelip. The infant couldn't be revived, and Cathy watched the mother walk into a lake and drown. It's known that various equines including horses and donkeys grieve the loss of others (for instance, see *Donkey: The Mystique of Equus Asinus* by Michael Tobias and Jane Morrison), so I didn't find this story to be inconsistent with what is known about these highly emotional beings.

I think it's too early to make any definite statements about whether animals commit suicide. Opinions vary, and some say animals don't have the same concept of death that we have, and so they don't know that their lives will end when they do something to stop breathing.

But this does *not* mean they don't grieve and mourn the loss of family and friends. What they're thinking when they're deeply saddened when another animal dies isn't clear, but it's obvious that a wide variety of animals suffer the loss of family and friends. Cathy's story made me rethink the question of whether animals commit suicide, and I hope this brief story opens the door for some good discussion about this intriguing possibility. As some of my colleagues and I have stressed, we must pay attention to stories and hope they will stimulate more research in a given area.

[ORIGINALLY POSTED ON JULY 22, 2012]

Grieving Animals:
Saying Good-bye to Friends and Family

EVERY NOW AND AGAIN a book comes along that not only deals with the behavior of a fascinating group of animals but also raises important questions about science in general and what sorts of information can be used to say that we really know something about this or that behavior.

A few months ago I read through the galley proofs of John Marzluff and Tony Angell's book *Gifts of the Crow* so that I could write a brief supporting statement. I couldn't put the book down, and just this week when I received the published version, I wound up reading through it as if I hadn't previously seen it. It's really that good. Marzluff and Angell are also writing essays for *Psychology Today* under the category "Avian Einsteins" (www.psychologytoday.com/blog/avian-einsteins) and offer fascinating stories and data about crows and other amazing birds. Crows, for example, make and use more complex tools than chimpanzees, are socially complex and incredibly adaptable, playfully frolic with others, and occasionally entertain themselves by snowboarding down a roof.

Gifts of the Crow is filled with wonderful stories and solid research data about these amazing corvids. The authors "base every thesis about their human-like behavior on how the brain of a bird is known to function." There's a lot of solid science between the two covers.

One aspect of this book I really like deals with the authors' handling of anecdotes, often written off as "just-so stories" with no credibility at all. Marzluff and Angell note that some researchers dismiss stories about animal behavior "because of laypeople's lack of formal training, lack of documentation, overinterpretation, and uncontrolled influences." They go on to write, "taken individually, such stories are anecdotal, but collectively they provide a unique body of information that stimulates scientific exploration and becomes an assemblage of possibilities."

I couldn't agree more, especially for behavior patterns that are difficult to observe and/or are rare, such as grieving ceremonies and other instances in which animals display amazing cognitive skills and emotional capacities. My colleague and NYU philosopher Dale Jamieson and I like to say "the plural of anecdote is data." We must pay attention to the accumulation of stories that have a similar ring. Marzluff and Angell weave the theme of skepticism throughout their excellent book, noting that all accounts, including those of "citizen scientists," must be given careful attention because the credibility of accounts of "rare and exceptional behaviors cannot be limited to the few specialized researchers who study corvids," and "science teaches us to be skeptical, especially of the fantastic."

I also like to stress that many observations that some of my colleagues call "surprising" aren't really all that surprising. Many of them study animals in situations where animals are unable to express their full behavioral repertoire because they live in unnatural social groups or small impoverished cages or enclosures. The only way we will come to a more complete understanding of what birds and other animals can do and what they feel is to study free-ranging animals.

Chapter 7 of *Gifts of the Crow* deals with passion, wrath, and grief. Animal grief is a hot topic, and as I reread this chapter I found myself once again reflecting on the ways in which nonhuman animals deal with the death of others, how they say good-bye. Raven expert and renowned biologist Bernd Heinrich also writes about this general topic in his new book *Life Everlasting: The Animal Way of Death*.

Years ago I observed what I call a magpie funeral. My friend Rod and I came upon a magpie corpse in the middle of a street in Boulder, Colorado, and watched as a succession of magpies very deliberately brought grass and laid it by the corpse, stood as if in vigil, and then flew off (I tell this story in *The Emotional Lives of Animals*). To date I've received numerous stories about these sorts of rituals, primarily for crows, ravens, and magpies, and one for starlings. To be sure, we need more data about how different animals grieve and mourn the loss of friends and family, but there is overwhelming evidence that individuals of many different species do.

Marzluff and Angell note that "crows and ravens routinely gather around the dead of their own species [but] rarely do they touch the body." When I wrote to John to congratulate him on the publication of his and

Tony's book, he sent me a story about a crow funeral that closely resembles what we saw in the magpies. Vincent Hagel, formerly the president of the Whidbey Audubon Society, wrote, "My good buddy and I were in his mother's kitchen as she prepared an after-school snack for us. Suddenly, she told us to quickly look out the kitchen window. Just a few feet from the house lay an obviously dead crow, and about twelve other crows were hopping in a circle around the body. After a minute or two, one crow flew off for a few seconds, then returned with a small twig or piece of dried grass. It dropped the twig on the body, then flew away. Then, one by one, the other crows each left briefly, one at a time, and returned to drop grass or a twig on the body, then fly off until all were gone, and the body lay alone with twigs lain across it. The entire incident probably lasted four or five minutes."

Clearly, when we pay attention to the observations and data of researchers and the stories of nonresearchers, we see other animals grieve and mourn the loss of friends and family. The database isn't just a motley of overzealous just-so stories offered by untrained animal lovers.

Skeptics need to keep an open mind about these events, and we must appreciate animals for who they really are and what they are capable of doing and feeling. Those who still think we don't really know if other animals are conscious or hold funeral services, for example, when existing data show they clearly are and do, should be eating lots of crow, metaphorically that is.

I ended a previous essay as follows, and more recent information is consistent with these conclusions: "Why do animals grieve and why do we see grief in different species of animals? It's been suggested that grief reactions may allow for the reshuffling of status relationships, or for the filling of the reproductive vacancy left by the deceased, or for fostering continuity of the group. Some theorize that perhaps mourning strengthens social bonds among the survivors who band together to pay their last respects. This may enhance group cohesion at a time when it's likely to be weakened."

Clearly we're not the only animals who possess the cognitive and emotional capacities for grieving and mourning the loss of others. Grieving and mourning rituals show that nonhuman animals are socially aware of what is happening in their worlds and that they feel deep emotions. They're sad and brokenhearted when family and friends die. Grief itself remains something of a mystery, for there doesn't seem to be any obvious adaptive value to it in an evolutionary sense. It doesn't appear to increase an individual's reproductive success. Whatever its value, grief is the price of commitment, that wellspring of both happiness and sorrow.

Animals give us many gifts, and all we have to do is open our senses and our hearts to these valuable life lessons. We learn much about ourselves when we recognize the treasures that other animals freely offer to us when we take the time to learn about their fascinating lives. Grieving and mourning say so much about the character of individuals of numerous diverse species.

[ORIGINALLY POSTED ON JULY 1, 2012]

A Fox, a Cougar, and a Funeral

I'M INCREDIBLY FORTUNATE to live among wild animals, but living in nature can have its downside, especially when confronting such majestic beasts as cougars or black bears.

I've had some close encounters with cougars, almost falling over a huge male as I walked backward to warn some neighbors of his presence. I met another cougar more recently, and discovered much about nature, although I've been studying coyotes and other animals for many years. There's just so much we don't know.

I was driving up my road late one evening when I saw a large tan animal trotting toward my car. Thinking it was my neighbor's German shepherd, Lolo, I stopped and opened my door to say hello, only to hear Lolo barking behind me. I was face to face with a male cougar. He stared at me, seemed to shrug his shoulders, and walked off. I slammed the car door shut and went home with all my senses on fire.

The next morning my neighbor said Lolo had found a fox carcass, so I went to look at it. The fox, a formerly healthy male, had clearly been killed by the cougar (I'll spare you the gory details), but his body was intact and partially covered with branches, dirt, and some of the fox's own fur. It looked as if the cougar had tried to cover his prey. I checked the carcass the next morning, and it was still partially covered and unchanged from the day before.

Two days later I headed out at first light to hike with my companion, Jethro. I wanted no more surprises. I looked down the road and saw a small red female fox trying to cover the carcass. I was fascinated, for she was deliberately orienting her body so that when she kicked debris with her hind legs, it would cover her friend, perhaps her mate. She'd kick dirt, stop, look at the carcass, and intentionally kick again. I observed this ritual for a short while.

A few hours later, I saw that the carcass was now fully buried. I uncovered it and saw that it had been decapitated and partially eaten. No one to whom I have spoken, naturalists and professional biologists alike, has ever seen a red fox bury another red fox. I don't know if the female fox was intentionally trying to bury her friend, but there's no reason to assume that she wasn't. Perhaps she was grieving and I was observing a fox funeral.

I have no doubt that foxes and other animals have rich and deep emotional lives. Back in 1947, a naturalist on the East Coast saw a male fox lick his mate as she lay dead, and the male also protected his mate quite vigorously. Perhaps he too was showing respect for a dead friend. I was lucky to have this series of encounters, for nature doesn't hold court at our convenience. Much happens in the complex lives of our animal kin to which we're not privy, but when we're fortunate to see animals at work, how splendid it is.

[ORIGINALLY POSTED ON JULY 22, 2009]

Humpback Whales Protect
a Gray Whale from Killer Whales

As MORE AND MORE DATA ARE COLLECTED, we're learning about the prevalence not only of cooperation, compassion, and empathy among members of the same species (see *Origins of Altruism and Cooperation*, edited by Robert Sussman and C. Robert Cloninger), but of instances of individuals of one species helping members of other species. Here are two fascinating recent examples.

In the first, three different species of whales were involved. In Monterey Bay, California, as a boat of whale-watchers looked on, a pod of killer whales attacked a baby gray whale. Not only did the baby's mother attempt to save her child, as we would expect, but a group of several other humpback whales seemed to intervene to fight off the killer whales, at times putting themselves in danger of being hurt. One story said this was "probably the first time such an event has been witnessed and recorded." The encounter lasted seven hours. Eventually the killer whales succeeded in killing the baby gray whale, but even afterward, up to seven humpback whales seemed to be trying to keep the killer whales from the dead baby, by trumpeting, pursuing the killer whales, "tail slashing," and exhibiting other signs of agitation and distress.

Clearly, there's a lot of cetacean cognition and brain power going on in this encounter, as well as what would appear to be empathy and altruism on the part of the humpback whales.

The article quotes cetacean expert Dr. Lori Marino, who teaches at Emory University:

> This is apparently a case of humpback whales trying to help a member of another cetacean species. This shows that they are capable of tremendous behavioral flexibility, giving even more credence to reports of cetaceans coming to the aid of human beings. They seem to have the capacity to generalize from one

situation to another and from one kind of being to another. Moreover, they seem to sympathize with members of other species and have the motivation to help.

One reason may be that humpback whales, and many other cetaceans, have specialized cells in their brains called Von Economo neurons ("spindle cells") and these are shared with humans, great apes, and elephants. The exact function of these elongated neurons is still unknown but they are found in exactly the same locations in all mammal brains for the species that have them.

What is intriguing is that these parts of the mammal brain are thought to be responsible for social organization, empathy, speech, intuition about the feelings of others, and rapid "gut" reactions. So the presence of these cells is neurological support for the idea that cetaceans are capable of empathy and higher-order thinking and feeling.

In either case these whales are apparently demonstrating a high level of sensitivity and concern (morality, if you will) that is laudable in any species.

In another example of an animal of one species helping a member of another species, a pit bull named Lilly was hit by a train while pulling her unconscious human companion, Christine Spain, off of the tracks. The train's engineer saw the dog pulling Spain away, but could not stop in time to avoid hitting the animal. However, even after being hit and suffering an injured foot and a fractured pelvis, Lilly stood guard over her human friend till help arrived. In a happy end to the story, Spain is fine and Lilly is recovering.

While these sorts of encounters are rarely seen, I'm sure that as researchers and others spend more and more time carefully observing animals in various situations, they'll see between-species aid more regularly. Rare or not, these encounters show clearly that animals are sensitive to the plight of others, they display empathy, and they surely are conscious beings.

[ORIGINALLY POSTED ON MAY 8, 2012]

Empathic Chickens and Cooperative Elephants: Emotional Intelligence Expands Its Range Again

THE MORE WE ACTUALLY STUDY ANIMALS, the more we learn about their emotional lives and cognitive skills. A few years ago a prestigious research group discovered that mice displayed empathy, but in the process they caused a good deal of pain to the mice being studied (see "Wild Justice and Moral Intelligence in Animals," page 195). Now we've just learned that chickens also feel one another's pain. A research group at the University of Bristol, using noninvasive methods, showed for the first time that domestic hens show a clear physiological and behavioral response when their chicks are mildly distressed. Mother hens and their chicks were exposed to puffs of air. When the air puff was directed at the hens, they reacted with signs of fear, becoming more alert and preening less. Their eye temperature also decreased. When their chicks were exposed to the puffs of air, the hens showed all these signs but also their heart rate increased and they made more clucking calls to their chicks, indicating they were concerned with what was happening to the youngsters.

Previous research has shown that chickens are very intelligent, so this new discovery is not all that surprising. For years, Karen Davis, president of United Poultry Concerns (www.upc-online.org), has been telling us how smart and emotional birds are and that they deserve far better treatment than they receive in food-processing facilities, truly torture chambers, around the world. Accumulating data from research on chickens (and other birds) support her views. Chickens kept in horrific conditions, such as in battery cages on factory farms, don't like it, and they also feel the pain and suffering of other chickens who are crammed into these incredibly inhumane prisons.

Elephants also are making news once again. We all know how smart and emotional these amazing beings are, and now, in a new study, we've learned they will cooperate with one another in order to obtain a reward. A report on the elephant study said that elephants were presented with a challenge:

to get food, two elephants had to pull on the ends of the same rope at the same time. Not only did they do this, the elephants waited for another elephant to come help knowing that there was no point to pulling the rope alone. "These findings suggest that the elephants had not simply learned to pull on the rope after their partner arrived at the apparatus. They seemed to understand that the cooperative task involved both animals pulling on a rope simultaneously. This puts their performance on a par with that of chimps and bonobos."

[ORIGINALLY POSTED ON MARCH 9, 2011]

Empathic Rats and Ravishing Ravens

ANYONE WHO'S KEPT UP with the latest and greatest about the cognitive, emotional, and moral lives of nonhuman animals knows "surprises" are being uncovered almost daily and that many nonprimate animals are showing intellectual and emotional capacities that rival those of the great apes. Today, I can write about some fascinating new results that caution against our tooting our "we're so special" horn too loudly or proudly.

Over the past few years we've learned much about the moral lives of animals (for instance, see *The Moral Lives of Animals* by Dale Peterson). Detailed studies have shown that chickens display empathy, and now we know rats do, too. According to a story in *Nature*, a study published today conducted by Inbal Ben-Ami Bartal, Jean Decety, and Peggy Mason working at the University of Chicago has provided the first evidence of empathy-driven behavior in rodents. Appearing in the prestigious journal *Science*, the results of this landmark study show that untrained laboratory rats will free restrained companions, and this helping is triggered by empathy. They'll even free other rats rather than selfishly feast on chocolate. Researcher Peggy Mason notes, "That was very compelling.... It said to us that essentially helping their cage mate is on a par with chocolate. He can hog the entire chocolate stash if he wanted to, and he does not. We were shocked."

A press release from the University of Chicago, which is accompanied by a video of the rats doing this, states:

> The observation, published today in *Science*, places the origin of pro-social helping behavior earlier in the evolutionary tree than previously thought. Though empathetic behavior has been observed anecdotally in non-human primates and other wild species, the concept had not previously been observed in rodents in a laboratory setting.... "This is the first evidence of helping behavior triggered by empathy in rats," said Jean Decety.... "There are a lot of ideas in the literature showing that empathy is not

unique to humans, and it has been well demonstrated in apes, but in rodents it was not very clear. We put together in one series of experiments evidence of helping behavior based on empathy in rodents, and that's really the first time it's been seen."

It's also very interesting that the rats were not trained to open the cage door. Inbal Ben-Ami Bartal noted, "These rats are learning because they are motivated by something internal. We're not showing them how to open the door, they don't get any previous exposure on opening the door, and it's hard to open the door. But they keep trying and trying, and it eventually works."

It's also important to note that the rats in the cage didn't have to experience unbearable physical pain for other rats to help them. In an earlier study in mice, researchers caused a lot of excruciating pain. As such, this new study on rats sets a wonderful precedent for future research on sentient and empathic animals. It's also safe to assume that numerous animals display empathy based on what we already know. As Jean Decety concludes in a very important paper on the evolution of empathy, "There is strong evidence that empathy has deep evolutionary, biochemical, and neurological underpinnings. Even the most advanced forms of empathy in humans are built on more basic forms and remain connected to core mechanisms associated with affective communication, social attachment, and parental care."

There's also another very important aspect to this study. Much research is showing that human and nonhuman animals are inherently compassionate and empathic (for instance, see Robert Sussman and C. Robert Cloninger, *Origins of Altruism and Cooperation*) and that it's really easy to expand our compassion footprint. Thus, the comments of Peggy Mason ring true: "When we act without empathy we are acting against our biological inheritance....If humans would listen and act on their biological inheritance more often, we'd be better off."

We can only hope these findings will be used to protect rats and other rodents from being used in horrific invasive research. Although it's been known for more than five years that mice display empathy, this has not been factored into a revision of the Federal Animal Welfare Act in the United

States. Rodents and many millions of other animals who comprise more than 99 percent of the animals used in invasive research can still be greatly harmed or killed "in the name of science." Only about 1 percent of animals used in research in the United States are protected by legislation, and the legislation is sometimes amended in nonsensical ways to accommodate the "needs" of researchers. For instance, in 2004, the Animal Welfare Act was amended so that the definition of "animal" specifically *excluded* mice and rats bred for research.

The desperation of science to rob animals of their sentience produces distortions that open the door for egregious and reprehensible abuse. In the *Nature* story, Garet Lahvis, a behavioral neuroscientist at Oregon Health & Science University in Portland, correctly notes, "We study animals to see what makes us uniquely human, but the findings of empathy in animals often force uncomfortable questions about how humans treat animals."

Now, what about ravens. Their fascinating story is almost anticlimactic but well worth telling. Previous research has shown that ravens will punish others who steal food from the group, and it's been suggested that they demonstrate moral behavior. Now, according to an article about a new study, we know that wild ravens in the Austrian Alps use "their beaks and body language to direct another raven's attention, usually a member of the opposite sex, to a specific object, marking the first time such complex gesturing has been documented in an animal outside of humans and their primate cousins." They often do this to start a relationship. Thomas Bugnyar, a coauthor on this study, wrote on his project website, "Understanding the social life of corvids may thus be critical in our attempt to understand primate cognition, since comparison between these groups may offer the unique opportunity to identify which cognitive abilities are common to social living." All in all, these discoveries and others demand that we keep an open mind on who other animals are and what they are capable of. As I and others have concluded time and time again, we need to debunk the myth of human exceptionalism once and for all. In other words, don't toot your horn too loudly or proudly. Other animals truly are amazing beings.

[ORIGINALLY POSTED ON DECEMBER 8, 2011]

Bonobos: Going Out of Their Way to Help Others

THE MORE WE STUDY OTHER ANIMALS, the more fascinating they turn out to be. Rapidly accumulating data show that other animals are far more caring, compassionate, and kind than we give them credit for, and according to a pair of revealing studies, this now includes highly social bonobos, often called pygmy chimpanzees (*Pan paniscus*).

The first research paper describes an incident in which a group of bonobos traveled long distances in order to successfully rescue a friend trapped in a snare. While other species often leave injured animals behind to die, the bonobos did not do this, and researchers thought this was most likely because their social groups are led by females.

A *New Scientist* article about the report described the incident as follows: "Last September, deep in the swamp forest of the Democratic Republic of the Congo, Nahoko Tokuyama of Kyoto University in Japan heard a scream. It came from a male bonobo whose hand was trapped in a snare. What happened next shows that bonobos (*Pan paniscus*) don't forget their lost friends.... As soon as the other group members realised the male was trapped, they gathered around him. One untangled the snare from woody ground vines, enabling the male to move. Another tried and failed to remove the wire. Later in the day, the bonobos returned to the dry forest to sleep. The injured male could not follow."

Yet the bonobos returned to the area the next day, traveling almost two kilometers out of their way for no other apparent reason than to find their injured group member. In the story, Amy Cobden, of Emory University in Atlanta, Georgia, said she had "never seen this behavior before." However, this wasn't surprising, since bonobos are known to be "very concerned for each other's emotional status."

A more detailed description of this remarkable event is given in the abstract for the original research paper:

> This is the first report to demonstrate that a large mixed-sex party
> of bonobos travelled a long distance to return to the location of a

snare apparently to search for a member that had been caught in it. An adult male was caught in a metallic snare in a swamp forest at Wamba, Luo Scientific Reserve, Democratic Republic of the Congo. After he escaped from the snare by breaking a sapling to which the snare was attached, other members of his party assisted him by unfastening the snare from lianas in which it was caught and licked his wound and tried to remove the snare from his fingers. In the late afternoon, they left him in the place where he was stuck in the liana and travelled to the dry forest where they usually spend the night. The next morning, they travelled back 1.8 km to revisit the location of the injured male. When they confirmed that he was no longer there, they returned to the dry forest to forage. This was unlike the usual ranging patterns of the party, suggesting that the bonobos travelled with the specific intention of searching for this injured individual who had been left behind. The incident described in this report likely occurred because bonobos usually range in a large mixed-sex party and try to maintain group cohesion as much as possible.

Then, another study — this one conducted by Duke University researchers Jingzhi Tan and Brian Hare with captive bonobos living at the Lola ya Bonobo Sanctuary (www.friendsofbonobos.org) in the Democratic Republic of Congo — has shown that, unlike chimpanzees, these great apes will share food with strangers.

In this novel set of experiments, bonobos were presented with a pile of food and then given the chance to release from other rooms a stranger, a group mate, or both individuals. Tan and Hare showed that bonobos will voluntarily donate food to strangers and give up a meal as long as there are social benefits that entail having the opportunity to interact with a stranger, but they also will help others get food even when there are no social perks. They conclude that prosociality ("voluntary behavior intended to benefit another") in bonobos "is in part driven by unselfish motivation, because bonobos will even help strangers acquire out-of-reach food when no desirable social interaction is possible."

These intriguing reports and experiments support the argument that we must be very careful when making claims about human exceptionalism when writing about animal minds and the cognitive and social skills of other animals (see "Animal Minds and the Foible of Human Exceptionalism," page 42). They also show that we must continue to conduct comparative research on many different species. In this case all species of chimpanzees do not show the same behavior patterns, and we might have wrongly concluded that food sharing and social tolerance are uniquely human or evolved later. In a *New York Times* story about his study, Tan notes, "If you only studied chimps, you would think that humans evolved this trait of sharing with strangers later.... But now, given that bonobos do this, one scenario is that the common ancestor of chimps, humans, and bonobos had this trait." We also do not know if individuals of other species — such as social carnivores like wolves, coyotes, or jackals, or perhaps domesticated dogs — display these patterns of behavior, so we must keep that door open as well.

In the abstract of their study, Tan and Hare conclude, "Other-regarding preferences toward strangers are not uniquely human," and they initially evolve "due to selection for social tolerance, allowing the expansion of individual social networks." They note that humans don't "possess a unique proclivity to share with others — including strangers." However, they do caution, following up on the work of Arizona State University's Kim Hill and his colleagues, that "it is likely that humans are unique for the ability to extend our ape-like prosociality even to the most costly of contexts. These extreme other-regarding preferences possibly rely on language and social norms making it unlikely that such preferences preceded the evolution of these socio-cognitive abilities."

[THIS ESSAY ORIGINALLY APPEARED AS TWO ESSAYS:
"Bonobos Rescue Friends in Need Because Females Lead,"
POSTED ON MARCH 15, 2012, and
"Animal Kindness: Bonobos Forego Food to Give to Strangers,"
POSTED ON JANUARY 8, 2013]

Do "Smarter" Dogs Really Suffer More Than "Dumber" Mice?

THE QUESTION I ASK IN THE TITLE of this essay centers on the idea that supposedly smarter nonhuman animals suffer more than animals who are not as intelligent. Indeed, many people who write about other animals make this assumption, as do those who develop and enforce policies on what sorts of treatment are permissible and those that are not. In the eyes of the US Federal Animal Welfare Act, animals such as mice and other rodents, birds, fish, and invertebrates deserve little if any protection from extreme abuse, and they are not even considered to be animals, despite the fact that we know that mice, rats, and chickens display empathy. Furthermore, their relevance to biomedical research is also seriously questioned. Thus, concerning the utility of animal models, Mark Davis, director of the Stanford Institute of Immunity, Transplantation, and Infection, has been quoted as saying, "Mice are lousy models for clinical studies." Many other researchers are also concerned that animal models are not all that useful in biomedical research (see, for example, *FAQs About the Use of Animals in Science* by Ray Greek and Niall Shanks).

In 1994 I published an essay titled "Cognitive Ethology and the Treatment of Nonhuman Animals: How Matters of Mind Inform Matters of Welfare." When I reread it this past week as I was writing a recent essay called "The Birds and the Bees and Their Brains: Size Doesn't Matter" (see page 151), I realized that some of the arguments I rejected back then about the relationship between intelligence and suffering are still being considered, even in light of a plethora of new data on the cognitive and emotional lives of other animals. Here I want to revisit briefly some of these claims given what we now know, based on more recent research, about animal cognition, emotions, consciousness, and sentience, and the capacity of other animals to suffer and to feel pain. My essential attitude is expressed in the abstract for my essay:

Anthropocentric claims about the ways in which nonhuman animals (hereafter animals) interact in their social and nonsocial worlds are often used to influence decisions on how animals can or should be used by humans in various sorts of activities. Thus, the treatment of individuals is often tightly linked to how they are perceived with respect to their ability to perform behaviour patterns that suggest that they can think — have beliefs, desires, or make plans and have expectations about the future. Here, I review some basic issues in the comparative study of animal minds and discuss how matters of mind are related to matters of welfare and well-being. Much comparative research still needs to be done before any stipulative claims can be made about how an individual's cognitive abilities can be used to influence decisions about how she or he should be treated. More individuals from diverse species whose lives, sensory worlds, motor abilities, and nervous systems are different from those of animals with whom we identify most readily or with whom we are the most familiar, need to be studied. As others, I stress the importance of subjectivity and common sense along with the use of empirical data in making decisions about animal welfare, and that subjective assessments should be viewed in the same critical light as are supposedly objective scientific facts. I also argue that whatever connections there are between an individual's cognitive abilities and what sorts of treatment are permissible can be overridden by that individual's ability to feel pain and to suffer. When we are uncertain, even only slightly, about their ability to experience pain or to suffer, individual animals should be given the benefit of the doubt. There is a great deal of uncertainty about the phylogenetic distribution of pain and suffering.

In the past twenty years since my essay was completed, there has been an explosion, if you will, in studies and data concerning the cognitive, emotional, and moral lives of animals. Numerous surprises have been discovered for individuals of species who were assumed to be not all that smart or sentient. In a nutshell, research has opened up the door to reconsider not only the nature of the cognitive, emotional, and moral lives of animals but also how much they suffer when they are mistreated. It's also become clear that the word "intelligence" needs to be reconsidered. Asking if a dog is smarter than a cat or a cat is smarter than a mouse doesn't result in answers that are very meaningful. Likewise, asking if dogs suffer more than mice ignores who these animals are. They do what they have to do to survive and thrive on their own terms, not according to ours or those of other animals.

Furthermore, a great deal of comparative research has now shown that what was once considered well-founded common sense — based on Charles Darwin's ideas about evolutionary continuity — about what animals know and feel has been borne out by numerous studies. For example, we share with other mammals and vertebrates the same areas of the brain that are important for consciousness and processing emotions. We need to abandon the anthropocentric view that only big-brained animals such as ourselves, nonhuman great apes, elephants, and cetaceans (dolphins and whales) have sufficient mental capacities for complex forms of consciousness and for enduring deep suffering. It's bad biology to rob animals of traits they clearly possess.

In 2012, a group of esteemed scientists put forth the Cambridge Declaration on Animal Consciousness (see "Scientists Finally Conclude Nonhuman Animals Are Conscious Beings," page 116), in which they concluded that "nonhuman animals, including all mammals and birds, and many other creatures" display consciousness. That doesn't mean that all consciousness is the same. And it also leaves the door open for speciesist arguments that there remain "higher" and "lower" animals and that the pain and suffering of "less intelligent" animals needn't concern us very seriously. Of course, I disagree, and the reasoning I presented in my 1994 essay holds true today. Since access to that essay is restricted, let me offer a relevant section of what I wrote then. (References for the sources it cites can be found in the Endnotes, page 343.)

When individual cognitive capacities are used for drawing lines along some arbitrary scale concerning what can and cannot be done to them, granting that an individual is conscious or capable of behaving intentionally and having thoughts about the future (for example) can greatly influence the treatment to which he is subjected. Using the word "stupid" to refer to domesticated animals (Callicott 1980, p. 30) when compared to their wild relatives can certainly influence how one treats an individual. Perhaps, as Szentagothai (1987, p. 323) notes: "There are no 'unintelligent' animals; only careless observations and poorly designed experiments."

What might be some of the implications of discovering that some animals are "not all that cognitive" — that they have relatively impoverished cognitive abilities and lives or that they have fewer memories and fewer beliefs about the future? First, we would have to show that these so-called cognitive "deficiencies" are morally relevant. Is having a sense of time and being able to foresee one's own death a morally relevant difference between humans and animals (Duncan 1993a, p. 7)? Second, it could be argued that although some individuals' cognitive lives are not as rich as those of other "more cognitive" animals, the limited number of memories and expectations that the former individuals have are each more important to them. Not allowing certain expectations to be realized is a serious intrusion on their lives, perhaps more serious than not allowing some expectations in animals with richer cognitive lives to be realized. As Gruen (1992) has pointed out with respect to death, a person who does not get home to write the play they have been thinking of and the dog who does not get to go for one more run by the river are both having desires thwarted to the same degree, totally.

Furthermore, as some have argued, if the memories of some animals are not well developed so that they live in the present and do not have the ability to know about the passage of time into the future, then their pains have no foreseeable end. Thus, I might know that my canid companion Jethro's pain might end in five seconds, but he cannot know this on this account (see also Duncan & Petherick 1991, p. 5,021).

Related to this line of reasoning is the observation that many animals, even those for whom we would be hard-pressed to suggest a rich cognitive life (e.g., lobsters), take what are called self-regarding steps (Hannay 1990, p. 154ff); they seem to try to remove themselves from situations that they find aversive, situations they seem not to prefer that resemble situations that normal human beings and other animals do not prefer either. Even if they do not imagine that there is something that is more pleasurable, and even if they are (some might say merely) removing themselves from a situation that is aversive, they seem to be showing some indication of displeasure and possibly pain. Not being able to imagine a brighter or cooler future does not mean that they are not in pain when they are dropped into hot water. They are acting as if they do not like the situation in which they find themselves, and they may be trying to remove themselves from it without having a subjective experience of pain or a thought about the future. Mason (1994, pp. 57–58) points out that there seems to be no good reason why self-awareness needs to be a prerequisite for suffering, why "the (self-aware) feeling 'I am suffering' [should] be considered worse than the (not self-aware) feeling 'Something truly terrible is happening.'"

Nonetheless, it is possible that there is a difference between a preference for cool water rather than hot water and having a preference to live. DeGrazia (1991) claims that if a struggle for survival is not accompanied by a particular mental state, then it fails to reveal a preference to live. DeGrazia's claim forces the following issue: we must be sure that there is not a particular mental state — perhaps a mental state with which we are unfamiliar — that is associated with a preference shown by an animal who we think is "not all that cognitive," and we must remember that this remains largely an empirical question. It is possible that some animals experience pain and suffer in ways that we cannot yet imagine, and it would be wrong now to conclude that their responses to various stimuli do not count in welfare decisions — that they are similar to the various tropisms shown by plants (see Lewis 1980 for a discussion of pain that concerns itself with the possibility that others who act nothing like we do when we feel pain nevertheless really do feel pain). As Bateson (1991) points out, it was rare in the past to find people taking seriously the possibility of insect pain, but now there is a lot of interest in this area (see also Orlans 1993). Despite their shortcomings (Duncan 1992, 1993a; see also Kaufman 1994), it is possible that preference tests that are developed for a broad spectrum of animals would help to shed some light on the phylogenetic distribution of sentience. This is a challenge for the future because when animals do not do what we expect them to do or when they do nothing, it is possible that they are not motivated by the situation that we create — there are as yet unknown factors that influence their behaviour (Rozin 1976; Cheney & Seyfarth 1993).

Now, the minimalist might want to argue that having a more impoverished life might be a morally relevant difference, but she can't have it both ways. If there are fewer memories or mental states, each of which matters more, then we have to be sure that we do not forget this in our moral deliberations. Removing a calf who is to become veal from his mother might be agony for the mother, for her calf is all she has at the moment. She cannot, it seems, anticipate having another calf in the future, but even if she could have this thought, this would not in any way justify removing her present calf. Furthermore, if my companion Jethro's pains are interminable for him, then causing him pain would be more serious than causing pain for someone to whom you could tell that it would only last for five seconds. But, intentionally causing him pain might still be wrong even if he could know that it would only last for five seconds.

For those who look to studies of humans in order to find some relevance for these sorts of arguments, there might be some strong connections. Consider humans who Dresser (1993) calls "missing persons"; those who are seriously demented and mentally disabled. These people have impoverished mental lives, but it is possible that each of their few memories is more important to them than many of the memories of unimpaired humans.

In the end, if many animals have some form of consciousness — that is, have some capacity for thoughts and emotions, as scientists now largely agree — the question becomes, do differences of degree matter to our ethical choices when it comes to animal welfare? More to the point, do the thoughts and feelings of "less cognitive" animals mean less to the animals themselves? Or, as I argued in 1994, might they in fact mean more? Just because one species of animal might have fewer memories or mental states, or live in the present and not have the ability to know about the passage of time, that doesn't mean they suffer less. Conversely, the pains of supposedly "smarter" animals are not morally more significant than the pains of "dumber beings." Solid science supports these ideas, and I stand by this conclusion.

[ORIGINALLY POSTED ON APRIL 7, 2013]

PART 7

WILD JUSTICE AND
MORAL INTELLIGENCE

Don't Blame Other Animals
for Our Destructive Ways

IT IS CLEAR THAT OTHER ANIMALS are conscious and emotional beings. But are they moral? Do they know right from wrong? This is a hot area of research, and comparative studies are showing that indeed they are and they do. In fact, we're learning that all animals, including humans, are far nicer and more cooperative than we previously imagined. One thing this means is that we shouldn't blame nonhuman animals for our destructive ways. As this part points out, nonhuman animals have been observed intentionally harming one another, but on balance humans clearly do much more intentional harm to their own species than other animals ever do to their own. Further, we also can learn a lot about compassion, empathy, and morality from observing other species. But finally, new research shows that across cultures humans are really much nicer than we ever give them credit for. It's a relative few who wage wars, kill people, and harm children. Most people in the world are nice, kind, and generous, just like their nonhuman cousins.

Wild Justice and
Moral Intelligence in Animals

DO ANIMALS HAVE A SENSE OF MORALITY? Do they know right from wrong? In our forthcoming book, *Wild Justice: The Moral Lives of Animals*, philosopher Jessica Pierce and I argue that the answer to both of these questions is a resounding "yes." "Ought" and "should" regarding what's right and what's wrong play important roles in the social interactions of animals, just as they do in ours.

Historically, others agree. Charles Darwin believed that animals, like humans, could be moral beings. He suggested that human morality is continuous with similar social behavior in other animals. Darwin paid special attention to the capacity for sympathy, which he believed was evidenced in a large numbers of animals. Darwin wrote, "Any animal whatever, endowed with well-marked social instincts...would inevitably acquire a moral sense of conscience, as soon as its intellectual powers had become as well-developed, or nearly as well-developed, as in man."

In the 1980s, Jane Goodall noted in her book *The Chimpanzees of Gombe*, "[I]t is easy to get the impression that chimpanzees are more aggressive than they really are. In actuality, peaceful interactions are far more frequent than aggressive ones; mild threatening gestures are more common than vigorous ones; threats per se occur much more often than fights; and serious, wounding fights are very rare compared to brief, relatively mild ones."

Consider the following scenarios. A teenage female elephant nursing an injured leg is knocked over by a rambunctious hormone-laden teenage male. An older female sees this happen, chases the male away, and goes back to the younger female and touches her sore leg with her trunk. Eleven elephants rescue a group of captive antelope in KwaZula-Natal; the matriarch elephant undoes all of the latches on the gates of the enclosure with her trunk and lets the gate swing open so the antelope can escape. A rat in a cage refuses to push a lever for food when it sees that another rat receives an electric shock as a result. A male Diana monkey who learned to insert a token into a slot to obtain food helps a female who can't get the hang of the trick, inserting the token for her and allowing her to eat the food reward. A female fruit-eating bat helps an unrelated female give birth by showing her how to hang in the proper way. A cat named Libby leads her elderly deaf and blind dog friend, Cashew, away from obstacles and to food. In a group of chimpanzees at the Arnhem Zoo in The Netherlands, individuals punish other chimpanzees who are late for dinner because no one eats until they're all present. A large male dog wants to play with a younger and more submissive male. The big male invites his younger partner to play, and when they play, the big dog restrains himself and bites his younger companion gently and allows him to bite gently in return.

Do these examples show that animals display moral behavior, that they can be compassionate, empathic, altruistic, and fair? Yes, they do. Animals not only have a sense of justice, but also a sense of empathy, forgiveness, trust, reciprocity, and much more as well.

One of the most compelling examples of animals having a sense of morality is the story of a female western lowland gorilla named Binti Jua (Swahili for "daughter of sunshine") who lived in the Brookfield Zoo in Illinois. One summer day in 1996, a three-year-old boy climbed the wall of the gorilla enclosure and fell twenty feet onto the concrete floor below. As spectators gaped and the boy's mother screamed in terror, Binti Jua approached the unconscious boy. She reached down and gently lifted him, cradling him in her arms while her own infant, Koola, clung to her back. Growling warnings at the other gorillas who tried to get close, Binti Jua carried the boy safely to an access gate and the waiting zoo staff. Binti Jua was widely hailed as an animal hero. She was even awarded a medal from the American Legion.

Scientific research has shown that mice display empathy — they feel the pain of other mice and change their behavior. In this compelling story, CeAnn Lambert, director of the Indiana Coyote Rescue Center, saw that two baby mice had become trapped in a sink and were unable to scramble up the slick sides. They were exhausted and frightened. CeAnn filled a small lid with water and placed it in the sink. One of the mice hopped over and drank, but the other was too exhausted to move and remained crouched in the same spot. The stronger mouse found a piece of food and picked it up and carried it to the other. As the weaker mouse tried to nibble on the food, the stronger mouse moved the morsel closer and closer to the water until the weaker mouse could drink. CeAnn created a ramp with a piece of wood and the revived mice were soon able to scramble out of the sink.

The social lives of many animals are strongly shaped by affiliative and cooperative behavior, as Jane Goodall wrote above for chimpanzees. Also consider wolves. For a long time researchers thought that pack size was regulated by available food resources. Wolves typically feed on prey such as elk and moose, both of which are bigger than an individual wolf. Successfully hunting such large ungulates usually takes more than one wolf, so it makes sense to postulate that wolf packs evolved because of the size of wolves' prey. However, long-term research by David Mech showed that pack size in wolves is regulated by social and not food-related factors. Mech discovered that the number of wolves who can live together in a coordinated pack is governed by the number of wolves with whom individuals can closely bond (the "social attraction factor") balanced against the number of individuals from whom an individual could tolerate competition (the "social competition factor"). Packs and their codes of conduct break down when there are too many wolves.

Fairness is also an important part of the social life of animals. Researchers Sarah Brosnan, Frans de Waal, and Hillary Schiff discovered what they call "inequity aversion" in Capuchin monkeys, a highly social and cooperative species in which food sharing is common. These monkeys, especially females, carefully monitor equity and fair treatment among peers. Individuals who are shortchanged during a bartering transaction by being offered a less-preferred treat refuse to cooperate with researchers. The Capuchins expect to be treated fairly. Research by Friedericke Range and her colleagues in Austria also shows that dogs expect to be treated fairly.

Dogs won't work for food if they see other dogs getting more than they do for performing the same task.

Animals are incredibly adept social actors: they form intricate networks of relationships and live by rules of conduct that maintain social balance, or what we call social homeostasis. Humans should be proud of their citizenship in the animal kingdom. We're not the sole occupants of the moral arena.

[ORIGINALLY POSTED ON JUNE 19, 2009]

"What Were Wars?"
Don't Blame Other Animals for Human Violence

HUMANKIND'S LONGTIME AND RAMPANT OBSESSION with making war is well known, as is the claim that, because we are animals, it's natural to behave in these violently destructive ways. John Horgan's 2012 book *The End of War* is a worthy read, in which he makes clear that war is a choice that some people make and is not part of who we (or other animals) are — war is not innate. Horgan argues, "I believe war will end for scientific reasons; I believe war must end for moral reasons." For others who agree with his general message, read *Beyond War* by Douglas Fry and *Winning the War on War* by Joshua Goldstein.

Regardless of mounting scientific evidence that nonhumans are predominantly cooperative, peaceful, and fair, and on occasion display social justice (see also *Born to Be Good* by Dacher Keltner), media hype portrays other animals as being far more violent and warlike than they really are. This includes the 2012 movie *The Grey*, which misrepresents wolves as violent hunters who harm humans. Why is it that blood, rather than peace, sells?

However, people who claim nonhuman animals are inherently aggressive and warlike are wrong. When they use information from animal studies to justify our own cruel, evil, and warlike behavior, they're not paying attention to what we really know about the social life of animals. Do animals fight with one another? Yes. Do they routinely engage in cruel, warlike behavior? Not at all. Numerous species display wild justice and carefully negotiate their social relationships, so that fairness, cooperation, compassion, and empathy are quite common.

In another essay called "Quitting the Hominid Fight Club," Horgan summarizes much of what is known about warfare in great apes and other primates. Horgan is especially concerned with what is called the "demonic male" theory that states "both male humans and chimpanzees, our closest genetic relatives, are 'natural warriors' with an innate predisposition

toward 'coalitionary killing,' which dates back to our common ancestor." Horgan summarizes what is known as follows: "All told, since Jane
Goodall began observing chimpanzees in Tanzania's Gombe National
Park in 1960, researchers have directly observed 31 intergroup killings, of
which 17 were infants.... [R]esearchers at a typical site directly observe
one killing every seven years.... [M]y criticism — and that of other critics I've cited — stems from science, not ideology. The evidence for the
demonic-males theory, far from extraordinary, is flimsy."

Warlike animals are the rare exception, not the rule, and this must be
factored into our own rationalizations and justifications for our seeming
obsession with making war. War is a choice, and nonhuman animals should
not be blamed for our destructive inclinations.

When we say to someone, "Oh, you're behaving like an animal," it's
actually a compliment rather than an insult. We need to work for a science
of peace and build a culture of empathy, and emphasize the positive, prosocial side of the character of other animals and ourselves. It's truly who
we and other animals are.

The quotation in the title of this essay is taken from Horgan's book,
and it should give us all hope for the future. Imagine the day when a child
asks, "What were wars?" This thought makes me sit back and smile, and it
is indeed a possibility.

[ORIGINALLY POSTED ON JANUARY 22, 2012]

Human-Like Violence Is Extremely Rare in Other Animals

IN THE DEPRESSING AND SAD WAKE of the ghastly tragedy in Newtown, Connecticut, on December 14, 2012, in which twenty-six people were killed, including twenty children, a number of people have asked me, "What can we learn about human violence from nonhuman animals?" I've written some on this topic before, but it's worth revisiting what we know about the social behavior of nonhuman animals and adding the new, detailed scientific research that has been discovered. In a nutshell, we shouldn't be blaming other animals for our violent and evil ways.

When discussing violent behavior in humans, newscasters and other people quite often refer to those who commit these acts as "animals" or say they're "acting like animals." However, this dismissal is based on a lack of knowledge about the latest scientific research, which clearly shows that individuals of many species are far more cooperative, peaceful, kind, compassionate, empathic, and nice than previously thought.

For instance, in an important 2010 essay, John Horgan summarizes current research about warfare in great apes and other primates (for a description, see "'What Were Wars?' Don't Blame Other Animals for Human Violence," page 199). Citing the research of Jane Goodall, he makes clear that such violence among nonhuman primates is extremely rare.

Along these lines, Robert W. Sussman, an anthropologist at Washington University in St. Louis, and his colleagues Paul A. Garber and Jim Cheverud, reported in 2005 in *The American Journal of Physical Anthropology* that for many nonhuman primates, more than 90 percent of their social interactions are affiliative rather than competitive or divisive. The upshot of this is that positive emotions lie at the core of "animal nature."

We're also learning a lot about moral behavior in very young children. For example, researchers who study child's play, like Ernst Fehr of the University of Zurich, and Anthony D. Pellegrini of the University of Minnesota–Twin Cities, have discovered that basic rules of fairness guide play, and that egalitarian instincts emerge very early in childhood. Indeed, while playing, children learn, as do other young animals, that there are right and wrong ways to play, and that transgressions of fairness have social consequences, like being ostracized. Research has also shown that six-month-old babies know right from wrong. And, of course, there's University of California psychologist Dacher Keltner's wonderful book called *Born to Be Good*, in which he shows that positive emotions lie at the core of human nature, just as they do for other animals.

An excellent 2013 book titled *War, Peace, and Human Nature: The Convergence of Evolutionary and Cultural Views*, edited by Douglas Fry, deals with many of these issues. In this book ethologist Peter Verbeek notes, "[W]e go to war not because we are naturally driven to do so, but because we choose to do so. A choice for war is linked to overcoming fear and empathy, and it is critically important to understand what biological, social-learning, and cultural factors take us there." Yes, animals fight with one another, but cruel, violent behaviors are extremely rare. Thus, we can learn a lot about who we really are from paying attention to what we are learning about the social behavior of other animals, and we can harness our own innate goodness to make the world a better place for all beings.

In my own interests in how we can rewild our hearts (see "Rewilding Our Hearts: Maintaining Hope and Faith in Trying Times," page 322) and better and more closely connect with nature, I argue that rewilding is all about being nice, kind, compassionate, empathic, and harnessing our inborn goodness and optimism. We all must work together at this. It's about time we focus on the good side of human and animal nature. As renowned primatologist Frans de Waal reminds us (such as in his books *The Age of Empathy* and *The Bonobo and the Atheist*), nature offers many lessons for kinder society. Blood shouldn't sell. There really is hope if we pay attention to what we know and push aside misleading sensationalist media that misrepresents us and other animals.

[ORIGINALLY POSTED ON DECEMBER 16, 2012]

The Moral Lives of Animals: What Did Herman Melville Have to Say about Animals?

A NEW 2011 BOOK HAS RECENTLY APPEARED that deserves wide attention. Dale Peterson's *The Moral Lives of Animals* considers a topic that is of great interest among a large number of scholars and lay people, namely, can nonhuman animals be moral beings?

This book follows a small number of other books on this general topic, including one of my own. In fact, in March 2006 I had dinner with Dale Peterson, the author of this well-written, well-researched, and forward-looking book. Dale was eager to tell me about his great idea for a new book and went on to outline his views about the moral lives of nonhuman animals. When he was finished I timidly told him that Jessica Pierce and I were in the final stages of writing a book on the same topic called *Wild Justice*, with, as it turned out, the same subtitle as his new book. Later, Dale told me he felt crestfallen, but I encouraged and assured him that there was plenty of room for more than Jessica's and my voice on this wide-ranging and controversial topic. I'm glad Dale went on to complete his own project because we come to the topic from decidedly different perspectives. And the more the merrier, since the discussion of moral intelligence in animals is in its infancy.

Peterson is well-qualified to write this book. He holds a PhD in English literature, and he has had twenty-five years of firsthand experience with a number of different animals around the world. He was educated in primatology during collaborations with renowned researchers Jane Goodall and Richard Wrangham, and he learned about elephants while writing about them (see *Elephant Reflections*), advised by well-known elephant expert Katy Payne (see *Silent Thunder*).

Peterson's latest book was born after an argument at a dinner party where someone seemed to suggest that animals displaying moral behavior was the stupidest thing he'd heard all day! I can relate to that experience. One colleague told me years ago that surely I had better things to do with my time because animals simply could not be moral beings or display moral sentiments. Animals surely didn't know right from wrong, and that was it, end of story. Clearly, these naysayers were and are wrong and are beginning to find themselves in an ever-growing minority. Almost daily we learn about elephants, wolves, dogs, rodents, and many other animals who care for one another by displaying compassion and empathy and who put others before themselves. We now know that mice and even chickens display empathy (see "Empathic Chickens and Cooperative Elephants: Emotional Intelligence Expands Its Range Again," page 178).

The Moral Lives of Animals is an eye-opening, original, wide-ranging, and ambitious book. Part one is concerned with where morality comes from. Peterson shows how morality can be understood as a gift of biological evolution. He is concerned with tracing evolutionary continuity and not inventing it where it doesn't exist, and throughout the book he does this in a careful and detailed way. Peterson offers a simple practical definition of morality: "The function of morality...is to negotiate inherent serious conflict between self and others." He notes that morality in animals could be homologous with human morality, having been derived from a common origin, and not merely analogous or due to coincidental similarities. Inherent in his definition are conflict and choice. Further, moral behavior isn't the same as niceness and doesn't necessarily promote egalitarianism. Animals can be fully moral rather than "premoral" or "proto-moral." I agree with these views, and as Jessica Pierce and I concluded in *Wild Justice*, we don't need to use hesitation quotes when we talk about the moral behavior of animals. They have the real thing.

Parts two and three center on what morality is. Peterson argues that there are nonlinguistic rules that evolved in response to social conflict and attachments. He examines the rules of morality in five different social situations — namely, authority, violence, sex, possession, and communication — and looks at attachments morality, which includes mechanisms promoting cooperation and kindness.

Part four is concerned with where morality is going. Here, Peterson envisions an increased importance for empathy that will serve nonhuman animals and human animals well. He hopes that in the future we will move toward "greater tolerance, higher wisdom, and a new condition of peace between humans and nonhumans alike."

Peterson's diverse background leads him to take a refreshingly novel and wide-ranging view of animal moral behavior by anchoring his arguments using Herman Melville's classic *Moby Dick*. In the novel, Ahab, who lost his leg to the albino whale Moby Dick, and his first mate Starbuck have different perspectives on the cognitive and moral life of whales. Ahab believes Moby Dick is "alive, aware, and morally responsible" and vows revenge. Ahab assumes what Peterson calls the "First Way" of thinking about animals — a "medieval vision of animal minds as intelligent entities constructed in a humanoid form — essentially underendowed human minds." Starbuck, on the other hand, adopts the "Second Way" of thinking about animals, in that he believes animals act from blind instinct and are not morally responsible for what they do. The Second Way of thinking is the Enlightenment vision often associated with French philosopher René Descartes, which proposes that only humans have minds. Animals are alive and experience sensations, but they are basically machines, so animals do not actually feel pain because they don't have mental experiences.

Peterson notes that both characters are wrong. Ahab is wrong because Moby Dick is not responsible as would be a human, and Starbuck is wrong because animals are not unfeeling things or objects. Peterson cleverly suggests triangulating these two views into a "Third Way" of thinking about animals. This perspective allows for the existence of animal minds but recognizes that they are "alien minds," that is, alien from human minds. The Third Way looks for real similarity and genuine dissimilarity between human and animals minds. Alien does not mean lesser, just "imperfectly comprehensible." Humans are not above and apart from other animals. I agree. Meanwhile, skeptics can't resort to Peterson's First or Second Way. They're too reductionistic and simplistic, and they fly in the face of what we now know about the emotional and moral lives of animals.

While Peterson writes about numerous different species, he also writes about his companion dogs Smoke and Spike. He notes of the relationship between himself and his dogs, "we are friends...in spite of evolutionary discontinuity and because of evolutionary continuity."

In the end we learn that while animals surely compete and on occasion harm one another, this is rare compared to more cooperative, empathic, prosocial interactions. Hand-to-hand combat can be dangerous for all involved; even if a dominant individual wins, they may at the same time lose. Animals are more peaceful, generous, and fairer than we give them credit for. For the most part, animal violence is directed outward, that is, outside the species — where the moral rules don't usually hold — or sometimes, for some species, within the species but outside the social group. An inhibition of violence within the social group is indeed one of the several functions of morality.

We need details of what animals do in the wild. We need to understand who they are and what they do in the context of their own lives, not ours. They display flexibility, in that the rules that apply to one group of chimpanzees or pack of wolves might not apply in others. Studies of wild animals are essential because captive individuals kept in impoverished conditions, social and otherwise, are unable to express their full behavioral repertoire, and we get a false picture of what they are capable of doing.

Peterson's book gives us a wealth of new and powerfully original ideas for future research and debate. It also shows us how animals are part of various landscapes, and we need to know who they are and what they know and feel and can do. We can learn a lot about ourselves and our relationships with the natural world by learning more about the other animals with whom we share Earth. They can be very good teachers if we allow them to be. They can show us how to have compassion and empathy for the natural world and why our troubled and wounded world could benefit greatly from these lessons. We are so fortunate to share Earth with such wonderful beings.

[ORIGINALLY POSTED ON MARCH 23, 2011]

Give Peace a Chance:
We Do Not Have to Go to War

I'VE WRITTEN A NUMBER OF ESSAYS about the importance of cooperation, fairness, compassion, and empathy in the evolution of social behavior in human and nonhuman animals. Now, a new book edited by Douglas Fry titled *War, Peace, and Human Nature: The Convergence of Evolutionary and Cultural Views* and an interdisciplinary meeting called "Obstacles and Catalysts of Peaceful Behavior," held in March 2013 at the Lorentz Center in Leiden, The Netherlands, show clearly that a science of peace is possible and that war is neither a human universal nor an ancient or an evolved adaptation.

This Leiden gathering was strongly international, and I was there to speak about social reciprocity, conflict resolution, and peacemaking in nonprimates and the importance of social play. This followed up on the book I wrote with Jessica Pierce called *Wild Justice: The Moral Lives of Animals*. Many animals work hard to cooperate to play fairly. And the basic rules for fair play in animals also apply to humans, namely, *ask first, be honest, follow the rules,* and *admit you're wrong*. When the rules of play are violated, and when fairness breaks down, so does play and peace.

Professor Fry's wide-ranging and encyclopedic book is truly a landmark compendium and a myth-buster. It's a must-read that deserves very close attention. Written by leading biologists, psychologists, anthropologists, sociologists, and geologists, the book is divided into six parts that provide a comprehensive look at the topic. It presents ecology- and evolution-based models of peace, and it looks closely at ancient nomadic, hunter-gatherer human societies as well as at primatological research to seek out the roots of cooperation and the modern forms of violence and conflict. The book ends with a proposal for creating a "Global Peace System." The amount of information and the documentation and references are staggering.

In the foreword, renowned primatologist Frans de Waal writes that "the evidence that we have always waged war is rather thin." Professor de Waal goes on to discuss the importance of research on topics such as reconciliation, conflict resolution, empathy, and friendships in nonhuman animals. He notes that while we do need to be concerned with human aggression, this concern "needs to be balanced with that other potential that we have, which is to make peace, get along, and develop societies based on cooperation. The idea that this is not part of human nature, that it is merely a thin moral veneer over an otherwise nasty biology, is massively contradicted by the contributions assembled here." Professor de Waal also has a new book, called *The Bonobo and the Atheist: In Search of Humanism Among the Primates*, which covers the biological origins of human fairness.

While it should be noted that other animals do indeed fight with one another, and on occasion seriously harm and kill one another, their behavior is predominantly prosocial (defined as "voluntary behavior intended to benefit another"). For more on this, see my essays "Human-Like Violence Is Extremely Rare in Other Animals," page 201, and "Wild Justice and Moral Intelligence in Animals," page 195. By some estimates, among many nonhuman primates, over 90 percent of their social interactions are affiliative rather than competitive.

In a recent interview, in response to the question "How does chimp behavior help us better understand human behavior?" world-renowned researcher and conservationist Jane Goodall answered, "Well, the part that always shocked me was the intercommunity violence among the chimps: the patrols and the vicious attacks on strangers that lead to death. It's an unfortunate parallel to human behavior — they have a dark side just as we do. We have less excuse, because we can deliberate, so I believe only we are capable of true calculated evil."

When it comes to morality and violence, the issue of intention, of calculated premeditation, is important. In his chapter in *War, Peace, and Human Nature*, called "An Ethological Perspective on War and Peace," psychobiologist and co-organizer of the Leiden meeting Peter Verbeek (who coined the term "peace ethology") notes, "[W]e go to war not because we are naturally driven to do so, but because we choose to do so…

and it is critically important to understand what biological, social-learning, and cultural factors take us there." To this end, Richard Hughbank and Dave Grossman, both of whom are retired from the US military, write an essay about the challenge of getting men to kill. In fact, it's not easy to get people to kill other people.

How to overcome the challenge of a human society built to wage war is the subject of ex-US Army Captain Paul Chappell's excellent book called *Peaceful Revolution: How We Can Create the Future Needed for Humanity's Survival*. Chappell writes, "Today ending war is necessary for the survival of humanity, yet those who perpetuate war control the society, government, military, corporations, many universities, and most of the money. What do we have on our side? The truth. Contrary to widely believed myths, it is not true that human beings are naturally violent. It is not true that war is inevitable. It is not true that war protects our way of life and makes us safe.... We can talk about how tragic war is, but unless we question its underlying assumptions and challenge its prevailing myths, war will continue."

If this sounds like something only "peace advocates" would say, Chappell quotes none other than General Douglas MacArthur: "[The abolition of war] is no longer an ethical equation to be pondered solely by learned philosophers and ecclesiastics, but a hard-core one for the decision of the masses whose survival is the issue.... We must have sufficient imagination and courage to translate this universal wish for peace — which is rapidly becoming a universal necessity — into actuality!"

Echoing Mr. Chappell and General MacArthur, Professor Fry writes in his conclusion to *War, Peace, and Human Nature*: "Human survival requires that nation-states give up the institution of war and replace it with a cooperatively-functioning global peace system — for the well-being and security of all people everywhere." Amen.

I hope that these new books by Douglas Fry and Paul Chappell, and the discussions at the Leiden meeting, will truly make us deeply reflect on the new paradigm, the science of peace, that is sorely needed and entirely possible. Let's not ignore our kind and beneficent nature.

Let's give peace the attention and chance it truly deserves. Nothing will be lost and much will be gained. Cooperation, empathy, and peace will prevail if we allow them to. Let's stop justifying war as inevitable because "that's who we are."

We do not *have* to go to war.

[ORIGINALLY POSTED ON MARCH 14, 2013]

PART 8

THE LIVES OF CAPTIVE CREATURES

Why Are They Even There?

BILLIONS OF ANIMALS are kept in various captive situations, ranging from laboratories to zoos and aquariums, from circuses and rodeos to our own homes. We keep animals for a variety of reasons: in the name of science, in the name of entertainment, in the name of food (see part 9), or because they're our companions. However, the lives of captive animals are often compromised. They may suffer from confinement, the lack of exercise, from being kept alone without friends, and from being mistreated (or deliberately "broken," as happens in circuses, so they do what's needed to entertain us). Here I'm primarily concerned with wild and domestic animals who are kept for purposes of entertaining humans. Today, there is increasing scrutiny of zoos and their purpose. Particularly in light of the uneven levels of animal care, the untimely deaths of zoo animals, and even the occasional death of their human caretakers, we must ask what zoos are really good for. I hope that this sample of essays shows that captive animals deserve much better treatment than they receive and that this should lead us to question why we hold them captive in the first place.

Zoos and Aquariums Do Not Accomplish What They Claim They Do

MANY PEOPLE VISIT ZOOS and aquariums (which I'll refer to as "zoos" for convenience) for a variety of reasons. While there are "better" and "worse" zoos, animals residing in captivity live highly compromised lives. They are often kept in very small cages and in unnatural groups without family and friends while suffering losses of freedom of movement and of the ability to control their own lives. Some can't get out of the public eye and are on constant display during visiting hours, during which time they eat, urinate, defecate, rest, sleep, and sometimes mate under constant scrutiny. Many are simply bored, and some, like African elephants, die at a significantly younger age than their wild relatives, as shown by a study published in the prestigious journal *Science*. In the study, elephants in captivity lived an average of nineteen years compared to fifty-six years in the wild. Major zoos also have had serious problems but have continued to receive accreditation from the Association of Zoos and Aquariums (AZA; www.aza.org).

Do zoos accomplish what they claim to do? No, according to a detailed 2010 study published in a peer-reviewed professional journal. Lori Marino, of Emory University, and her colleagues conducted a research project to assess the claims of a study performed by the AZA on why zoos matter, and they report in their abstract as follows:

> Modern-day zoos and aquariums market themselves as places of education and conservation. A recent study conducted by the American Zoo and Aquarium Association (AZA) (Falk et al., 2007) is being widely heralded as the first direct evidence that visits to zoos and aquariums produce long-term positive effects on people's attitudes toward other animals. In this paper, we address whether this conclusion is warranted by analyzing the study's methodological soundness. We conclude that Falk et al. (2007)

contains at least six major threats to methodological validity that undermine the authors' conclusions. There remains no compelling evidence for the claim that zoos and aquariums promote attitude change, education, or interest in conservation in visitors, although further investigation of this possibility using methodologically sophisticated designs is warranted.

The study by Professor Marino and her colleagues clearly shows that zoos fall short on their claims that seeing animals in these facilities has long-term positive effects on people's attitudes toward other animals. There is no evidence that many people make any useful monetary contributions or use their visit to a zoo to have any positive effect on the animals who they see, even though they say that visiting a zoo made them appreciate animals more. Thus, we need to revisit the very reasons why zoos exist: why should animals be kept in these places and often shipped here and there as if they're objects for purposes of mating or adding to an already existing collection? And why should people visit them rather than watch videos of wild animals, observe the animals with whom they share their homes, or simply take walks in nature and enjoy the fauna and flora they see, hear, and smell?

[ORIGINALLY POSTED ON APRIL 13, 2010]

"Faux" Animals in Cages Deserve Much Better

I'm NOT A FAN OF ZOOS and aquariums, but for now at least they're not going away. Zoos and aquariums don't really do much if anything for education and conservation, they ship animals around as if they were mere objects, they reduce the life span of their residents, and places like SeaWorld are notorious for mistreating animals and for the death of their residents and humans (for instance, see *Death at SeaWorld* by David Kirby). Yet they persist in many shapes and sizes and in varying quality. In fact, zoos really do very little or nothing for the individuals who live there or for other members of their species. Indeed, many people, including experts in the fields of animal behavior and conservation biology, argue that the animals living in zoos and aquariums are "fabricated" or "faux" animals and are not at all representative of their wild relatives. Be that as it may, zoos are here to stay at least for a while.

I just read an interesting interview in *National Geographic* with zoo expert David Hancocks, which was sent to me by my friend Hannah Jaicks, about the need to revolutionize zoos. As long as zoos exist, there is so much that can and must be done to vastly improve and enrich the lives of the beings who are forced to languish in concrete or aquatic cages. Despite the claim of some of my colleagues that "good" people don't work in zoos, it's clear that many people who really care about animals do indeed choose to work in zoos, and the animals are lucky they're there. I've had students delay going to graduate school so that they could continue to work in zoos, so that the animals with whom they had bonded would be well taken care of and not have to get used to or stressed out by the presence of a new keeper. Meanwhile, other friends could have gone on to higher-paying jobs but chose to continue to work in zoos because they felt badly for the animals for whom they were responsible.

David Hancocks is one those people who chooses to work in the zoo industry while tirelessly working for the resident animals. Often it's not an easy job. There are some zoo professionals who claim they care for the animals but their behavior belies these claims — they separate and ship animals around and engage in breeding programs that do nothing for the individuals or species involved. For them and others, money rules and animal well-being gets mere lip service.

Some snippets from the interview with David Hancocks include:

If zoos gave serious attention to education, we should surely see much greater variety in their collections, to help them better focus on biodiversity; if they were serious about conservation, they would give much more attention to local species; and if they truly wanted their visitors to develop better understandings of the natural world, they would be showing and interpreting the really small life forms....

In this regard it is disturbing to note studies showing that the present coordinated breeding program for elephants is doomed to failure. Yet zoos persist in making loud and persistent claims that they are centers of elephant conservation, and, as the AZA has risibly declared, are critical to their survival....

What zoos have decided to do instead is to design animal enclosures (they call them "habitats") that look vaguely naturalistic, but in which the animals have no contact with anything natural. None of their senses are stimulated by the typical zoo-built enclosure. Everything they touch except their food and feces is unnatural: trees made of concrete or plastic; floors made to look natural but formed of unyielding concrete (or, occasionally, tan-bark or hard-packed dirt, each as useless to the animals as concrete). The animal spaces are very often as barren as the old menagerie cages. Visitor spaces, meanwhile, are typically bewildering and visually chaotic spaces that vaguely resemble a mix of suburban park environments and the *Tarzanesque* appearance of Hollywood B-grade movies. Worryingly, all these modern zoo exhibits are usually designed by specialized professionals....

I recently attended a symposium on "The Future of Zoos."

The opening statement on its program stated that zoos today are "dominated by multispecies displays that strive to replicate entire ecosystems." Dominated? Entire ecosystems? This is the same sort of nonsensical hubris that the AZA continually parades, making such claims as, "The survival of the world's endangered species *pivots* on the conservation and education efforts of modern zoos." [Emphasis added in original.] This mindset is the greatest stumbling block to zoo progress.

Zoo animals are lucky to have friends like David Hancocks. I, like, many others, would like to see zoos phased out, but as long as they're around, we must do all we can to improve and enrich the lives of their residents. A revolution is sorely needed so that the animals who are held in various sorts of cages can live with more respect and dignity.

[ORIGINALLY POSTED ON MARCH 15, 2012]

"Zoothanasia" Is Not Euthanasia: Words Matter

A RECENT ESSAY in the *New York Times* has made me rethink why zoos exist and what they're really good for. The title of this essay, "When Babies Don't Fit Plan, Question for Zoos Is, Now What?" also made me realize how the animals who find themselves living in zoos are totally at the mercy of the humans who control their lives. My colleague Jessica Pierce also wrote about this essay and told me she wasn't radical enough in that she really isn't "for zoos." She encouraged me to write more on this touchy and very controversial subject.

The *New York Times* essay begins: "Zookeepers around the world, facing limited capacity and pressure to maintain diverse and vibrant collections of endangered species, are often choosing between two controversial methods: birth control and euthanasia. In the United States, the choice is contraception. Chimps take human birth control pills, giraffes are served hormones in their feed, and grizzly bears have slow-releasing hormones implanted in their forelegs. Even small rodents are included."

However, in countries other than the United States, it's a different story. In Europe, for example, "some zookeepers would rather euthanize *unneeded* offspring after they mature than deny the animal parents the experience of procreating and nurturing their young." In the quote, I added emphasis to the word "unneeded" because, frankly, the use of this word makes me sick to my stomach. These animals aren't objects but rather sentient beings who are "unneeded" simply because the zoos don't need them. How anthropocentrically arrogant and insensitively heartless it is for these people to take this view. I also was sickened to see an abstract of a paper by Paul Andrew, curator of the Taronga Zoo in Sydney, Australia, in which animals are referred to as being surplus to the genetic needs of a zoo's program.

Consider what happens at the Copenhagen Zoo. In the *New York Times* story, according to Bengt Holst, director of conservation, "We have already taken away their predatory and antipredatory behaviors. If we take away their parenting behavior, they have not much left." Using this reasoning, the *Times* reports, European zoos "generally allow animals to raise their young until an age at which they would naturally separate from parents. It is then that zoo officials euthanize offspring that do not figure in breeding plans."

Killing animals in zoos because they don't "figure into breeding plans" is not euthanasia, it's "zoothanasia," and it is a most disturbing and inhumane practice. Using the word "euthanasia" seems to sanitize the killing, at least for some people, and makes it more acceptable. While one might argue that many if not all animals in zoos suffer, killing animals who aren't needed isn't mercy killing. It's really a form of premeditated killing. Furthermore, by using "that" rather than "who" to refer to "offspring" in the quote above, the *Times* continues to objectify animals. Of course, referring to animals as if they're objects can make it easier to kill healthy animal children.

In my view there's something very wrong with this picture. People who supposedly love animals and want there to be more of them choose to kill them because there are too many of them. The animals are innocent victims of human arrogance and quite often greed.

In this story, I also learned about another phrase thrown around by zoo administrators, "management euthanasia." One former zoo director goes as far as to say, "I am not saying management euthanasia is wrong.... It is just not the best solution." I thoroughly disagree. There is something very, very wrong with this egregious practice. It should really be called "mismanagement zoothanasia." Zoo administrators should surely be held accountable for reckless breeding practices that lead to this.

The *New York Times* essay is filled with lame rationales for killing unneeded or surplus animals. Consider this discussion about the timing of killing unneeded animals. "Even when zoos wait to euthanize animals until their parents have had a chance to raise them, questions can come up. It might seem suspiciously convenient for zoos to destroy an animal just after it has completed its most adorable phase — given that baby animals are a top zoo attraction. But Dr. Holst emphasized that the timing is dictated by nature. Zookeepers know it is time when the young leopards start picking fights with their mother. 'It may be painful for us,' he said, 'but more natural to them.'"

Oh, please! How can anyone who knows anything about animals claim that killing them because they pick fights is natural? Would he also kill his or another dog who fought with others?

We also learn that it's okay for animals who are "genetically useless" to be killed. Lesley Dickie, executive director of the European Association of Zoos and Aquaria, called the killing of the offspring of a hybrid male tiger at Zoo Magdeburg in northern Germany "courageous." The zoo director and three employees were prosecuted for violating the euthanasia law, but they received suspended sentences. Of course, this was *not* euthanasia.

There's ample evidence that zoos do not contribute much if anything to education or conservation (see "Zoos and Aquariums Do Not Accomplish What They Claim They Do," page 213), a conclusion that's even supported by the Association for Zoos and Aquariums, despite claims to the contrary. Given that animal lives are discussed as if the individuals are unfeeling and unneeded or surplus objects, it's no surprise that there are many reasons many people are against zoos. For further discussion about why zoos must go, please see Dale Jamieson's essay "Against Zoos."

Zoos, as long as they exist, must be for the animals who are forced to live there, not for the people who visit or run them. We really need some radical changes now that emphasize *the importance of every single animal living in captivity*. Glib excuses for killing any individual must be countered, and zoo personnel (and others, including those who write for the media) must refer to animals as who they really are, not as disposable, unneeded, or surplus objects "that," for example, it's okay to kill.

Phasing out zoos in favor of sanctuaries where individuals can live out their lives with respect and dignity should be the focus of future efforts to enrich and honor the lives of the numerous animals who find themselves languishing in captivity. Allowing animals to be treated, and even killed, as if they were mere objects should not be tolerated. Each of us must work to end this egregious practice. The compassionate conservation movement (see "Ignoring Nature No More: Compassionate Conservation at Work," page 303) is one such move in the right direction.

[ORIGINALLY POSTED ON AUGUST 9, 2012]

Elephants in LA Zoo
Aren't Happy or Content, Says Judge

IT'S BECOMING CLEARER and clearer that zoos and aquariums are not good homes for animals. SeaWorld has all sorts of problems (see "Deaths at Sea-World: Animals Are Dying to Entertain in This SeaJail," page 223), and now we've just learned that the Los Angeles Zoo isn't all it claims to be. As Michael Mountain reports on his Earth in Transition blog, Los Angeles judge John A. Segal concluded, "All is not well at the Elephants of Asia exhibit at the Los Angeles Zoo."

This is a landmark decision that should be widely applauded and publicized. More and more, as with the compelling case against SeaWorld, it's not only professed animal advocates who are sick and tired of the horrific ways in which animals are treated when held in captivity for entertainment. Judge Segal wrote, "Contrary to what the zoo's representatives may have told the Los Angeles City Council in order to get construction of the $42 million exhibit approved and funded, the elephants are not healthy, happy, and thriving."

As Michael Mountain notes, this pricey and inadequate exhibit has nothing to do with the Asian elephants who live there: Billy, Tina, and Jewel. It has everything to do with entertainment, the results of which won't do anything for the elephants who are held captive in conditions that don't even remotely resemble the way in which these magnificent animals live in the wild. For example, the elephants get shocked if they go near the trees or grass in their natural-looking cage, since they may destroy them. Further, keeping these elephants captive provides no benefit at all for their wild relatives.

The conditions in which the elephants are forced to live and the claims of the zoo about how well they are doing were very dismaying to the judge, as they should be to everyone who reads about this total waste of money. Billy was also trained to stand on his back legs to entertain visitors.

So, just as for the unfortunate animals at SeaWorld and other similar places, entertainment is the name of the game as animals are trained to perform stupid and unnatural tricks that are utterly disrespectful of who these amazing beings truly are.

While the judge didn't tell the zoo to get rid of the exhibit and send the elephants to a sanctuary, where they could live out their lives in dignity, it's clear this incredible decision puts the onus on zoos to come clean about how they actually treat their residents and what they really do for them and their wild relatives. Of course, spokespersons for the zoo disagreed with the judge's decision, but it's clear that cruelty and misleading claims about what zoos do for animals can't stand the spotlight, and indeed they should never, ever be ignored.

I always say we must continue to be optimistic. As time passes, more and more people, including those who make decisions that really make a difference, will see zoos for what they really are and work to change them, so that someday the animals who are held in these facilities will be able to live out their lives absent abuse.

[ORIGINALLY POSTED ON JULY 26, 2012]

Deaths at SeaWorld:
Animals Are Dying to Entertain in This SeaJail

DEATH AT SEAWORLD: *Shamu and the Dark Side of Killer Whales in Captivity* by David Kirby is an outstanding book. I titled this short essay "Deaths at SeaWorld" because, in fact, many animals, human and non-human, have died at this "carefully managed facade." *Death at SeaWorld* is one of the most important books, if not the most important book, ever written on the horrific plight of captive cetaceans. Kirby systematically dismantles the arguments used to justify keeping these incredibly intelligent and sentient beings in aquatic cages.

The praise for award-winning investigative journalist David Kirby's book is outstanding and comes from well-recognized animal advocates and also from places that often remain neutral on issues of animal abuse and animal protection. For example, renowned primatologist and conservationist Jane Goodall wrote, "As David Kirby so eloquently documents in this timely work, killer-whale captivity only benefits the captors. It is impossible to read *Death at SeaWorld* and come to any other conclusion." Louie Psihoyos, Academy Award-winning director of *The Cove* (www.thecovemovie.com) wrote, "Entertaining, engaging, and enraging — the fairy tale fantasy that the captivity marine mammal industry has spun for the unwary public is expertly unraveled in this nonfiction crime thriller." And Ken Balcomb, director of the Center for Whale Research, exclaimed, "One helluva book! David Kirby provides the most complete and accurate account of what I perceive as a transgression of morality toward the animal kingdom — the slavery of orcas, supreme beings in the aquatic world."

Reviewers for the mainstream press also praised *Death at SeaWorld* as a "great book," including the *Wall Street Journal*, the *Columbus Dispatch*, and *Library Journal*. It's rare for such a book to get wide-ranging unqualified support from such a diverse audience. This is because this book is very well-written, extremely well-documented, and timely.

In a nutshell, Kirby, a *New York Times* bestselling author, exposes the dark side of SeaWorld's treatment of animals, focusing on killer whales or orcas, and shows clearly that numerous animals at SeaWorld have been and are horrifically abused and chronically stressed. They're force-fed antibiotics, vitamins, and antacids; have their teeth removed with power drills; are left to mourn on their own after having their young taken away from them; and are masturbated for sperm. Most die in their teens and twenties, far younger than their wild relatives, and around 15 percent of all orcas held in collections in SeaWorld have been involved in serious acts of aggression against trainers. To date there are no records of wild orcas seriously injuring or killing a person. Trainers are also kept ignorant of risks, and there's poor recordkeeping. For example, "minor" behavioral issues such as whales mounting trainers, which frequently result in injury, go unreported. Indeed, in 2010, SeaWorld was fined seventy-five thousand dollars by the Occupational Safety and Health Administration for three safety violations, including one classified as willful, after animal trainer Dawn Brancheau was killed.

In a discussion of the egregious practices of SeaWorld, I wrote an earlier essay called "Tilly's Willy: In the Name of Science?," page 225, in which I recounted the story of how this awesome being was repeatedly masturbated so that his sperm could be used to make more orcas. We now know that many of his descendants are kept at SeaWorld to breed, often with one another, as if they're living in a "whale mill."

What good does SeaWorld do? Very little. SeaWorld conducts little scientific research and does little or nothing for the conservation of wild orcas.

SeaWorld is really a SeaJail. It's a whale mill, and they should be ashamed of how they keep highly sentient beings and for continuing to deceive an unknowing public about what they really do and why they do it. Simply put, SeaWorld abuses amazing animals, forces them to breed and perform stupid and unnatural tricks, never allowing them to retire, all in the name of money. They've been caught and fined before, and let's hope that this careful scrutiny continues.

[ORIGINALLY POSTED ON JULY 22, 2012]

Tilly's Willy: In the Name of Science?

FOR YEARS I'VE BEEN WRITING about various aspects of animal behavior, focusing more recently on their emotional and moral lives, conservation strategies, and the horrific ways in which animals in captivity are treated.

In February 2010 I wrote about Tilikum (a.k.a. Tilly), a wild-caught killer whale who attacked and killed a trainer at SeaWorld. This wasn't the first time Tilly had killed a human. Tilly had been taken from his pod at about two years of age in 1983. Now, twenty-eight years later, Tilly is back on display and continues to be a very successful stud, used in the same way that puppies in a puppy mill are used to make more dogs. In effect, Tilly is part of a profit-motivated "whale mill," the result of which is to produce more whales who will languish and be abused in captivity, for entertaining humans by performing stupid tricks.

While the confinement of Tilly and other orcas (and many other animals) in and of itself is as regrettable, demeaning, and disrespectful as can be, I just learned that humans go into the water to play with Tilly's willy so that he produces semen. I was shocked. How could I not know this, as I've been studying and writing about animals for decades? While some people from SeaWorld deny that this is done, former SeaWorld scientist John Hall disagrees, as do others who have worked at this aquarium. One article about this includes a video of the process (see Endnotes, page 346), as humans casually engage in what could be called whale whacking. Great, get a job working with whales kept in prison and then pleasure them purportedly "in the name of science" but really "in the name of money." Captive whales such as Tilly make no contribution to useful knowledge about his species, despite the spurious claims that captive animals educate people and increase their contributions to conservation efforts.

Did you know this happened? I wonder what the people who play with Tilly tell their friends about what they do for a living. Perhaps something like, "Well, you know, I'm helping conserve orcas by — you know — by helping him — by helping him — hmm — by helping him make more orcas who'll spend their lives in a small cage, tormented and bored out of their amazing minds, and perhaps go crazy just like him."

Are you as surprised as I am? Please write to SeaWorld and ask them to stop this practice now because these requests can make a difference. Surely we don't need any more captive orcas. Leave Tilly's willy alone! Free his willy.

[ORIGINALLY POSTED ON APRIL 16, 2011]

Rewilding Animals: Going Home at Last

I WOKE UP THIS MORNING to some very good news for some animals. Damian Aspinall, who has taken over two wildlife parks founded by his father more than fifty years ago in the Kent countryside in England, has decided to release some animals back into the wild. Mr. Aspinall has come to loathe zoos, as they really accomplish little if anything in terms of education and conservation, and over the next few months he plans to release forty animals of various species, including langurs, gibbons, and black rhinos.

Zoos often claim they make significant contributions to conservation, but in fact very few individuals have ever been released back into the wild after they've lived in captivity. To quote Mr. Aspinall in a *Daily Mail* story: "If I had my way, I'd close down 90 percent of all zoos tomorrow.... They are nothing more than jails. People argue they are educational — well, stuff education! You can learn far more from a David Attenborough film than going around a city-centre zoo.... Just walk around any of these city zoos and be appalled! They shouldn't be allowed to exist. They are a necessary evil, and if we are going to have them, there should be a law that they have programmes to protect the wilderness and reintroduce animals to the wild. Otherwise you just have a collection of animals being kept for the enjoyment of man — and I don't think animals should be kept for our enjoyment."

Animals in captivity can be seen as more or less wild, depending on how they wound up in the cages in which they live. If they were brought into a zoo from the wild, there is still "wildness" in them, and if they were born in a zoo, they still have wild genes. One of the comments attached to the *Daily Mail* article made a gross error about the nature of these animals, and it's worth noting because many others also make the same mistake. The comment reads, "They are not wild animals. They are domesticated. They will probably be dead within a month."

The animals living in zoos and who are to be released are *not* domesticated individuals. Some may be *socialized* but as I've pointed out elsewhere, domestication is an evolutionary process, and the animals in zoos aren't domesticated as are companion dogs and cats (see "Going to the Dogs Is a Good Idea: It's Not a Dog-Eat-Dog World," page 79). So, a captive wolf might be a socialized individual but a domesticated wolf is a dog.

Of course, these sorts of projects are risky endeavors, but one could well argue that they're worth trying because lives in captivity are severely compromised. The animals are on display for our pleasure and entertainment, not for theirs. As these projects are undertaken, we will surely learn more and more about how to release animals and have them survive. It's about time we try to free some animals from a life in captivity. Like other reintroduction projects, such as moving wolves back into Yellowstone, there are risks (some wolves did die for the good of their species, and some were injured). We can only hope that these projects will be done with great care and that we'll learn from them for future endeavors. We're always weighing relative harms, and being in captivity is rather a large harm.

By making serious attempts to rewild animals, we can also rewild our hearts and appreciate just who these amazing beings truly are. Bravo, Damian, and all those who are working to rewild animals.

[ORIGINALLY POSTED ON JUNE 17, 2012]

Rewilding Dolphins:
Good News for Tom and Misha

IT'S A PLEASURE TO REPORT GOOD NEWS in a world where animal abuse is far too common. I recently learned about a success story that is unfolding concerning the release from captivity of two bottlenose dolphins, Tom and Misha, after having spent years in captivity. Both were wild-born. The project is sponsored by the Born Free Foundation (www.bornfree.org.uk). In May 2012, CNN reported, "Within 48 hours, satellite transmitters showed that Tom and Misha had traveled more than 100 miles, and they were observed hunting fish as a team and interacting with other wild dolphins."

Estimated to be around twelve years old, Tom and Misha spent about six years in a filthy pool in a Turkish resort after being caught in the Aegean Sea. When they attracted the attention of conservationists, they would only eat dead fish who were offered by humans. They didn't recognize fish as food.

Born Free is offering updates about Tom and Misha, who have now gone their separate ways. Here's the latest: "Thursday 17th May — This morning, Tom left the waters off the island of Samos, where the team were observing him, and headed east back into Turkish waters. The latest satellite hit indicated he was approximately 15 km east of the island. Meanwhile Misha is still travelling separately, and his last satellite hit today indicated he was south of Bodrum." Let's thank everyone who is working on this wonderful project.

Reintroduction projects are extremely ambitious and risky, and they usually are not successful, so let's wish Tom and Misha the best of luck, as they still face major challenges. And let's hope that this rewilding project serves as a model for releasing other animals from captivity, where they surely do not belong. As we rewild nonhuman animals, we can rewild our hearts at the same time as we rejoice in their freedom. Reading about Tom and Misha made my day.

[ORIGINALLY POSTED ON MAY 17, 2012]

Whipping Horses Doesn't Work

HORSE RACING CAN BE HARD ON THE ANIMALS who are used to make money and entertain those who find this to be a worthwhile activity. However, serious injuries often occur when these animals are pushed beyond what they normally are capable of doing, even if few of these injuries are fatal. In May 2008, people around the world were horrified when Eight Belles had to be "put to sleep" on the track after she broke both front ankles during a running of the Kentucky Derby. Usually this goes on behind the scenes after some horses are run to death or experience serious injuries so they're no longer moneymakers. But this poor horse was in so much pain, it would have been adding insult and indignity to injury to make her wait to be killed behind closed doors.

As we know, horses are incessantly whipped while they're racing, but new research from the University of Sydney shows that "whipping horses is pointless and does not make a difference in the outcome of the race." The summary from the peer-reviewed published paper reads as follows:

Concerns have been expressed concerning animal-welfare issues associated with whip use during Thoroughbred races. However, there have been no studies of relationships between performance and use of whips in Thoroughbred racing. Our aim was to describe whip use and the horses' performance during races, and to investigate associations between whip use and racing performance. Under the Australian Racing Board (ARB) rules, only horses that are in contention can be whipped, so we expected that whippings would be associated with superior performance, and those superior performances would be explained by an effect of whipping on horse velocities in the final 400 m of the race. We were also interested to determine whether performance in the latter sections of a race was associated with performance in the earlier sections of a race. Measurements of whip strikes and sectional times during each of the final three 200 metre (m) sections of five races were analysed. Jockeys in more advanced placings at the final 400 and 200 m positions in the races whipped their horses more frequently. Horses, on average, achieved highest speeds in the 600 to 400 m section when there was no whip use, and the increased whip use was most frequent in the final two 200 m sections when horses were fatigued. This increased whip use was not associated with significant variation in velocity as a predictor of superior placing at the finish.

Thus, traditional thinking is shown to be outmoded. Rosanne Taylor, dean of the faculty of veterinary science at the University of Sydney noted: "Science has the ability to challenge our views of what is otherwise considered the norm. This result is a good example of how evidence can inform the way we work with animals to promote their optimal performance and welfare. In this instance, the future well-being of Australian racehorses is looking brighter, because we now better understand that horses give their best when they are not whipped, before the 400m mark, positioning themselves for a win or place."

Let's hope these important findings find their way into how horses are treated around the world.

[THIS ESSAY ORIGINALLY APPEARED AS
"Whipping Horses Doesn't Work and New Observations of Grief
in Chimpanzees," POSTED ON FEBRUARY 2, 2011]

Rise of the Planet of the Apes Shows That Real Primates No Longer Need to Be Used in Movies

THE 2011 MOVIE *Rise of the Planet of the Apes* (www.riseoftheplanetofthe apes.com) can easily serve as a conduit to get people interested in important issues concerning animal protection. In the past, real animals have been used to make movies, and on many occasions they have been abused, even if it was not the intention of the people who were using them. However, on some occasions animals were intentionally abused and intimidated — "broken" is the term used — so that they would do exactly what the filmmakers wanted. Some even died as a result of their mistreatment. Even a movie set can be unsettling to an animal. They don't like the bright lights and noise of a typical set, and even when their basic needs are taken care of, they'd rather be left alone.

Rise of the Planet of the Apes, like *Avatar*, shows clearly that no longer do we even have to consider using real animals to make movies about the amazing beings with whom we share our planet. Created using the latest technology to produce computer-generated apes, Caesar, the star of this forthcoming movie, looks and acts like a real chimpanzee, and it's wonderful that not a single chimpanzee had to be used to show viewers what it's like to be a chimpanzee. Caesar's various and wide-ranging emotional states are beautifully portrayed, and at times I asked myself what was this chimpanzee feeling about being used this way, only to remind myself that Caesar wasn't a real animal. We should be happy that there is a lot of work being done to protect animals in entertainment, and this new movie will surely go a long way toward ending the use of animals in film.

[ORIGINALLY POSTED ON APRIL 13, 2011]

Buddy the Chimpanzee Killed in Nevada Because He Wasn't Really a Pet

WILD ANIMALS ARE DANGEROUS and should not be kept as pets. Consider the tragic story of CJ and Buddy, two chimpanzees who lived in a home in Nevada. When discussing the need for regulations on the private possession of exotic pets in Nevada or elsewhere, it's important to see the jungle for the trees.

CJ and Buddy, the two chimpanzees who escaped from a residential Clark County neighborhood in July 2012, were treated as pets, but they were and always remained highly sentient wild animals. In a natural situation, chimpanzees typically remain with their mothers, nursing, playing with siblings, and learning to forage until they are about eight years old. A mother chimpanzee in the wild patiently teaches her young vital skills such as hunting, foraging, and using tools, as well as the subtleties of their community's culture.

But the story of CJ and Buddy followed a drastically different course. Born at a chimpanzee breeding facility in Texas, ripped from their mothers and sold shortly after birth, dressed in baby clothes and pampered as virtual children, CJ and Buddy were propped up in front of cameras and thrust into the spotlight, and then, too powerful to handle after just a few years, eventually locked away in a backyard cage. Such treatment would drive a person mad, and it drives a chimpanzee bonkers. We know that captive chimpanzees and other animals suffer from a wide variety of mood and anxiety disorders.

When you understand that an adult chimpanzee is many times stronger than any human and has the capability to crush bones with his jaws, you see the animal the Clark County officer was forced to shoot dead that fateful July morning when CJ and Buddy ran amok. CJ's life was undoubtedly shattered as she watched Buddy, the only companion she had ever had, die, and it is because of this trauma that she likely acted out again, escaping two more times following her escape with Buddy.

Yet it is only because of this tragedy that CJ's luck turned around, and she is headed to a sanctuary where she will make new friends in a more suitable environment. It's the best outcome for her, but it's a very rare outcome for most pet primates who are cast into roles as surrogate children or household pets. When pet primates reach sexual maturity and begin powerfully acting out, many are locked away in backyard or basement cages, dumped at shoddy roadside zoos, pseudo-sanctuaries, backyard menageries, or breeding facilities. These sentient, emotional, and intelligent animals, who can live to be sixty years old, often spend those years wasting away in a cage, slowly losing their minds. Others, seeking an escape from the profound and relentless boredom, make a mad dash for freedom, which, as was the case for Buddy, almost always ends badly.

And chimpanzees are not the only primates kept as pets who are capable of inflicting serious injuries; smaller primates also pose a significant danger. Even those individuals who have been subjected to painful tooth extractions can inflict serious bruising and break skin, and they can all spread parasitic, bacterial, and viral infections. Macaque monkeys, popular in the pet trade, naturally carry the herpes B virus that is often fatal to humans. Health risks are so serious that people in Canada who work with primates are not allowed to donate blood for fear of spreading known and unknown diseases.

There have been hundreds of dangerous incidents involving captive primates, many kept as pets. Scores of children have been injured by pet monkeys, many requiring hospital treatment while worried parents wait to hear from doctors if they've contracted any infectious diseases. Then, consider the tragic story of the Connecticut woman whose face was torn off by her friend's pet chimpanzee named Travis in February 2009.

Travis was a pet chimpanzee living in a town in Connecticut who uncharacteristically and brutally attacked a friend of his human companion, and after the attack, he was fatally shot by police. In some stories about this in the popular press, Travis was referred to as a "domesticated chimpanzee." This is a complete misrepresentation of who he was. Travis was accustomed to drinking wine and using a WaterPik to brush his teeth, and while this may sound "cute," asking a chimpanzee to do these things is an insult to who they are. Domestication is an evolutionary process. Through this process, animals such as our companion dogs and cats undergo substantial behavioral, anatomical, physiological, and genetic changes. Travis was a *socialized* chimpanzee who usually got along with humans, but he was not a domesticated being. He still had his wild genes, just as do wolves, cougars, and bears who live with humans. Tragedies like this occur when wild animals are treated as if they're humans. In stories about the incident, it was also said that there was no known provocation that would have spurred Travis to attack, but this ignores the basic fact that he was a wild animal, and wild animals do *not* belong in human homes. They can be highly unpredictable (consider other attacks by famous animals on their handlers), and they should be allowed to live at sanctuaries that are dedicated to respecting their lives while minimizing human contact. Let's hope that this tragic situation serves to stimulate people to send the wild friends who share their homes to places that are safe for all.

Let's also not forget the massacre of exotic animals in Ohio in October 2011, in which over fifty captive exotic animals were released right before the man who lived with them killed himself. At least forty-nine of the animals were subsequently killed by police, including seventeen lions and Bengal tigers. It took a public disaster and embarrassment over a lack of policy to awaken Ohio lawmakers. At the time the animals were released and killed, Ohio had no regulations concerning the keeping of exotic animals as pets, but now they do.

Unfortunately, Nevada has set itself up for situations like the Clark County escape and even worse scenarios. Without restrictions regarding the private possession of dangerous wild animals, law enforcement officers will never know if their day will involve holding off a rampaging gunman or trying to stop a neurotic ape. Maybe the Clark County incident will help serve as an impetus for change.

By leaving Nevada as one of only six states in the nation without restrictions for private ownership of exotic animals, Nevada lawmakers are playing Russian roulette with public safety, and a pet chimpanzee might as well be holding the trigger.

[ORIGINALLY POSTED ON AUGUST 24, 2012]

PART 9

WHO WE EAT
IS A MORAL QUESTION

HUMANS PAY VERY CLOSE ATTENTION to the food they choose to eat. I call this a "moral question" because the animals who wind up in our mouth are sentient beings who quite often suffered enormously on the way to our stomach — either on factory farms and in slaughterhouses where they see, hear, and smell others get slaughtered, or when they're writhing on the deck of a boat or a dock after they've been pulled from their watery homes. Animals aren't objects. When I give lectures and very gently remind people that they're eating formerly sentient beings, it often gets very quiet because we're so accustomed to asking "What's for dinner?" not "Who's for dinner?" After these discussions I've had people tell me they'll never eat animals again. I fully realize that our meal plans raise many difficult questions that we wish would just go away, but they won't, and each of us needs to be responsible for the choices we make. It's easy to show in a compassionate and gentle way how a vegetarian or vegan diet can work for just about everybody.

Animals' Lives Matter:
Sentience and Feelings Count

NONHUMAN ANIMALS have many of the same feelings we do and share the same neural structures that are important in processing emotions. So, why do we unrelentingly slaughter sentience? Animals experience contagious joy and the deepest of grief, they get hurt and suffer, and they take care of one another. They have a point of view on what happens to them, their families, and their friends. Nonetheless, in innumerable situations, their lives are wantonly and brutally taken in deference to human interests. The activity that claims the lives of far more individuals than all other venues combined is eating them, and it's here where each of us can make an effortless and graceful difference. We can expand compassion and at the same time save environments and enjoy better health.

Consider this: If it takes you five minutes to read this essay, more than 250,000 animals will have been slaughtered for food in the United States alone; that comes to about 27 billion animals a year. Then, at the slaughterhouse, it takes less than thirty minutes to turn a cow into a steak, during which time these sentient beings continue to suffer interminably. They also see, hear, and smell other cows on their way to becoming a burger. As one slaughterhouse worker once noted of food animals, "They die piece by piece." In her wonderful essay "Am I Blue?" Alice Walker wrote, "As we talked of freedom and justice one day for all, we sat down to steaks. I am eating misery, I thought, as I took the first bite. And spit it out."

We not only eat millions of mammals but also billions of birds, fish, and invertebrates. As I relate in my book *The Animal Manifesto*, we know fish and lobsters feel pain, and their response to painful stimuli resembles that of humans. In a nutshell, fish don't like being hooked and lobsters really don't like being dropped into hot water.

There are innumerable things we can do to make the world a better and more peaceful and compassionate home for all beings. We can protest the abuse of animals in education, research, circuses, zoos, and rodeos, and we can stop wearing and eating them. We can stop killing animals whose land we stole and learn to coexist with them. After all, this land is their land, too. We can alert kids that their turkey was once a bird, their bacon and sausage was once a pig, and that their hamburger was once a cow. It's amazing how few children know this, and when they discover that they're eating Babe, even without knowing how the animal suffered, they're often incredulous. Kids know animals aren't "things."

Naming animals also is a good way to decrease the distance we construct and the alienation that follows when we think of animals as things or numbers, rather than as individual beings. I once heard about a crayfish who went home with a student after a class in which kids observed the behavior of these fascinating crustaceans (who, like lobsters, feel pain). The woman who told me the story wasn't sure what to do with her new tenant, but after the crayfish was named Bubbles, it was impossible to think of doing it any harm, including eating it. We name our companion animals, so why not name the other animals with whom we have contact?

We're immersed in an "animal moment," and globally there's an increasing amount of interest and activism by people who want to make a difference, by people who have had enough of the unthinkable cruelty to which we subject billions of animals a year. Animal nations are made up of individuals who are treated as second-class citizens and whose lives are routinely taken as long as they serve human ends. We slaughter, silence, and squelch sentience with little more than a fleeting thought and with indignity. While we may not be able to define dignity, we all know when we lose it, and so do the animals.

It's really easy to make a positive and noble difference in the lives of animals, and we can all begin right now. You don't have to go out and protest or found a movement. You can just stop eating other animals and make an immediate difference with your next snack or meal. No need to go "cold turkey" on meat; do it slowly and steadily so it's a progressive and lasting change. It's really that easy. This isn't radical activism, is it? We can make a huge positive difference by cutting back on carnivory. If you're an environmentalist, it's impossible to justify eating factory farmed meat, which is notorious for causing irreversible local and wider environmental damage. But consider your own health as well, since there's a price to eating red meat. According to a 2009 essay in the *New York Times*, "a new study of more than 500,000 Americans has provided the best evidence yet that our affinity for red meat has exacted a hefty price on our health and limited our longevity." So why eat it? There are numerous healthy, nonanimal alternatives that don't destroy the environment or the lives of other animals.

It's pretty straightforward. We must respect and love other animals as our fellow beings on this planet that we all want to share in peace. We must stop abusing animals now, not when it's convenient. We must expand the size of our compassion footprint. No more lame excuses. As Barbara Cook Spencer notes, when we abuse animals, we debase ourselves. When we show kindness to animals it's a win-win situation for all because compassion begets compassion; compassion for animal beings spills over to compassion for human beings. Wouldn't the world be a better place with more compassion and far less easily avoidable cruelty? Every human being can make more humane choices as she or he goes through each day.

[ORIGINALLY POSTED ON JULY 1, 2009]

Who We Eat Is a Moral Question:
Vegans Have Nothing to Defend

A DECEMBER 2009 COLUMN in the *New York Times*, "Sorry, Vegans: Brussels Sprouts Like to Live, Too," presents some interesting ideas to ponder concerning our food choices, but it has little to do with what is scientifically known about vegetables and other plants. In places this essay reads as if it's a convenient excuse, and not a very good one, for those who choose to eat animals to continue to do so. Rather than being "a small daily tragedy that we animals must kill to stay alive," as suggested in this essay, I find meat eating an extremely inhumane act that must be curtailed, and one that can be easily terminated with insignificant changes in our daily eating habits.

As I point out in *The Animal Manifesto*, when we're making decisions about our meals, we need to ask, "*Who's* for dinner?" not "*What's* for dinner?" There is no doubt that animals suffer and cry out for help when they're being prepared for meals — from the way they're raised, transported to the torture chambers of factory farms, handled when awaiting their own slaughter, and having a bolt driven into their brain, far too often inefficiently, so that they're not instantaneously rendered unconscious as existing laws require. In 2009, the strong passage of Proposition 2 in California (in which 63 percent of voters voted to "improve the welfare of factory farm animals") and federal legislation protecting "downer" cows and banning their use in food shows that people really do care about the suffering of animals who are served up as meals. The suffering of sentient animals in slaughterhouses around the world is indisputable and reprehensible and a sad comment on the choices humans make.

Now, what about brussels sprouts and other vegetables? Do they scream and suffer when they're wok-fried? There is no credible evidence that plants are sentient and suffer and feel pain or that they have a conscious desire to live. Vegetables don't suffer when they're prepared for meals, wok-fried, steamed, or otherwise cooked. Plants show intriguing and sophisticated tropisms — automatic reflexive responses to various environmental conditions — and do communicate with one another, but they don't have intentions and desires as do many animals. Thus, it's not valid to claim that a brussels sprout or carrot does not aspire to be wok-fried as a cow or pig might not aspire to be tortured in a slaughterhouse. Claims about animal sentience are not overblown or speculative, whereas claims about sentience in plants are entirely speculative.

Other questions also need to be pondered as we decide who to put in our mouth. Factory farms cause enormous environmental damage, and this must be factored into our gustatory decisions. So, even if people don't give a hoot about animal suffering and death, they must consider what their choices are doing to the environment, local and otherwise. In many countries, 50 percent or more of greenhouse gases come from cow gas, and the use of water and land for the production for unneeded meat is huge compared to the amount of land and water needed to produce non-animal meals. For example, it's estimated that by 2025 about 64 percent of humanity will be living in areas of water shortage. The livestock sector is responsible for over 8 percent of global human water use, 7 percent of global water being used for irrigating crops grown for animal feed. In New Zealand, 34.2 million sheep, 9.7 million cattle, 1.4 million deer, and 155,000 goats emit almost 50 percent of the country's greenhouse gases in the form of methane and nitrous oxide. Animals are living smokestacks. People are now talking about the "carbon hoofprint" to refer to the large amount of greenhouse gases released into the atmosphere by the livestock industry. As a *New York Times* story reported, "Producing a pound of beef creates 11 times as much greenhouse gas emission as a pound of chicken and 100 times more than a pound of carrots, according to Lantmannen, a Swedish group."

According to a *New York Times* essay titled "Rethinking the Meat-Guzzler," "Global demand for meat has multiplied in recent years, encouraged by growing affluence and nourished by the proliferation of huge, confined animal feeding operations. These assembly-line meat factories consume enormous amounts of energy, pollute water supplies, generate significant greenhouse gases and require ever-increasing amounts of corn, soy and other grains, a dependency that has led to the destruction of vast

swaths of the world's tropical rain forests.... The world's total meat supply was 71 million tons in 1961. In 2007, it was estimated to be 284 million
tons. Per capita consumption has more than doubled over that period. (In
the developing world, it rose twice as fast, doubling in the last 20 years.)
World meat consumption is expected to double again by 2050." These are
daunting and haunting figures that spell doom for much fertile habitat.

Even the United Nations' Nobel Prize–winning scientific panel on
climate change urged people to stop eating meat because of the climatic
effects of factory farming. It's been calculated that the carbon footprint of
meat-eaters is almost twice that of vegetarians. Commercial meat production is not sustainable.

So, let's be serious about food choices and ask that our critics also be
serious about their tongue-in-cheek criticisms. We can easily reduce suffering and increase our "compassion footprint" by being vegetarians and
vegans. Of this there is no doubt. We're all responsible for the decisions we
make. We vegans don't have to defend or apologize for our humane and
ethical choices. If in the future we learn that some plants are sentient, we
will have to change our ways, but as yet I'm happy to be a vegan and don't
feel guilty for eating a nonprotesting brussels sprout.

[ORIGINALLY POSTED ON DECEMBER 27, 2009]

Dead Cow Walking

DECEMBER 21 IS NATIONAL HAMBURGER DAY. It's interesting that a dead cow on a bun is called a hamburger rather than a cowburger, so I looked up the origin of the word. I discovered that historically beef and other meats served on a bun were called "Hamburg steaks" because of their association with Hamburg, Germany. This popular meal first appeared on an American menu in 1826. But, regardless of what you call it, a Big Mac, le Big Mac, a Royale with cheese (as in *Pulp Fiction*), or a Whopper, a hamburger sandwich is essentially a dead cow on a bun. This is so whether it's grilled or barbequed, square or round, filled with holes or other ingredients — such as flour, vegetable protein, or ammonia-treated defatted beef trimmings (really!) — or topped with assorted condiments like ketchup, mustard, mayonnaise, or seasonings that enhance or mask its taste, rendering the burger palatable. And you can be sure that the cow who provided the meal into which you're sinking your teeth suffered immensely during his journey from grazing to his home in a bun. The plate on which this unnecessary meal is sitting is a platter of death.

This might sound harsh, but those are the facts, even if the cow was one of a very lucky few who walked up Temple Grandin's purportedly humane "stairway to heaven." Dr. Grandin is famous for making the living conditions of cows more humane, but only an incredibly tiny fraction of a percentage of cows who contribute to the more than 14 billion hamburgers eaten yearly in the United States benefit from these niceties, and their lives are still filled with misery and untold pain and suffering before they're killed on their way to your mouth. A "better" life on a factory farm isn't close to being marginally "good" (see "My Beef with Temple Grandin: Seemingly Humane Isn't Enough," page 248). Surely, nobody would choose to send his or her dog to a factory farm.

Here are some more facts associated with one's choice to eat dead cows. Cows are sentient mammals who are very intelligent. They worry over what they don't understand and have been shown to experience "eureka" moments when they solve a puzzle, such as how to open a particularly difficult gate. Cows communicate by staring, and it's likely we don't understand their very subtle ways of communicating. They also form close and enduring relationships with family members and friends and don't like to have their families and social networks disrupted. Nor do they like to be subjected to the reprehensible conditions to which they are exposed during their transport to the factory farm (or CAFOs, concentrated animal feeding operations) and their short stay at these filthy and inhumane facilities. They also suffer not only their pains but also the pains of other cows who are their short-term roommates on the way to one's plate.

Cows also carry numerous diseases they acquire while being prepared to become burgers, many of which are easily passed on to humans (for a summary of scientific research, see the work of renowned physician Michael Greger, www.drgreger.org). Confinement at high densities at agribusiness factory farms requires that cows be given antibiotics and hormones, and pesticides are also freely used. It's known that slaughterhouse workers may develop acute and chronic lung disease, may suffer musculoskeletal injuries, and may catch zoonotic infections (ones that transmit from animals to human beings and vice versa). Consumers also can suffer from the chemicals to which cows are subjected to control the spread of disease on filthy factory farms. Mad cow disease that causes variant Creutzfeldt-Jakob disease (vCJD), a fatal dementia, also is a major problem, as is swine flu. A burger can turn out to be very dangerous to one's health. Let's also not forget the regular *E. coli* outbreaks and the numerous recalls of hundreds of tons of cow meat infected with feces. Millions of Americans are infected and thousands die each year from contaminated animal "food" products. For more on why one can safely say "eat a cow at your own risk," see *CAFO: The Tragedy of Industrial Animal Factories*, edited by Daniel Imhoff.

Even if you dismiss the ethics of eating a cow or the possibility of getting seriously ill, consider the well-documented and deleterious environmental impacts of factory farms. Even the United Nations has issued a concern about the environmental impacts of factory farming, which are direct effects of rampant and unnecessary animal cruelty (for more details, see "Who We Eat Is a Moral Question: Vegans Have Nothing to Defend," page 242). Clearly, the numerous and serious problems associated with eating burgers isn't a matter with which only organizations such as People for the Ethical Treatment of Animals is concerned, or some radical point of view. The scientific facts speak for themselves. The benefits of making humane and ethical choices are evidence-based, supported by impartial and solid research.

So, what can we do? Each of us can make more ethical, compassionate, healthier, and environmentally friendly choices. Let's not have December 21 be a day that actually celebrates *unnecessary* and intense pain, suffering, and death — *unnecessary* because no one *has* to eat a burger. Excuses such as "Oh, I know they suffer, but don't show me because I love my burger" only add cruelty to the world. You're eating animals who do really care about what happens to them and to their friends. Indeed, as one of my friends who works "in the industry" has told me time and again, when you're eating meat, you're eating misery. And, most likely, you're also eating filth and disease.

Rather than eating a dead cow on National Hamburger Day, let's celebrate the shortest day of the year and the upcoming New Year with a pledge to add more compassion to the world and to reduce unnecessary cruelty by choosing not to eat the same old burger. You still can go to most burger joints: order a healthy vegetarian or vegan meal instead and know you're not only saving cows and the planet but also adding compassion to a severely wounded world. By replacing mindless eating with mindful compassionate eating, each of us can really make a positive difference that will benefit ourselves and future generations, our children and theirs, who depend on our goodwill, as they will inherit what we leave in our wake.

[ORIGINALLY POSTED ON DECEMBER 10, 2010]

My Beef With Temple Grandin:
Seemingly Humane Isn't Enough

TEMPLE GRANDIN IS AN ICON, an "anthropologist on Mars" as she aptly puts it, in a book of the same name by renowned neurologist Oliver Sacks, whom I had the extreme pleasure of meeting a few months back. We did not talk about Dr. Grandin, but we chatted about a wide-ranging number of topics, including if nonhuman animals hallucinate. Dr. Sacks's book newest book *Hallucinations* was just about to be published, and he was keenly interested in this topic. I said it's highly likely that other animals hallucinate, basing my reasoning on Charles Darwin's ideas about evolutionary continuity.

In an all-too-brief April 2013 interview in the *New York Times* titled "Temple Grandin on Autism, Death, Celibacy and Cows," which was based on her new book called *The Autistic Brain: Thinking Across the Spectrum*, Dr. Grandin reflects on a number of issues. She clearly is a wide-ranging thinker who is willing to talk about diverse issues, including autism and capital punishment, without hesitation.

Let me say right off that I applaud Dr. Grandin's quarrelsome, frisky, and sometimes irreverent nature and her down-to-earth take on many complex issues. One area in which Dr. Grandin and I continue to disagree centers on the slaughter of cows and other animals for food.

Dr. Grandin prides herself on making the lives of farm animals "more humane." She calls the ramp she's designed to make their lives better until the bitter, harsh, and heartless end the "stairway to heaven." Years ago, here's what she wrote about this stairway:

"One night when the crew was working late, I stood on the nearly completed structure and looked into what would become the entrance to heaven for cattle. This made me more aware of how precious life is. When your time comes and you are walking up the proverbial stairway, will you be able to look back and be proud of what you did with your life? Did you contribute something worthwhile to society? Did your life have meaning?"

As romantic and inviting as that sounds, it's really a bit too poetic for me because in reality it's just a ramp to death, and most often an undignified and brutal death at that.

I first addressed this in a February 2010 essay called "Going to Slaughter: Should Animals Hope to Meet Temple Grandin," and some of these thoughts bear repeating here:

> Does Temple Grandin actually make the lives of factory farmed animals better because they are treated in a more humane way because of her research? I think, to be fair, that perhaps some animals — likely a tiny fraction of the animals who go to slaughter — may have slightly better lives than they otherwise would, but let's face it, no animal who winds up in the factory farm production line has a good or even moderately good life, one that we would allow our dogs or cats to experience. In fact, their lives are marked by constant fear, terror, and anxiety. So, "slightly better" isn't "good enough" and I'd like to see Grandin encourage people to stop eating factory farmed animals and call attention to the fact that none of the ways in which they are currently treated even borders on what should be acceptable and humane. "Humane slaughter" allows for interminable pain, suffering, and death and simply must be stopped. Efficiency standards vary for "bolting," a technique that is supposed to end an animal's life immediately and "humanely" because of the damage done to the individual's brain, and the likelihood that the trip to the slaughterhouse and waiting in line to be killed are even borderline humane are so low you wouldn't head to work if you had such a small chance of getting there alive. The American Veterinary Medical Association's 2002 panel on euthanasia approved bolting "if done properly."

In the interview in the *New York Times* (NYT), three of Dr. Grandin's (TG) responses concerned with killing cows caught my eye. I've responded to each.

NYT: You have used your ability to empathize with cattle to design humane slaughterhouses. Given that you're asked to imagine how they feel on the way to their deaths, I'm surprised you eat meat.

TG: Nature's very harsh. There is nothing about how nature kills things that is kind. When cattle are raised right, they have a really good life. When they go to the meat plant now, they just walk up the chute; it's no more stressful than going to the veterinary chute.

Yes, nature can be very harsh, but natural predators do not consider what's "right" from "wrong" in their predatory ways. There are no nonanimal alternatives, as there are for humans. They are natural-born killers, and while we can all wish that nature didn't evolve as it did, that's what predators and prey are faced with. And what does "a really good life" really mean? It means that perhaps a very few cows have a better life than cows who don't benefit from their walk up the "stairway to heaven." However, their lives aren't all that good, really, and in the end they are killed for predominantly unneeded meals no matter if they had supposedly fewer moments of pain and suffering. There's no doubt that their pain and suffering mean as much or more to them as ours do to us. For more on this topic, see my book *Wild Justice* and the essay "Do 'Smarter' Dogs Really Suffer More Than 'Dumber' Mice?" (page 186).

NYT: I know you think in pictures. When you're looking at a steak you're about to eat, do you think about the cow in the slaughterhouse?

TG: Oh, yes. If I know where it comes from, then I see the plant, because I know all the plants. I'll go, "That's Cargill," or, "Oh, that's National," or, "That's Tyson."

Oh my, while I know Dr. Grandin says she cares about the cows who die for food... would it be different if she referred to the animals by name — "that's

Mary or that's Harry"? I should hope so. Among the major problems is that these highly sentient beings become mere objects in the wholly unnatural, heartless, and reprehensible food chain that characterizes factory farming. Calling animals by name and recognizing them as individuals fosters a much closer connection, and we should hope it would make abusing them much more difficult or impossible.

NYT: And it doesn't spoil your appetite?

TG: No. I also think about the hyenas ripping the guts out of something, and that did not happen to that steak. The way the wolves kill things is not that nice. Cats will kill you first, but wolves just rip you open and dine on live guts.

As for this last answer, I stand by what I wrote above in response to the first exchange.

Would you walk up a "relatively" humane stairway or into a "seemingly" humane pen only to be killed?

[ORIGINALLY POSTED ON APRIL 14, 2013]

Going "Cold Tofu"
to End Factory Farming

DURING THE PAST SIX MONTHS I've been fortunate to go to a number of wonderful, inspirational, and highly educational meetings on topics ranging from animals in religion to animal protection in Asia, the importance of play for children, great ape conservation, and most recently ending factory farming. A common theme to all of these gatherings and my main role is to talk about animal emotions and animal sentience. Animal emotions and sentience figure largely into *who*, not what, we choose to put in our mouth. The lives of factory farmed animals are filled with unrelenting terror, pain, and suffering.

Food is central to our existence, and our choices in food influence the quality of ecosystems, human health, and the lives of billions of animals who needlessly suffer because of our eating habits. Farm Sanctuary's (www.farmsanctuary.org) recent meeting dealing with ending factory farming brought together numerous people from many different walks of life who want to end the torture and slaughter of animals on the heartless assembly lines of factory farms, also known as concentrated animal feeding operations (CAFOs; see "Dead Cow Walking," page 245). Some think it's necessary to eat animals and animal products to be healthy, but it's not.

There are many views on why we should stop consuming animals and animal products, especially those from factory farms.

Some are concerned about the environmental effects of slaughterhouses, whose waste literally decimates ecosystems and pollutes water and air. For example, according to Farm Sanctuary, "the quantity of waste produced by farm animals in the U.S. is more than 130 times greater than that produced by humans. Agricultural runoff has killed millions of fish, and is the main reason why 60 percent of America's rivers and streams are 'impaired.' In states with concentrated animal agriculture, the waterways have become rife with pfiesteria bacteria. In addition to killing fish, pfiesteria causes open sores, nausea, memory loss, fatigue, and disorientation in humans. Even groundwater, which takes thousands of years to restore, is being contaminated. For example, the aquifer under the San Bernardino Dairy Preserve in southern California contains more nitrates and other pollutants than water coming from sewage treatment plants." The facts are there, and it's not hype or sensationalism to claim that factory farms decimate ecosystems worldwide and on the local level decrease property values. The stench alone from factory farms would make a house near one of these facilities a poor choice. The list goes on and on. An excellent summary of the wide-ranging detrimental effects of factory farming can be found in Gene Baur's excellent book *Farm Sanctuary*. Simply put, if you're an environmentalist, you shouldn't be eating factory farmed meat.

In addition to environmental destruction, it's clear that eating factory farmed animals and animal products is incredibly unhealthy compared with a more plant-based diet. For more information, visit the website of Dr. Michael Greger (www.drgreger.org) and read his book *Bird Flu*. As with concerns about the ecological effects of factory farms, being concerned about the wide-ranging and serious negative health aspects of eating factory farmed animals isn't mere vegan-hype but rather supported by detailed scientific research.

There is no reason at all ever to eat factory farmed animals. Even if one wants to eat animals and animal products, there are numerous alternatives available in communities around the world. Some would like to see the world become vegan, a wonderful goal to which to aspire and just about as equally unrealistic, at least for now. But this *doesn't* mean we can't make significant inroads into reducing ecological devastation, food-related diseases, and animal suffering, and it's simple to do.

It's really easy to cut down on, and perhaps eventually cut out, animals from one's diet. There's no reason to do it rapidly, by going cold turkey, if that doesn't work for you. But it's simple to do by going more slowly, going "cold tofu" as I like to call it. One can gradually eliminate animals and animal products so that the transition to a healthier diet that reduces environmental devastation, illness, and animal suffering becomes an easy habit to follow.

So, I ask you to try a number of different things. Simply refuse to eat factory farmed animals or animal products. When ordering an animal meal at a restaurant or buying food at a store, ask where the meat came from and don't ever buy factory farmed products. If you eat, for example, five cheeseburgers a week, make a pact with yourself to cut back slowly and replace them with a vegetarian or vegan alternative. Each person will choose different meal plans, and a slow transition will likely result in more permanent changes than a rapid one, at least for some people.

Clearly, there are many reasons why it's not okay to kill animals for food. Each of us can make a positive difference in the quality of ecosystems, our own health, and the lives of billions of other animals by changing who we choose eat. There are also many economic incentives. We're at a pivotal moment in world history, and there's no doubt that the earth can no longer sustain the increase in human population and our overconsuming and destructive ways. As I write this the seven billionth human has just been born. In the future there will be many more mouths to feed.

Each of us can add more compassion to the world by not eating factory farmed animals and ending factory farming. This is an indisputable fact, so please, let's begin today. Your choice of your next meal can make a difference. And after you stop eating factory farmed animals, being a "conscientious carnivore" means entirely phasing out animals and animal products from your diet, and that is also simple to do.

[ORIGINALLY POSTED ON OCTOBER 31, 2011]

Brain Scans Show Vegetarians and Vegans Are More Empathic Than Omnivores

EVERY NOW AND AGAIN we discover that some of our beliefs are supported by scientific research. As reported by Farm Sanctuary, recent research using functional magnetic resonance imaging (fMRI) shows that "vegetarians and vegans appear to have more of an empathetic response to both human and animal suffering.... FMRI brain scans showed that the areas of the brain associated with empathy (such as the anterior cingulate cortex and the left inferior frontal gyrus in this study) were more activated in vegetarians and vegans compared to omnivores when all three groups were shown pictures of human or animal suffering. Written questionnaires on empathy, in both this and other studies, seem to confirm higher empathy levels in vegetarians and vegans (Preyo and Arkiwawa, 2008; Filippi et al., 2010)."

I've been thinking about this general topic and relationship for a long time, and I agree with the conclusion of the essay in which these results are reported, namely that "most animal advocates also care deeply about a broad spectrum of social justice and humanitarian causes." I've always believed that "compassion begets compassion" and easily crosses species lines. I welcome more research in this area from both social scientists and neuroscientists.

[ORIGINALLY POSTED ON JULY 12, 2012]

Killing Other Animals for Food
Does Not Make Us Human

I JUST READ AN INTERVIEW called "Killer Cuisine" that made me think about who we are in the grand scheme of things. It also made me a bit ill. The interview is with Georgia Pelligrini, author of *Girl Hunter: Revolutionizing the Way We Eat, One Hunt at a Time*, who decided to go out and kill animals and write about the epiphany she experienced when killing a turkey: "Killing the turkey was sort of my watershed moment; it sort of woke up a dormant part of me. So many horrible things happen in our industrial food system and I wanted to explore what it meant to step outside the traditional way of procuring meat, and really go back to the way we used to do it. I wanted the experience of participating in every single part of the process — from the field to the plate — *and to make sure that there was no suffering* [emphasis added], that every part of the animal was used and used with integrity. I wanted to pay the full karmic price for the meal." There's lots of "I's" here, but what about "them," the animals whom she kills? There are two sides to the bullet, the hunter and the hunted, and this "It's all about me" attitude is an insult to the animal beings who are killed.

I do agree that factory farming should be stopped immediately, but Pelligrini's claim that the turkey she killed didn't suffer is absurd. Stalking animals causes immense suffering for those who are stalked, and even if there were no suffering, what gives her the right to kill an animal for a thoroughly unnecessary meal? Even if people stalk animals but don't try to kill them, the animals suffer greatly. Just seeing a potential predator, and hunters are viewed as predators, is stressful. Patrick Bateson, at the University of Cambridge in England, found red deer stalked by dogs showed stress responses similar to those experienced when animals were anxious and scared. Deer showed high levels of cortisol and the breakdown of red blood cells, indicating extreme physiological and psychological stress. Stalked deer also displayed excessive fatigue and damaged muscles. Non-stalked deer and those shot without prolonged stalking didn't show similar stress responses. There's no reason to think that birds would respond any differently.

Clearly, animals don't like the emotional distress, anxiety, and fear of being stalked, and neither do humans. Stalked animals may also spend less time feeding, resting, and protecting young. The stalker's intentions, malevolent or not, are unimportant to the animal, and there often is much collateral damage to family and friends of the targeted individual.

In her book, Ms. Pelligrini writes, "If you want to feel what it is to be human again, you should hunt, even if just once." Hmmm. I feel rather human and find hunting to be offensive, especially when it's for a meal that's not needed. She also finds hunting to be "emotional, spiritual, intense." What is spiritual about killing another being? Once again, the point of view of the hunted is totally ignored. Does she think the turkey or other animals feel good about providing an unneeded meal to a human predator?

As I wrote above, there's lots about the hunter in these discussions, but little about the hunted. The implications of these claims, for few are really detailed arguments, imply much about perceived human exceptionalism and speciesism, in which we conveniently place ourselves above other animals in importance, and in which animals are valued only for what they can do for us but not for their own inherent or intrinsic value (an excellent discussion of this is Lori Gruen's *Ethics and Animals*).

It's important to get the issues about hunting out for discussion. Others who have been vegetarian or vegan also become born-again meat-eating zealots when they change their ways and write as if there's no other way to live or to be human (another book like this is *The Mindful Carnivore* by Tovar Cerulli). They write self-serving flowery prose about their personal and spiritual journeys, claiming that it's human and almost an out-of-body experience to kill other animals. Killing other animals is just fine for them and everyone should do it. But what about the animal whose life was taken because the human decided it was okay to do it? And what about the other animals who suffer the loss of family and friends? We need to factor in their points of view as well.

[ORIGINALLY POSTED ON MARCH 17, 2012]

Babe, Lettuce, and Tomato:
Dead Pig Walking

ON A RECENT TRIP TO TORONTO, Canada, to celebrate World Animal Day (www.worldanimalday.co.uk) with Jill Robinson, founder and CEO of Animals Asia (www.animalsasia.org), I first went to a protest organized by Toronto Pig Save (http://torontopigsave.org), a group founded by Anita Krajnc. This wonderful grassroots organization is made up of compassionate people who are devoted to saving pigs from being tortured and slaughtered for food. They focus on Quality Meat Packers, a slaughterhouse located near downtown Toronto, the horrific and pungent stench of which fills the local neighborhood. If residents and others could also hear the unrelenting squeals of pain and bear witness to the incredible inhumanity of killing these pigs, I'm sure many would do something to end the horrific practice of turning live sentient pigs into ham, bacon, and sausage.

I like pigs. A few years ago I had the great pleasure of meeting Geraldine, a rescued potbellied pig, on a visit to Kindness Ranch, a sanctuary that rescues and rehabilitates former laboratory animals. Geraldine behaved as a companion dog, leaning into me as I rubbed her back and flipping over on her back as I rubbed her belly. I couldn't imagine how anyone could do anything that would cause her to suffer. We can learn a lot of positive lessons from pigs about loyalty, trust, friendship, compassion, and love if we open our hearts to them. Calling someone a pig is really a compliment.

Pigs are very intelligent, highly social, and deeply emotional animals. They display many different personalities. There's even scientific research that shows that pigs can be optimists or pessimists depending on whether they live in enriched environments or in places where there's continuous stress and suffering. Pigs are sentient beings who are capable of suffering incredible pain. They not only suffer their own pain, they also see, smell, and hear the pain of others. We grossly underestimate animal suffering, and many argue that their pain is worse than ours in that they don't know when it's going to end. It's interminable, and they can't rationalize it. All they know is what they're feeling at the moment, and it's endless psychological and physical abuse. My encounters with pigs haven't always been as pleasant as my meeting with Geraldine. What I saw, smelled, and heard in Toronto when a truckload of squealing pigs stopped where we were protesting was deplorable and heart wrenching.

A few weeks before my trip to Toronto, I was most unpleasantly surprised by a pig roast right on the Pearl Street Mall in my hometown of Boulder, Colorado. The guy running it proudly stood in front of a pig on a spit inviting people to come see a pig and then eat her. When I heard him say to a little boy, "Come see a pig that was killed this morning," I wondered what the boy would do when he saw the scorched carcass turning slowly over a fire. He looked briefly, and as he turned away he simply said, "That's a dead pig and I won't eat it." Another youngster exclaimed, "That stinks!" Good for them. Unfortunately other youngsters laughed at the rotating body, as did their parents. But often it was an uncomfortable, defensive laugh, and some people walked away and shook their head from side to side, possibly because they just didn't want to see whom they ate in the flesh. Imagine if the pig were a dog. When some people learn that I go to China to work with Animals Asia in their moon bear rescue program, they ask, "How can you go there? That's where they eat dogs and cats." I simply say that I just left the United States where people routinely eat pigs, cows, chickens, and millions of other sentient beings.

Few people really know about the horrific treatment of the food they casually put in their mouth. I'm sure if you asked a youngster if they'd like a Babe, lettuce, and tomato sandwich, it would stimulate a lot of discussion, one that many wish to avoid. I'm also sure if you ordered a Babe, lettuce, and tomato sandwich at a restaurant, the incredulous waitperson would ask, "You want a what?" Paul McCartney once said, "If slaughterhouses had glass walls, everyone would be a vegetarian." He's right. One could no longer dismissively say, "Oh I know they suffer, but I love my bacon."

The words we use to refer to other animals often distance us from who they really are. Dead pigs are called ham, bacon, and sausage, and dead cows become meat, steaks, and hamburgers. They're wrapped in packages that make it impossible to know who they used to be. Carrie Packwood Freeman, who teaches at Georgia State University, points this out in "This Little Piggy Went to Press." I'm sure restaurants would never put "pig, lettuce, and tomato" or "cow on a bun with fries" on their menu, since some or many people would then refuse to eat them.

As I was standing at the Toronto protest, a truckload of pigs going to market appeared, and the stoplight turned red just as the truck showed up. For the next few minutes I stared into the eyes and faces of pigs on their way to being killed for unneeded human meals. Transport is part of the highway of torture. After being raised on cramped and filthy pig farms, they're loaded onto a truck for their inhumane trip to the slaughterhouse, where they're brutally and mercilessly killed. On the crowded truck and before they're slaughtered, they're unrelentingly terrified. When I looked into the eyes of the pigs, I could feel their pain and panic. Their ears were flopped forward, their faces drawn, and their unrelenting squeals of protest pierced the air. The cacophony of protests brought tears to my eyes. Their behavior pierced my heart. How could anyone do this to these amazing beings? I could hear them asking to be freed from this reprehensible treatment. If these pigs were dogs, I'm sure people would vehemently protest their treatment.

Most people don't know the plight of the animals who they eat. We must remember that food animals are formerly sentient beings who were unnecessarily tortured and killed for our palate. There's no reason at all to eat pigs. Indeed, there's no reason to eat other animals. We can all easily expand our compassion footprint by making more humane choices concerning who we eat. It's simple to do, and I humbly ask everyone to remove pigs and other animals from their diet. This is not a radical move. Simply say "no thanks" when someone offers you one form of animal or another. If you actually saw, heard, smelled, and felt, firsthand, the incredible pain and suffering that food animals endured before they arrived on your plate, you'd be horrified and more likely to change your choices of food. You're essentially eating pain.

By bearing witness to the pain and suffering of other animals, to show that this is a true state of affairs, a social movement can be born. I know none of you would ever place your dog in the same situations, so why allow pigs and other beings to be treated in these thoroughly inhumane ways? It simply makes no sense.

[ORIGINALLY POSTED ON OCTOBER 9, 2011]

Is Eating Dogs Different
from Eating Cows and Pigs?

ALL FORMS OF ANIMAL SLAUGHTER can be avoided by creating stronger laws and vigorously enforcing them and by the choices we make. Just today I learned about the cancellation of a dog-eating festival that was supposed to be held in Jinhua, Zhejiang Province, China. Of course, I find the idea of a dog-eating festival to be disgusting and am appalled by it, but as one of the people interviewed in a news story notes, "I am opposed to the cancellation. Eating dogs is no different than eating chickens, sheep, or pigs." They're right. In my recent essay concerning eating pigs (see "Babe, Lettuce, and Tomato: Dead Pig Walking," page 258), I mentioned that some people wonder why I ever go to China, since people eat dogs there. And I reply the same way: Why is eating dogs different from eating cows and pigs at a barbecue or in a restaurant in the United States? For one, we don't see the actual painful process of how pigs and cows become meals.

Offensive as eating dogs is, we must be consistent in our choices of food. Seeing dogs cramped into tiny cages on a truck isn't much different from seeing pigs and cows stuffed into transport trucks or chickens jammed into battery cages. I've seen them all, and they bring tears to my eyes. It's easy to feel the terror and suffering of all of these animal beings, and their reprehensible treatment is a blight on human nature.

While this dog festival was canceled, it's highly likely there will be others that will actually happen. Deep thanks to all of the people who are working to stop them. And while they're doing all they can do in a very difficult situation, we can also make a difference simply by facing our food choices head-on and by being consistent about who winds up in our mouth. It's much easier for us to do this than for the people in China to accomplish what they're trying to do.

[ORIGINALLY POSTED ON OCTOBER 20, 2011]

Vegans and Oysters:
If You Eat Oysters, You're Not a Vegan,
So Why the Question?

SHOULD VEGANS EAT OYSTERS? Should vegans eat any animals or animal products? No. However, Christopher Cox disagrees, and in an April 2010 *Slate* essay, he tries to argue that even strict vegans should feel comfortable eating oysters by the boatload. Humans have come up with various terms to reflect their choices of who, not what, we choose to put in our mouth. And one thing is clear — the *term* vegan means no animals or animal products wind up there. So, if you choose to eat oysters, you're not a vegan, and we can close up shop and move on to other matters because this isn't really a valid question. This isn't to be arrogant, some sort of idealistic zealot, or judgmental. Words need to mean something. If you eat oysters, you're not a vegetarian, either. The last time I looked, oysters were animals, not plants or by-products.

Many people choose their diet based on ethical principles. Sentience, the capacity to feel pain and suffer, frequently is the main reason people "go vegetarian or vegan." In his essay, Cox writes, "Moreover, since oysters don't have a central nervous system, they're unlikely to experience pain in a way resembling ours — unlike a pig or a herring or even a lobster." However, we don't know this is so. And it's not important if oyster pain or the pain felt by any other animal resembles ours. They have their own pain, and their pain matters to them. People also vary in their pain thresholds, and it would be wrong to conclude that someone doesn't feel pain because they don't express it in the usual way.

For all we know, oysters might feel pain. For a long time people thought fish didn't feel pain, but we now know that isn't so (see "Crabs and Fish Feel Pain: Expanding the Circle-of-Sentience Club," page 156). A 2010 book titled *Do Fish Feel Pain?* by the renowned scientist Victoria Braithwaite shows clearly that fish do suffer and feel pain, as do many other animals who were thought not to. Braithwaite concludes, "I have argued that there is as much evidence that fish feel pain and suffer as there is for birds and mammals — and more than there is for human neonates and preterm babies."

There are a number of issues that need to be considered in who we eat. Should pain be the hook on which we hang our decision to eat another animal? Should we simply not eat other animals because they exist — because they're alive — and we really don't need to eat them, anyway? Factory farming without suffering isn't acceptable, either.

We should give animals the benefit of the doubt. Cox sort of agrees, but not really, because he believes it's improbable that oysters feel pain, so even vegans should go ahead and let some slide down their throat. I disagree, and if you're vegan, you wouldn't eat oysters, anyway. As with many ethical decisions, we can easily find ourselves on a slippery slope that conveniently expands the range of animals we eat because we don't know for sure they feel pain. The argument that we really don't know something is a bit too facile for my liking.

We need to be serious about our food choices and ask that our critics, even "the converted," also be serious and avoid tongue-in-cheek criticisms. Right now I'm happy to be a vegan, and that means no oysters for me.

[ORIGINALLY POSTED ON JUNE 11, 2010]

PART 10

WHO LIVES, WHO DIES, AND WHY

Redecorating Nature,
Peaceful Coexistence, and
Compassionate Conservation

WHILE I WAS ATTENDING A MEETING in Oxford, England, in September 2010 about the growing field called "compassionate conservation," I came to realize that the basic question with which many of my colleagues and I are concerned is "Who lives, who dies, and why?" As humans, we can do just about anything we choose to do, and along with this incredible power comes incredible responsibilities to do the best we can for other animals and their homes. Power does not mean license to do whatever we like because it suits us just fine. I live in the mountains outside of Boulder, Colorado, and I am fortunate to have many nonhuman neighbors, including cougars, black bears, red foxes, coyotes, and a wide variety of small mammals, birds, lizards, insects, and snakes. I choose to live where I do, and I must do all I can to coexist in peace and harmony with these wonderful animals. As you'll read below, I've had some close and dangerous encounters of the lion kind and have had to change my ways so that my nonhuman neighbors and I can all live together. If I choose to, I can move, but my animal friends can't just pick up and move because their living rooms aren't mobile.

The late theologian Thomas Berry stressed that our relationship with nature should be one of *awe*, not one of *use*. Individuals have inherent or intrinsic value because they exist, and this alone mandates that we coexist with them. They have no less right than we do to live their lives without our intrusions, they deserve dignity and respect, and we need to accept them for who they are. Yet through a combination of habitat loss and climate change, we are in the midst of the sixth great extinction of species — what's called the anthropocene — in which we are the major cause of this incredible loss of biodiversity.

Simply put, there are far too many of us. Many people don't like to talk about our human tendency to overproduce, but at the core that's the major problem. Among my worst fears is that I'll wake up one day and wonder where have all the animals gone. Even if we do make immediate changes, numerous animals will still perish, but we can make a positive difference right now with little effort. We need to rewild our hearts and build corridors of compassion that include all beings. We need to treat animals better or leave them alone.

Close Encounters of a Lion Kind:
Meeting Cougars, Foxes,
Bears...and Bear Poop

BECAUSE MY LIVING SPACE ENCROACHES on the terrain of mountain lions and many other carnivores — including coyotes, red foxes, and black bears — the likelihood of meeting one of these beasts is fairly high. Red foxes entertain me regularly by playing outside of my office or on my deck. I've been lucky to have many such unplanned encounters with various animals, for nature doesn't hold court at our convenience. Much happens in the complex lives of our animal kin to which we're not privy, but it's a truly splendid moment when we're fortunate to see animals at work. Mountain lions, like black bears and foxes, also visit my home with little or no hesitation. They seem extremely comfortable sharing my home range with me, having habituated to my presence over the years. Technically, I was the one who moved into their home. Somebody redecorated the lions' habitat by building my house smack in the middle of their living room.

It's not surprising, then, that I've had some very close encounters with my feline neighbors, including the time I almost fell over a huge male as I walked backward to warn some of my neighbors of his presence. On a warm July day years ago, I arrived home thoroughly exhausted after racing my bicycle for three hours in Denver, only to learn that a mountain lion had killed a deer up the road from my house and was still lurking in the neighborhood. Some of my neighbors had small children, so I hiked up the road to tell them what had happened, each step causing my fatigued legs to ache. When I got to the first house a few hundred yards west of mine, I saw my neighbor on his porch and yelled to him that there was a lion around and that it would be a good idea to keep his kids home. Just as I turned to walk toward the next house, I came face to face with a large male lion — so close that we could easily have shaken hands. Of course, I was terrified and ran up the hillside, wearing clogs, yelling all the way, "There's a lion here, there's a lion here!" The lion just stood there watching me run, thank goodness. Later I learned that he had stashed his kill, a large mule deer buck, down below where I'd made his acquaintance. Luckily, I didn't cross the path between him and his catch. I'm sure that's why he didn't chase me — that and the fact that he had a full belly, having eaten, we later estimated, about twenty pounds of fresh deer.

Later, when I told some people what had happened to me, some had the audacity, though they were well-intentioned, to tell me that it was stupid of me to run. They informed me that it's best to tell the lion who's boss by yelling and screaming and shaking your fist or some object — like a tree branch — at him. As a field biologist who had by then studied coyotes for years, of course I knew that it was best to intimidate a lion, not run from him or her. But I must say that when I looked a cougar in the eye from about two feet away, instinct took over. Fleeing trumped remaining and trying to convince him that I wasn't scared. I was. I think that if I weren't dehydrated from having been in a bike race earlier that day, I'd have peed my pants. Had I done so, I suppose it would have been interesting to see the lion's reaction. Of course, with his keen sense of smell, there can be no doubt that the lion knew that I was quivering inside, regardless of my serendipitously empty bladder. I remember going to sleep that night imagining a headline in the local paper saying something like, "University of Colorado Carnivore Expert Who Ran from a Cougar Gets Maimed — What Was He Thinking?" Now, that would have been hard to live down, wouldn't it?

A few years later I met another lion. Late one evening I was driving up my road, and I saw a large tan animal trotting toward my car. Mistaking it for my neighbor's dog, I stopped and stepped out of my car to say hello, only to discover the animal was a male mountain lion. He stared at me and then walked off. I jumped back in my car, slammed the door shut, peeled out, drove home, and walked to my house with all my senses on fire. I was really scared, although not as frightened as I'd been when I'd met the lion up my road years ago. The next day, my neighbor alerted me to a red fox carcass nearby, and when I investigated this a few days later, I witnessed what could only be described as a fox funeral (I tell this story in "A Fox, a Cougar, and a Funeral," page 174).

Three years after this series of fascinating encounters, I heard a scraping noise outside of my bedroom window at about two in the morning. I didn't see anything, but as I was peering out I heard a mournful, high-pitched cry. Later, as the sun rose, I went out to see what had happened and discovered a long path laden with deer hair and blood etched into my sandy driveway. I subsequently learned that a lion had dragged a large male mule deer he'd killed about fifty yards down the road, across a grassy field, and then down my driveway, where he cached his victim for a later delight. I found myself wondering what the deer felt before the kill. While I find it almost impossible to step back and look at events like this with total objectivity, as many a scientist would, I do see them as reflecting cycles of life "out there in the natural world." So, while I surely feel for the fox or the deer, I also marvel at the predatory skills of mountain lions and other highly evolved "natural-born killers." Killing for food is how they make their living, so someone has to pay the price for being at the wrong place at the wrong time.

Nature is not always pretty, nor are lions to be blamed for killing for food. That's the way it is, although I wish that this wasn't the case. Having run from a lion myself, though, I have to say that it's certainly easier to put myself in the fox's shoes. No one to whom I have spoken, including naturalists, people who live among wild animals, or professional biologists, has ever seen a red fox bury another red fox and very few have seen a mountain lion kill a fox. However, a neighbor of mine told me that he'd seen a red fox "flying across his porch." Seconds later, he saw a mountain lion in serious pursuit of his early morning snack. I'd seen the lion about thirty minutes earlier, just above my friend's home.

Did the fox think he could outrun this large and tenacious predator? As an ethologist, the questions that motivate my own research are "What is it like to be a given animal?" and "What does it feel like to be that individual?" Because I've spent decades studying animal emotions, it was natural for me to empathize with the fox and imagine that he must have felt incredible fear as he tried to outfox the lion, perhaps looking for possible escape routes that the larger animal couldn't follow, or running here and there, cutting small circles that the lion couldn't keep up with.

What's also interesting is that while I frequently see red foxes around my home, they've been very rare this spring. On the other hand, three times in the past few weeks I'd sensed a lion nearby. In the past, whenever I've sensed the presence of a lion, I saw one later on. You just know they're there; you can really feel them lurking about. And if we *know* they're there, so do foxes and other animals who spend far more time and energy avoiding these magnificent predators.

My personal encounters with animals continue. A few years ago a black bear casually played with a plastic bottle on my deck, and I almost missed a plane because he wouldn't leave. When he finally decided to move on, I ran to my car and just made the plane. And when I returned ten days later, there was a fresh pile of bear poop right at my front door, one that hadn't been there a few hours earlier according to someone who had been at my house. Clearly the bear was telling me that this is his home, too, and it's okay for me to be there as long as we can live together. Just last week a parade of wild turkeys marched up the hill east of my house, squawking incessantly and paying no attention to me at all. The day before a red fox came to my door, looked at me, turned around, and peed on a tree, once again telling me this is his home, too, and I better not forget it! Meanwhile, lizards do their infamous push-up displays, telling me that this is their land as well.

We need to make every effort to coexist with the animals who visit our homes, and build corridors of compassion and coexistence so that we all can live in harmony. We need to make sure that urban environments are friendly to animals, and animals must be incorporated into urban planning; for example, see *Green Urbanism Down Under* by Timothy Beatley and Peter Newman and the documentary *The Nature of Cities* (www.the natureofcities.org). When we do, we can learn so much about who "they" are and who we are. We are so fortunate that these animal beings allow us to learn about their lives and to live in their homes.

[ORIGINALLY POSTED ON APRIL 4, 2010]

Being "Mad about Wildlife" and Redecorating Nature

I'M CONSTANTLY ASKED about how to survive with the animals into whose homes we've wantonly trespassed as we incessantly redecorate nature. More and more people say they want to "return to nature" and live among other animals, but many decide that actual coexistence comes at too much of a cost when the animals become "pests." So, the human intruders (and we are indeed an invasive species) decide how they're going to share space, and far too often the native residents or those who have lived in a particular area for years on end — the animals themselves — get the short end of the stick, so to speak. They're relocated, trapped, poisoned, or shot.

As the very animals who were at first attractive become annoying, they're treated as disposable things rather than as living beings. The Humane Society of the United States (www.humanesociety.org), along with many other organizations, has long been interested in the "problem" of urban and suburban wildlife, and a new publication called "Living with Wild Neighbors in Urban and Suburban Communities" is now available. A snippet from the introduction is very informative:

> In recent decades, our cities and suburbs have grown and taken over rural areas. Many wild species take advantage of conditions they find — the conditions we created.
>
> We unwittingly created ideal habitat in our cities and suburbs for many wild species. If you could ask a Canada goose what the perfect place to live looked like, she would describe a golf course. While we think of white-tailed deer as forest dwellers, they actually prefer edge habitat — places where woods meets open areas, common in modern suburbs and along our highways.
>
> City dwellers and suburbanites usually have limited experience with wildlife before an issue comes up. They often don't understand why a problem occurs and rarely have experience with

similar conflicts. They look for an easy "silver bullet" solution which almost never exists.

A common misconception is that getting rid of the animals will get rid of the problem. The reality is that nature abhors a vacuum: Removing animals simply allows the remaining animals to reproduce more successfully and invites more in to fill the empty space. Effective solutions need to address the conditions that attract animals into conflict with us.

This particular publication deals mainly with human conflicts with Canada geese — who sometimes are poisoned or shot because they poop on golf courses — white-tailed deer, beavers, and coyotes, but there's no dearth of information available for how to coexist humanely and ethically with many other urban dwellers.

We all make choices about where to live, and we need to take into account the lives of the animals we've affected or are going to bother when we redecorate their homes. Many neighborhoods show concern for their local fauna. A few weeks ago on a bicycle ride up to the small town of

ON A BICYCLE RIDE NEAR JAMESTOWN, COLORADO, I WAS THRILLED TO SEE THIS SIGN THAT LOCAL RESIDENTS HAD ERECTED TO PROTECT LOCAL FOXES.

Jamestown outside of Boulder, Colorado, I saw a sign asking drivers and cyclists to slow down so that the local foxes would be safe. And the town of Superior, Colorado, has formed a partnership with the California-based Project Coyote (www.projectcoyote.org) to promote a project for peaceful coexistence of people with coyotes.

I've also had black bears try to enter my house and keep me confined inside because they liked hanging out on my outdoor porch. One large male bear had the audacity to leave a huge pile of poop near my front door because I'd asked him to leave so I could get to the airport on time (see "Close Encounters of a Lion Kind: Meeting Cougars, Foxes, Bears...and Bear Poop," page 267). Another large male casually walked onto my porch as I was eating dinner. He was about six feet away, so I ran into my house and closed the screen door. He walked over and tried to slide it open. I told him that this was my dinner as I slid the glass door closed, and he walked off as if nothing had happened. I didn't think my vegan fare would be of interest. I got a nice picture of him leaving and sauntering slowly to a house down the road, where he immediately went to sleep under a hammock.

That's the way it is where I and many others choose to live, and I welcome my wild neighbors to come back anytime. I love seeing them and knowing they're around. Nonetheless, I've had to change my habits from time to time, but that's because I've chosen to live in their living rooms. As I write this essay, there's a beautiful mama bear and her two cubs living around my house. She's been around for at least two years. Just yesterday two other adults joined her, and now there are five gorgeous bears hanging out on their land. All of the people on my road are incredibly excited to have these magnificent bear beings around, and we constantly share photos and videos about their meanderings.

Part of rewilding ourselves and our hearts (see "Rewilding Our Hearts: Maintaining Hope and Faith in Trying Times," page 322) is to embrace the animals with whom we share space and time and to appreciate that when we have to change our ways it's an indication that we know we are indeed sharing space with other beings who care very much about what happens to them, their family, and their friends. If you're not willing to make these changes, and you choose to ignore nature, then perhaps it's

MAMA BEAR AROUND MY
HOUSE; 2 CUBS ARE ABOVE
HER IN THE TREE

best not to live where magnificent animals roam and try to survive. I've often asked realtors to be up front with people when showing them homes or lots where wild animals live.

People often tell me they're "mad about wildlife," and I've come to see this phrase as having a double meaning. When people say they're mad about wildlife and love wild animals and then harm them, often causing intense suffering and death, I always say I'm glad they're not mad about me. Our fickleness causes great harm. It's an arrogant and anthropocentric double-cross to choose to move into areas where wild animals are known to live and then compromise their lives.

I find it challenging to figure out how to coexist with my wild neighbors so we can all live safely and in peace, and I know many others do, too. We can learn a lot about other animals and ourselves when we appreciate just who our wild neighbors are. For instance, see the book *Companions in Wonder* by Julie Dunlap and Stephen Kellert. Youngsters can learn valuable lessons about other animals and nature, and we can all be companions in wonder, as we share experiences and explore our wonderful planet.

[ORIGINALLY POSTED ON JUNE 5, 2012]

Animals and Cars:
One Million Animals Are Killed
on Our Roads Every Day

IN *THE GRAPES OF WRATH*, John Steinbeck shares a heartrending account of a turtle's struggle to climb up an embankment toward a highway, only to be avoided by a compassionate woman and subsequently struck intentionally by an aggravated motorist. The turtle escaped with his life, but this scenario is far different from the one in which wildlife lives today. Encountering fragmented habitat, noise pollution, decreased and compressed territory and home-range size, and ever-distracted speeding motorists, wildlife living close to and using roadways are losing their struggle for survival. For the last century, automobiles and the roads they require have been the dominant force shaping the modern American landscape. There are more cars per capita in the United States than in any other nation in the world.

As human activity increases with soaring overpopulation and an increasing number of vehicles, more than one million animals die each day on roads in the United States. Road mortality is the leading cause of vertebrate deaths in the United States, surpassing hunting within the last thirty years.

When we consider the sheer number of animals who die on roads, we need to consider seriously how we so easily and regularly influence the lives of other animals. We must bring more compassion to the world. Operating some 200 million vehicles on our roads daily, our insulated industrialized culture keeps us disconnected from life beyond our windshields. Automobiles are a "development of eye consciousness rather than foot consciousness," according to James Hillman. By understanding this, we can return to a sense of *foot consciousness*, aligning ourselves with the rhythm and speed at which wildlife travels by slowing down and paying attention to our driving habits at no cost to ourselves.

The reasons we need to change our behavior are simple. Current rates of wildlife road mortality are neither sustainable for biodiversity nor a healthy reflection of our interactions with the environment and the animals who try to coexist with us. Our driving habits demonstrate the prevailing unconscious state in which we move about. Driving mindlessly and ignoring lifeless bodies on roads decreases our humanity and lends itself to a culture of indifference.

The western United States, replete with abundant landscapes, healthy ecosystems, and rich biodiversity, is highly vulnerable to human impacts. In our home state of Colorado, for example, road mortality is unsustainable: migrating pronghorn antelope deaths increase with road development, around three thousand deer are killed annually, and migrating elk, black bears, cougars, coyotes, and foxes show increasing losses. The detrimental impact of roads on Colorado's wildlife populations has been documented by Kevin Crooks and his colleagues, who noted that tens of millions of vertebrates are killed on roadways each year, including an estimated half to 1.5 million deer in the United States alone. Road kill rates for certain species may exceed natural causes of mortality due to predation and disease.

We also need to pay attention to our driving habits because animal-vehicle collisions influence human safety. Crooks and his colleagues report that nationally, about twenty-nine thousand injuries and two hundred fatalities occur each year along with associated costs of around $1 billion in property damage. They also reported that the number of animal-vehicle collisions in Colorado more than doubled between 1998 and 2004, making special note of those occurring in Durango.

In June 2010 mitigation efforts undertaken in Colorado to decrease wildlife road mortality resulted in the passage of a law called the *Wildlife Crossing Zones Traffic Safety Law* (Section 42-4-118, C.R.S.). This law requires the Colorado Department of Transportation to work with the Division of Wildlife to identify "Wildlife Crossing Zones" where signs will be posted, including the costs of fines for speeding in identified areas. However, legal measures should not be the only means by which we address our driving habits. We should care about the damage we do and not simply ignore the huge number of lives lost on our roads.

We should also consider expanding our compassion footprint to include nonhuman animals with whom we cohabit and into whose living rooms we moved as we redecorated nature. There's no personal cost to doing this. Regardless of one's motivation, religious affiliation, ethos, or sensitivities, animals who use roads are not intrusions nor should they be considered surprises. Indeed, they dwell alongside us and should also have a place in our heart. Increasing our compassion and expanding our awareness of their presence can be accomplished by simple means. Not only will wildlife benefit, but we may also improve our own well-being; compassion begets compassion. By increasing compassion for others and ourselves, we may also enhance our appreciation of the interconnectedness of magnificent and fragile webs of life. As we conduct ourselves in the public sphere, we can even become "compassion agents" — individuals with expanded awareness acting on behalf of animals in the vehicular community, eliciting more attention for animals with very little effort.

Simple solutions are readily available. These include removing a struck animal and calling for veterinary care or removing a carcass to prevent injury or death to opportunistic species who try to feed on it, alerting other drivers to the presence of road kill, and driving more mindfully — slowing down and "smelling the roses." Each of us can act individually to decrease avoidable losses on the road. By participating in practices to enhance mindfulness — including meditating, slowing down intentionally, reducing behind-the-wheel distractions, expanding peripheral vision, and improving our knowledge of local wildlife and their seasonal, diurnal, and nocturnal movement patterns — we will help decrease wildlife deaths on the roads. What is required of each of us is an understanding that the kinetic boundaries serving to delineate human and nonhuman life need to be transcended to encompass respect for all beings.

Several factors influence our attitudes, values, and beliefs. Direct experience, early childhood education, cultural ethos, and education all influence the complicated and challenging relationships we have with nonhuman animals. Biologist E. O. Wilson offered the notion of "biophilia," our "innately emotional affiliation of human to other living organisms." In short, our connection with nature, according to Wilson, is ancestral and psychological. Appreciating this perspective gives rise to the feeling of interconnectedness that gives us a deep sense of animal suffering.

Acknowledging that one million animals die each day on roadways can lead to feelings of helplessness. Many people feel exasperated, creating a "Why care?" attitude. Flooded with indifference or bereft in hopelessness, many turn away from their ability to positively impact the environment and resident animals. For the overwhelmed, the uninterested, the disempowered, or the unconvinced, appreciating that each of us can make a positive difference in the lives of others may prove an implausible concept in light of our present environmental predicaments. But we *can* make a difference with simple acts of kindness and increased empathy and compassion.

Altering our driving habits so that we pay more attention to what we're doing will increase peripheral vision and expand our awareness. Enhancing our knowledge of animal behavior including their movement patterns or simply slowing down to decrease stopping distances is often sufficient to effect a different outcome in the presence of a galloping coyote, a meandering deer, a soaring ferruginous hawk, or a slow-moving snake or turtle. Understanding that an opportunistic coyote, fox, hawk, or magpie will be picking up the day's road kill and be unaware of approaching vehicles also can save lives. Animals will also on occasion go out into a road and try to move the carcass of a friend or group member. Common sense and paying attention to the natural history of the animals with whom we share space will go a long way toward decreasing easily avoidable mortality on the roads. Facilitating the crossing of mating amphibians, escorting baby creatures across rural roads, and erecting descansos (roadside markers of fatal events; Spanish for "place of rest") to acknowledge animal deaths will all help raise awareness and encourage people to drive with wildlife in mind.

Our felt sense of animal suffering may be cultivated further through specific practices suggested by ecopsychologists that build on an acknowledgment and understanding of our interconnectedness with a multitude of webs of life. Central to this ethos is overcoming the human/nature disconnect inherent in modern culture. This approach is simple and entails providing individuals with direct experiences that cultivate empathy and compassion for wildlife, including those crossing roadways. Practices include watching prairie dogs living near a highway to comprehend the challenges of living alongside an asphalt-ridden landscape frequented by cars and trucks traveling at speeds of more than 70 mph and sitting beside a mountain highway at dusk to understand that a drink of water from a creek requires heightened acoustical and visual acuity so as to be aware of a speeding motorcycle. Placing ourselves where potential victims reside and where lifeless bodies typically go ignored helps us comprehend the cognitive, behavioral, and emotional challenges of wildlife.

Finally, let's consider youngsters anxious to get behind the wheel. As part of driver's education, in addition to being taught that motor vehicles can be weapons of mass destruction and that they must drive mindfully, youngsters should be taught about the wildlife they'll encounter on the roads. They can be taught that raccoons are highly curious and not street-savvy and most likely will be encountered at dusk. We can also teach them about the ritual autumnal gathering of food and nesting materials by Abert's, Grey, and European brown squirrels, or let them know that the presence of one deer signifies a small herd nearby and that a carcass in the road will likely be another's meal. By becoming more biologically and environmentally sophisticated, youngsters will learn about local ecosystems and the other species who also reside there, hopefully stimulating awareness for when it is critically needed — when they're behind the wheel.

Wildlife moves at their own pace. They are no match for the speed of our vehicles and the mindlessness and inattention with which we drive. Whatever our approach, finding ways to reach inward so that we feel an animal's experience will enhance our understanding of who these animal beings are and increase our awareness of the challenges they face as they try to adapt to different landscapes.

Simply put: *Slow down for wildlife, slow down for us all.*

[Note: This essay was cowritten with Denise Boehler, who studied this topic for her master's degree in ecopsychology from Naropa University.]

[Originally posted on July 21, 2010]

Should We Kill Animals
Who Presumably Attack Humans?

A FRIEND OF MINE JUST ALERTED ME to a *Slate* essay in which author Jackson Landers claims we should kill animals who kill humans. Throughout the article Landers refers to nonhumans as "that" and "it," but clearly the animals about whom he writes are sentient beings and should be referred to as "who."

Landers is a hunter who spent a year and a half hunting and eating invasive nonhuman species throughout North America, the details of which are chronicled in his book *Eating Aliens*.

Landers's *Slate* essay is a bit too sensationalistic and fast for my liking. He begins with a story about an alligator who bit off an arm of a teenager in a river in southwest Florida, and he also writes about Australian "crocodile hunter" Steve Irwin who was killed when a stingray's barb pierced his heart. Next he writes about "man-eating" predators, noting along the way that attacks really are rather rare — "hunting humans is not normal behavior among predators." Landers also writes about a huge crocodile named Gustave living in Burundi who presumably had eaten as many as three hundred people as of 2008.

One of Landers's claims is that if the rare "man-eater" is killed, it will be good for others of their species. This suggestion, and that's all it is, sounds interesting, but detailed data about the conservation benefits of killing are lacking.

Furthermore, we don't really know if there are repeat killers. Landers writes: "These repeat performances are typical among man-eaters of many species. Bears, lions, tigers, leopards, alligators, crocodiles, cougars. Possibly sharks as well, *assuming* [my emphasis] the 1916 attacks that inspired *Jaws* were in fact the work of a single shark. The man-eater is exceptional. It isn't a normal predator. The idea that the man-eater is an innocent totem of nature while man is the guilty interloper simply does not hold up to scrutiny."

Once again, Landers provides no data for his claim that there really are repeat performers. Indeed, I've asked people about this many times because of my own long-term interests in the behavior of predators who very rarely harm human beings.

We are the most invasive species who has ever roamed Earth, redecorating nature willy-nilly with little regard about the lives of the other animals into whose homes and lives we've trespassed. When we choose to live or go where dangerous animals live, there is a risk involved.

I'd be the first to agree that there are chance encounters with predators when we roam about in their living rooms, having personally had some very close calls with black bears and cougars who live around my house. But I wouldn't ever want the individuals I met harmed or killed because they harmed or killed me, and I have never seen any data that suggest that killing them would help others of their kind.

Landers conclusion is a bit over the top. He writes: "Unless the species' numbers are so low that genetic diversity is in immediate danger, there is no advantage to letting an animal like Gustave live. The consequences of leaving a man-eater in the wild, whether it is the brown bear that devoured Timothy Treadwell or the gator that swam off with Kaleb Langdale's arm, are terrible for nearly everyone concerned."

Really? Did the bear who killed Timothy Treadwell and his female partner or the alligator who attacked Kaleb Langdale have a previous record of attacking humans?

The reason for letting these animals live, including *presumed* "man-eaters," is that they were doing what comes naturally to them, as horrific and sad as the results of their tragic attacks are. I am *not* saying what they did is just fine, but if they're caught and *reliably identified*, I'd like to see them go to a place where they can live out their lives rather than be killed. Reliable identification of wild animals has always been a problem in these and other scenarios, and we need to have more than mere guesses when the life of an animal is on the line. That individuals "get the taste for blood" after attacking a human seems to be one of those myths that lives on and on.

The growing field of compassionate conservation (see "Ignoring Nature No More: Compassionate Conservation at Work," page 303) deals with the questions "Who lives, who dies, and why?" and "Should we kill in the name of conservation?" These and other questions that involve taking an animal's life deserve more than Landers's cursory analyses and decidedly anthropocentric garble, which are filled with suppositions. Killing an animal never benefits "everyone" concerned.

[ORIGINALLY POSTED ON JULY 14, 2012]

Murder, Inc.:
Wildlife Services Brutally Kills
Millions of Animals with Your Money

FROM TIME TO TIME I've written about the many horrific and heartless ways in which Wildlife Services brutally maims and kills millions of animals, including "collateral damage" — that is, domestic dogs and many other animals who happen to get in the way of their reprehensible and interminable slaughter. Now, a three-part series by Tom Knudson of the *Sacramento Bee* on the clandestine activities of this government agency (written with the help of Brooks Fahy, executive director of Predator Defense, www.predatordefense.org, and others) exposes Wildlife Services *using irrefutable facts* that should motivate everyone to publicly decry their killing ways. You can also preview the 2012 documentary *Wild Things*, produced by the Natural Resources Defense Council. To provide balance to Wildlife Services' killing ways, this movie "introduces a new generation of progressive ranchers in the US and Canada who are using nonlethal methods to protect their cattle and sheep from predation. These ranchers reject the idea (dating back at least to America's westward expansion) that the only good predator is a dead one."

Formerly called Animal Damage Control (or ADC, which could also stand for Animal Death Corp.), this group of wildlife foes, which I dub Murder, Inc., has tried to operate outside of public scrutiny, but they can no longer do so. If you doubt their underhanded and intentionally clandestine ways, consider this quote by Dennis Orthmeyer, acting state director of Wildlife Services in California, in the *Sacramento Bee* articles: "We pride ourselves on our ability to go in and get the job done quietly without many people knowing about it." As Camilla Fox, executive director of Project Coyote (www.projectcoyote.org), notes, "If people knew how many animals are being killed at taxpayer expense — often on public lands — they would be shocked and horrified."

Here is a summary of some of Wildlife Services' egregious activities, according to the *Sacramento Bee*:

> With steel traps, wire snares, and poison, agency employees have accidentally killed more than 50,000 animals since 2000 that were not problems, including federally protected golden and bald eagles; more than 1,100 dogs, including family pets; and several species considered rare or imperiled by wildlife biologists.
>
> Since 1987, at least eighteen employees and several members of the public have been exposed to cyanide when they triggered spring-loaded cartridges laced with poison meant to kill coyotes. They survived — but ten people have died and many others have been injured in crashes during agency aerial gunning operations over the same time period.
>
> A growing body of science has found the agency's war against predators, waged to protect livestock and big game, is altering ecosystems in ways that diminish biodiversity, degrade habitat, and invite disease....
>
> In all, more than 150 species have been killed by mistake by Wildlife Services traps, snares, and cyanide poison since 2000, records show. A list could fill a field guide. Here are some examples:
>
> Armadillos, badgers, great-horned owls, hog-nosed skunks, javelina, pronghorn antelope, porcupines, great blue herons, ruddy ducks, snapping turtles, turkey vultures, long-tailed weasels, marmots, mourning doves, red-tailed hawks, sand hill cranes, and ringtails.

The body count includes more than 25,000 red and gray foxes, 10,700 bobcats, 2,800 black bears, 2,300 timber wolves, and 2,100 mountain lions. But the vast majority — about 512,500 — were coyotes.

Aerial gunning is the agency's most popular predator-killing tool. Since 2001, more than 340,000 coyotes have been gunned down from

planes and helicopters across sixteen Western states, including California
— an average of 600 a week, agency records show.

According to WildEarth Guardians (www.wildearthguardians.org),
between 2004 and 2010, Wildlife Services killed over 22.5 million animals
to protect agribusiness. The agency spends $100 million each year, and
Wildlife Services' job is to "eradicate" and "bring down" wolves, coyotes,
mountain lions, bears, prairie dogs, and other wild animals.

In 2010, Wildlife Services killed 5 million animals (this number does
not include the thousands of birds Wildlife Services has since admitted to
poisoning in 2010), including 112,781 mammalian carnivores such as coyotes, wolves, bobcats, cougars, badgers, and bears.

It's *not* radical to openly oppose the hideous killing by Wildlife Services. WildEarth Guardians has sued Wildlife Services, Project Coyote has
an action alert to stop the killing of wildlife on public lands and to ban
predator poisons, and the American Society of Mammalogists, a prestigious professional organization, has formally criticized Wildlife Services.

Clearly, the killing ways of Wildlife Services have not worked and
indeed will never work because their methods don't take into account what
we know about the behavior and ecology of the animals whom they wantonly murder. Professional biologists who don't typically get involved in
these sorts of causes agree that Wildlife Services' war on wildlife will never
work. The facts speak for themselves.

[ORIGINALLY POSTED ON MAY 3, 2012]

Recreational Hunting:
Would You Kill Your Dog for Fun?

KILLING OTHER ANIMALS FOR RECREATION amounts to killing them for fun. I realize that many of the issues centering on sport hunting are highly contentious, but they need to be discussed openly. For those who choose to kill animals in the name of whatever serves their purpose, including conservation, if you wouldn't do it to your (or a) dog, why do it to other sentient beings?

Recreational or sport hunting and fishing are very popular activities. The US Fish & Wildlife Service keeps track of the number of people who hunt and fish in the United States, which totaled over 46 million in 2011.

Trophy hunting also is a form of recreational hunting. One example of this egregious activity that made the news in 2012 involved Donald Trump's rich sons, Eric and Donald Jr., who wrote off their killing sprees during pricey canned hunts in Zimbabwe in the name of conservation by claiming their activities save animals and habitats and help local people. How much fun it must be to pay a lot of money to kill animals in these staged encounters. Of course, rich kids aren't the only people who kill animals for fun, either recreationally or for trophies to hang on their walls.

Most people who hunt do not do it with conservation in mind. Many do it for unneeded food or clothing, whereas others do it for fun, or what some claim is quality family time. Hunting for food or clothing that aren't needed really amounts to sport hunting. And, hunting is not especially "efficient" in terms of animals being killed painlessly. Some people argue that it's okay to kill in the name of conservation. Individuals of invasive species (or species more appropriately called "out of place species," according to my Australian colleague Dr. Rod Bennison in his discussion of "ecological inclusion") are often killed, as are animals who humans decide are "pests."

Compassionate conservation is a growing global movement. One of the goals of compassionate conservation is to focus on the importance and value of *individual* nonhuman animals. This is because those people interested in animal welfare are drawn to the animals themselves, whereas those people interested in conservation and environmental ethics concentrate more on species of animals, animal populations, and ecosystems. Individuals are considered dispensable to achieve certain goals.

Focusing on larger entities such as species, populations, and ecosystems is a fundamental driver of conservationists. Those motivated by concerns about animal welfare argue against killing individuals, whereas conservationists accept that killing individuals might be permissible "for the good of the members of the same or other species." The guiding principles of compassionate conservation seek to create common ground between those who are concerned with the well-being of individual animals and those who are concerned more with conservation.

People all over the globe are extremely concerned that humans continue to move incessantly into animal habitats and redecorate nature. Once they've moved in, people often label the animals as "pests" when the animals act as the beings they are. Compassionate conservation considers both human and nonhuman animals and how to work out solutions that are satisfactory to both. Often it is not possible to attain these goals, and there usually are trade-offs that have to be made in the "real world."

One trade-off for some people — not all, but still far too many — involves needlessly killing other animals recreationally because they're pests; they kill for fun in the name of conservation. For example, this is happening with the iconic kangaroo and dingoes in Australia. In the United States the war on wildlife results in the reprehensible and inhumane slaughter of millions upon millions of sentient beings, including wolves and coyotes, each and every year (see "Murder, Inc.: Wildlife Services Brutally Kills Millions of Animals with Your Money," page 283). In some instances the animals are tortured in the most egregious ways, such as a trapped wolf being used for target practice; sanctioned coyote killing contests; and a "squirrel slam," which even has a children's category, run by the Holley Fire Department in upstate New York.

Another disgusting activity that occurs "down under" is called "pig dogging," which involves the savage killing of feral pigs by humans after they're located by packs of pig dogs. Some call pig dogging "arguably the cruellest and most brutal form of hunting still permitted in Australia today." I warn you that reading or watching videos about this reprehensible and brutal form of recreational hunting will ruin your day! Nonetheless, some support this so-called sport, and some call themselves "responsible" pig doggers. Many in Australia, including government agencies, label this as responsible and effective conservation. I'll leave it to you to decide if they have a case.

The authors in my book *Ignoring Nature No More: The Case for Compassionate Conservation* argue that humans, including conservationists, have been ignoring nature for too long, and this is something that has to change right now, not when it's "more convenient." For example, elephant poachers in Kenya have now been educated to protect the elephants, swapping their payments for killing for payments for protecting these magnificent animals. The compassionate conservation movement is really a social movement with a broad number of supporters. It is clear that it is our nature to be kind, empathetic, and compassionate. And individual animals certainly count on the goodwill of big-brained, big-footed, and invasive humans to take their lives seriously.

For compassionate conservation, the first premise is "First do no harm," and the second is that *individual* lives count. By following these guidelines it will be easy for people to expand their compassion footprint, to rewild their hearts, and to stop killing animals for fun or for some misguided premise of saving the environment or for protecting threatened or endangered species. Slaughtering sentience is wrong.

Again, I know that many of the issues I and others raise about sport hunting and killing in the name of conservation are highly contentious, but nothing is to be gained by pretending that people agree about the ethics of killing other animals for recreation or for conservation and that it's just perfectly okay to engage in this activity without a care in the world.

Regardless of how sticky the issues are for some people and how passionate they can get, killing for fun and killing in the name of conservation should not be accepted as if they're the only shows in town. If you wouldn't do it to your dog, why would you choose to do it to other sentient beings?

[ORIGINALLY POSTED ON FEBRUARY 9, 2013]

Are Fluffy Pandas Worth Saving
or Should We Let Them Go?

IN A PREVIOUS ESSAY I wrote about the plight of captive-bred pandas and the recent birth and almost immediate death of one of these charismatic mammals at the National Zoo in Washington, DC. Giant pandas surely are cute and pull at people's heartstrings — one video of a baby panda sneezing has more than 155 million hits — but my impression is that most people who find these endangered mammals to be seductively alluring do not know what sort of life they are destined to live.

This past Friday (February 22, 2013) giant pandas once again appeared in the major news media, this time on *Rock Center* on *NBC News*. The show was called "Are Giant Pandas Worth Saving?"

I call your attention to this show and the interviews Kate Snow held with Dr. Sarah Bexell and British wildlife expert Chris Packham because I found it to be very well-balanced, and it made me revisit some of the material about which I'd previously written. Dr. Bexell is the director of conservation education at the Chengdu Research Base of Giant Panda Breeding (www.panda.org.cn/english) and coauthor with Professor Zhang Zhihe, director of the same facility, of the very important book *Giant Pandas: Born Survivors*.

Dr. Bexell and her colleagues see the panda as an iconic animal worth saving, although she and others know there are very difficult, challenging, and frustrating questions that need to be addressed, whereas Mr. Packham does not think the panda is worth saving. He notes, "I think we have to make tough choices....I think that, ultimately, we have to be pragmatic as well as sentimental. You know, we can't allow our heart to rule our conservation head....And if we channel this much into just one species, then many others, which could be far better helped, many other, not just species, but communities and ecosystems could be better protected at the expense of one fluffy, cuddly bear." Similarly, noted conservation psychologist and *Psychology Today* blogger Susan Clayton writes, "So, I like pandas as much as anyone. But at some level I can't help wondering what we're saving them for. Just as tourist attractions?"

Dr. Bexell notes, "I think pandas are symbolic. We all love them. We all want to share the earth with them. And if we truly cannot save space for giant pandas, what does that say about us as a species? And how could we ever have hope for any of the others if we can't save the one that we profess to love the most?"

The captive breeding of animals who will spend the rest of their lives in cages as supposed "ambassadors of their species" or purportedly to raise money for conservation projects (though some funds are generated) raises many questions. And I come down more on the side of Mr. Packham. We need to make tough choices and might as well face up to the task at hand. I don't see captive breeding and keeping animals in cages as a way to rewild our hearts or to rewild other animals.

I know we are all attracted to cute, fluffy, and cuddly, but I am much swayed by a quotation from one of the world's foremost conservation biologists, Harvard University's Edward O. Wilson. Professor Wilson wrote, "If all mankind were to disappear, the world would regenerate back to the rich state of equilibrium that existed ten thousand years ago. If insects were to vanish, the environment would collapse into chaos."

In an essay called "Another Inconvenient Truth," Elizabeth Bennett, of the prestigious Wildlife Conservation Society (www.wcs.org), points out that we're really not very good about protecting charismatic species, so there's not that much hope for those who aren't eye-catching. More and more researchers are taking the view that we can't fix everything and that we need to make choices about who to save and who to let go. In an Internet survey conducted by the University of York's Murray Rudd of 583 conservation scientists, 60 percent agreed that criteria should be established for deciding which species to abandon in order to focus on saving others. Meanwhile, 99 percent agreed that a serious loss of biodiversity is "likely, very likely, or virtually certain."

Professor Wilson's vote for the less notable but more ecologically important species always makes me think about the choices we make in conservation projects. I really believe that, even when people differ, most are truly committed to making the world the best place it can be at a time when we are recklessly and selfishly destroying our magnificent planet at an unprecedented rate, wantonly and impetuously decimating wondrous and magical webs of nature, and heartlessly and mercilessly killing countless animal beings of myriad species. The biodiversity crisis that is a result of our overproducing, overconsuming, and incredibly invasive ways not only threatens other species but also negatively affects us all.

We can't save all species, and in the future we'll have to make some tough choices. Informed discussions are sorely needed, and ignoring the critical and difficult questions that arise will get us nowhere. Indeed, it will work against us, other species, and the integrity of ecosystems we are trying to save.

[ORIGINALLY POSTED ON FEBRUARY 24, 2013]

Using Hamsters to Save Ferrets:
The Need for Compassionate Conservation

SHOULD HUMAN BEINGS feed golden hamsters to black-footed ferrets? This provocative question (and for some, an unanticipated query) leads to many others about how we interact with nonhuman animals. Our relationships with animals are confusing, paradoxical, frustrating, challenging, and force us to consider who we are, who "they" are, and how and why we *choose* to interact with them in the ways we do. When push comes to shove, human interests usually trump those of other animals, as we are a selfishly dominating species.

As a focal point for dealing with deliberations about how we interact with animals, we have chosen to use reintroduction projects, in which an attempt is made to reintroduce individuals of a given species to areas where they once thrived. These projects often involve balancing the interests or right to life of individuals of one species with those of another, and balancing the interests of individuals with concerns for the integrity of entire populations, species, or ecosystems.

A number of ethical questions arise that warrant serious consideration because we, human beings with large brains, self-centered importance, and a tendency to be thoroughly and uniquely invasive, can do anything we want to other animals and their habitats. It is inarguable that ethics must be firmly implanted in conservation biology even if these discussions move us outside of our comfort zones and even if it means that some projects must be put on hold temporarily or forever. Many conservationists are concerned about the widespread loss of critical habitat as we redecorate nature. The well-being of animals is often less emphasized. But we must remember that loss of habitat is not only an environmental matter; it also influences animals and so gains the attention of animal advocates.

Some of the questions that need to be examined by the broad-based group of people interested in conservation biology include: How do we reconcile the interests or rights of *individual* animals with the health or integrity of larger entities such as populations, species, and ecosystems? Can we really "re-create" or "restore" ecosystems? Should individuals be traded off for the good of their own or other species? Should individuals of a prey species be used to train the hunting skills of predatory animals who are candidates for reintroduction?

Here we focus on the last question. However, we operate on the assumption that it is difficult if not impossible to re-create or restore ecosystems to what they were in the past, and we realize that reconciling the rights of individuals to exist — even if it means that species and ecosystems might go extinct — would require a much longer discussion in which many others are involved.

The question "Should individuals of a prey species be used to train the hunting skills of predatory animals who are candidates for reintroduction?" raises issues with which we are specifically concerned regarding the importance of recognizing that the lives of individual *animals* matter. Consider the black-footed ferret recovery program (www.blackfooted ferret.org). To prepare these endangered captive-bred predators to hunt in the wild, people working in this program provide the ferrets with live black-tailed prairie dogs and golden hamsters. The hamsters are bred specifically for this purpose. Their fate is sealed, though their deaths are not easy. Surely these sentient rodents endure pain and suffering when they are sought by the ferrets, especially hamsters who encounter a poorly trained or poorly skilled hunter. And surely their fear is immense, as they are placed in enclosures with predators who are trying to kill them. One needs only to watch their defensive behavior and look into their eyes. You'll sense the same fear as you would in a terrified dog.

In email correspondence, the people responsible for managing the ferret-hamster encounters stated, "In 2008 we fed out approximately 3,200 hamsters and in 2009 we fed out approximately 4,100 hamsters. They are fed out either live (70%) or dead (30%) depending on supply. Hamsters are euthanized using CO_2 as approved from the American Veterinary Medical

Association Guidelines on Euthanasia. All hamsters are produced at the Ferret Center."

So, in one recent two-year period, 7,300 hamsters were "produced" — bred to be killed — and fed to the ferrets. Of this number, about 5,100 were offered alive to these developing predators. In addition to the hamsters, in 2008 and 2009 a reported 2,466 prairie dogs were supplied to the ferret program by various sources. Sixty percent of these animals were fed alive to the ferrets.

What do you think about feeding hamsters and prairie dogs to black-footed ferrets? Did you know that this was done? Consider that the hamsters were bred *solely* for the purpose of being killed by the often inexperienced, fumbling ferrets. Is the use of the helpless hamsters as training bait permissible? Do their lives count less than those of the ferrets? Given that hamsters are sentient mammals who share with us the same neural structures that are important in processing emotions in the limbic system, what do you think they feel as they are fed live to the ferrets? These animals also have keen senses of smell and hearing, and therefore it is likely they are aware of the suffering of other hamsters who are being killed by the ferrets. A study published in 2006 in the prestigious peer-reviewed journal *Science* showed that mice are empathic rodents who feel the pain of other mice, and many other animals also display empathy.

We consider the use of hamsters and prairie dogs to be impermissible. We are *not* anti-black-footed ferrets, but pro-hamsters, speaking on their behalf. The project is unacceptable as long as live animals are used as bait.

What can be done to save hamsters and train ferrets? Humane alternatives such as the surrogate, inanimate models used to study the development of predatory behavior in African dwarf mongooses by the German ethologist Anne Rasa could be developed, as could inanimate models used to study antipredatory behavior in yellow-bellied marmots by UCLA biologist Daniel Blumstein. These alternatives would not only be more humane, because sentient animals would not have to be used, but also much more economical.

If humane nonanimal alternatives were used to train the ferrets, other questions still need to be considered, such as why would we want to reintroduce animals such as black-footed ferrets in the first place? Are they that important to the ecosystems in which they used to live or are to be reintroduced? Could the enormous amounts of money and time devoted to this project be used in more productive ways? It has been estimated that when only released surviving ferrets are considered, the cost may be as high as one million dollars per animal.

It is in the best traditions of science to ask questions about ethics. Ethical discussions can enrich us all, and we are not alone in calling for these exchanges. In September 2010 there will be a much-needed conference on Compassionate Conservation (www.compassionateconservation.org) in which these and other questions will be discussed and debated. Biologists John Vucetich and Michael Nelson argue in their excellent paper titled "What Are 60 Warblers Worth? Killing in the Name of Conservation" that human activities that cause intentional suffering and death in the name of conservation demand careful scrutiny. Unfortunately, such issues are rarely discussed.

We agree that open discussion on these and other questions is sorely needed. For example, why do people who get upset at the abuse of other animals permit the use of hamsters? If you had a hamster friend, would you allow him or her to be used in this project? How about a dog or a cat? If you are an ethical vegetarian or vegan, how do you defend the intentional breeding and killing of hamsters as meals for ferrets? Why are hamsters different from cows or pigs? Some who support eating meat argue that because the animals have had a chance to have a "good life" before they are killed it is permissible to slaughter them. This line of reasoning (with which we disagree) does not apply to the hamsters.

The use of hamsters also offers an uninspiring and confusing message for children, future ambassadors for a more compassionate and peaceful planet. There are no ethical principles of which we are aware that could be offered in humane/conservation education that would allow hamsters or other animals to be used to train predators.

We realize these are difficult questions, but that does not mean they should be avoided. They will not go away if we ignore them, and indeed they should not be pushed aside. In his book *A World of Wounds*, renowned ecologist Paul Ehrlich stressed that people who hold opposing opinions need to engage in open discussion with well-reasoned dissent. Positions should be questioned and criticized, not the people who hold them. Personal attacks preclude open discussion because, once someone is put on the defensive, fruitful exchanges are impossible, at least for the moment.

We are not trying to be antiscience or "radical." Indeed, we strive for the time when asking these questions would be mainstream, and the radicals would be the ones who allow such programs to persist. We also need to strive for consistency. If we find it offensive to use dogs for research, or cows or pigs for food or clothes, then why is it permissible to breed hamsters solely to be killed? We fully recognize that ethics might mean the demise of some projects forever, or that they have to be put on hold until more humane alternatives are developed, something that could be done in the ferret recovery program.

It is *individuals* who count when we consider how we treat other animals. It is individuals — not species — who personally feel pain and suffer. Animals aren't mere resources or property. We must respect their dignity and their lives. We suggest that the guiding principles for conservation projects and all of our interactions with animals should be: (1) do no intentional harm, (2) respect all life, (3) treat all individuals with compassion, and (4) tread lightly when stepping into the lives of other animals.

These principles form the foundation of a global moral imperative to expand our compassion footprint to which we all should aspire. We can rewild our hearts, build corridors of compassion and coexistence, and all animals, including ourselves, will benefit. We do not own the world, and when we ignore this fact it is to our peril and loss. We suffer the indignities we impose on other beings. If we are not part of the solution, we contribute to the problems.

The harm done to hamsters violates the above principles because it constitutes premeditated and intentional harm. Therefore, it is unacceptable. While we are concerned with the fate of populations, species, and ecosystems, we argue that humane and ethical alternatives must be developed if projects in which animals are intentionally harmed are to continue.

We look forward to further discussions with others who share our interests, including those who hold other views.

[Note: This essay was cowritten with David Crawford, who has worked for many years on a wide variety of issues centering on animal protection, including Animal Help Now (www.ahnow.org).]

[ORIGINALLY POSTED ON APRIL 30, 2010]

Bill and Lou:
Who Lives, Who Dies, and Why

BILL AND LOU ARE TWO OXEN who have lived and labored in obscurity for the past ten years on the campus of a small college, Green Mountain College (GMC), in a small town in a small state, Poultney, Vermont. Recently, college officials announced that as a reward for their long years of service on the college's working farm, Bill and Lou would be slaughtered and served as oxenburgers to students. They would serve as a lesson in sustainability and tradition.

So, why has the story about their impending slaughter rapidly attracted international attention? It's because Bill and Lou are sentient, feeling individuals, with unique personalities, who are condemned to death because they are too old to work, and there is a very simple humane alternative to their slaughter. VINE, a sanctuary near GMC, has offered to have them live there for free.

The case of Bill and Lou is not just of local interest. Our relationships with other animals are extremely challenging and paradoxical. Bill and Lou's story is a perfect example of how nonhuman animals depend on the goodwill of human animals for their very lives. We are the most powerful force on Earth, and every second of every day we're making decisions about who lives and who dies. In Bill and Lou's case, people who have chosen to kill them argue that because they're old and because they've been close and inseparable friends for so long, when one dies the other would terribly miss their workmate and that would be too much for the survivor to handle. Lou has a recurring injury, so some at GMC claim both of them should be killed at the same time. This decision is too convenient, fast, and daft. Would people do this to their companion dogs? Of course not. They would make sure the survivor would have the best life possible. So why do it to oxen?

Some at GMC also argue that sustainability is the main issue, but the one-dimensional rhetoric of sustainability, as a colleague puts it, makes for a very weak and impersonal argument. It's estimated Bill and Lou will produce about a ton of beef that otherwise would come from animals living on horrific factory farms, also known as concentrated animal feeding operations (CAFOs), that have well-known and significant negative ecological impacts including air, water, and land pollution. Why use CAFO meat at all?

Because Bill and Lou will have to eat grass during their retirement years and growing and maintaining grass requires water, some say it's best to kill them for reasons of ecological sustainability. It's unlikely they will live very long even in a sanctuary. However, if they were healthy and could work, they also would consume resources. Sure, they would also be helping to produce resources, but at some point all living beings will likely consume more than they produce for a wide variety of reasons. The sustainability argument is ludicrous because we're talking about only two oxen, not a herd of oxen.

Some people argue that the resistance to killing Bill and Lou centers on one's meal plan, be it carnivory, vegetarianism, or veganism, and that keeping them alive is really an argument for getting rid of animals in our diet. This isn't necessarily so, and it shifts the attention away from the fact that oxen are highly emotional and sentient beings, and this is the unnecessary slaughter of two special animals. And it's not euthanasia, or mercy killing, as some claim, because neither Bill nor Lou is suffering untreatable pain, according to my sources.

Bill and Lou are a special case. They've worked selflessly for GMC, they are the best of friends, and they have the opportunity to live out their lives in peace and safety. They deserve to live after GMC decides they're no longer useful. The decision to kill them shows how sentient beings are viewed as things, as mere property, to be used by humans for human ends. The details of their case, including that Bill and Lou are unique individuals, are lost in the muddle of impersonal ecological and philosophical arguments. Bill and Lou should be allowed to live a good life until death do them part, and then the survivor should be given the best life possible. Let heartfelt compassion be used to do something for them as special friends.

Those who favor killing Bill and Lou also argue there is a strong educational lesson. However, think of how much could be learned by factoring deep compassion and their close friendship with GMC and for one another into the fate of Bill and Lou. Showing flexibility would be a most valuable lesson. The world isn't linear or black-and-white. There are many ethical lessons here for those who teach humane and compassionate education.

Cruelty can't stand the spotlight, which is why Bill and Lou, supposed friends of the college, individuals with unique stories, have touched the hearts of people around the world. Killing them is an unacceptable "thank you" for who they are and for all they have done.

Note: Lou was killed in late 2012, but Bill was still alive as of March 2013.

[ORIGINALLY POSTED ON OCTOBER 21, 2012]

Saving Sentience:
Homeless Animals
Need All the Help They Can Get

DOGS, CATS, AND OTHER MAMMALS who are also favored companion animals often find themselves homeless. Indeed, millions of animals who also are companion animals are homeless. While it's difficult to know just how many homeless animals there are, it's been estimated by the ASPCA (www.aspca.org) that "approximately 5 million to 7 million companion animals enter animal shelters nationwide every year, and approximately 3 million to 4 million are euthanized (60 percent of dogs and 70 percent of cats). Shelter intakes are about evenly divided between those animals relinquished by owners and those picked up by animal control. These are national estimates; the percentage of euthanasia may vary from state to state."

Stray animals also need to be taken into account. It's impossible to know how many stray dogs and cats there are in the United States, but it's been estimated there may be as many as 70 million stray cats. I've been told by more than one person that about 75 percent of all dogs in the world are stray or homeless. I haven't been able to verify this number, but even if it were halved, it would be a large and unacceptable number. In the United Kingdom alone, more than 120,000 stray dogs were picked up over a recent twelve-month period with more than 7,500 having to be "put down." The number is on the rise. In Detroit, Michigan, there are at least 50,000 stray dogs. The numbers are staggering and sickening, and we can do something about this horrible situation.

Clearly, there's a major problem with homeless and stray animals worldwide. Many people are more concerned with dogs and cats who find themselves without a safe home in which to live and thrive, but of course other animals are also homeless, including hamsters, gerbils, guinea pigs, rabbits, and a wide variety of birds, fish, reptiles, and amphibians. These are all conscious beings who care about what happens to them, and they deserve much better care.

I just received a notice from the group called Advancing the Interests of Animals (www.aianimals.org) that August 18, 2012 is International Homeless Animals Day. They list a number of ways we can help these homeless individuals. These include:

- Adopt, don't buy. Animals in shelters and at rescue groups are waiting for you to give them a loving home! Pet store and online animals are usually sick and come from large and awful commercial breeding facilities. Don't support this cruelty.
- Spay/neuter your companion animal(s) and encourage others to do the same!
- Donate or volunteer at your local animal shelter or rescue group(s).
- Foster. Become a foster parent to a dog or cat and help find them their forever home.
- Help strays in your community! Carry food, water, and a leash and adjustable collar in your car.
- Educate yourself about homeless animals and all the ways you can alleviate their suffering. Understand the problems with dog and cat overpopulation and what you can do to help.

Each of us can make a difference in the lives of these needy beings and help to make their lives far better than they are. Saving sentience is really easy to do, and I encourage everyone to do what they can.

[ORIGINALLY POSTED ON AUGUST 13, 2012]

Ignoring Nature No More:
Compassionate Conservation at Work

COMPASSIONATE CONSERVATION is a rapidly growing interdisciplinary and international movement that I've written about in some previous essays. The first and highly successful meeting focusing on compassionate conservation was held in Oxford, England, in early September 2010; the next gathering was held in Chengdu, China, in June 2011; a workshop was convened in London, England, in November 2012; and in February 2013, Dr. Daniel Ramp and I gave lectures on this topic at the University of Technology in Sydney, Australia.

The gathering in Sydney was called "Compassionate Conservation: Is Recreational Hunting Defensible?" My talk was titled "First Do No Harm: Would You Kill Your Dog for Fun?" and Daniel Ramp's was called "Shooting Our Mouths Off About Conservation." Indeed, the topic of compassionate conservation is so important that there will be a symposium on this topic organized by Chris Draper of the Born Free Foundation (www.bornfree.org.uk) at the International Congress for Conservation Biology (www.conbio.org) in Baltimore, Maryland, on July 24, 2013.

The original meeting, sponsored by the Wildlife Conservation Research Unit (www.wildcru.org), the Born Free Foundation, and others, focused on a number of major themes, including nonhuman animal welfare and the conservation of wild animals, captive animal welfare and conservation, conservation consequences of wildlife rescue, rehabilitation and release, and the international trade in live wild animals. It is essential that field workers focus on protecting *individual* animals during their research.

The organization Compassionate Conservation (www.compassionateconservation.org) has put together the following "guiding principles":

Recognising that wild animals, whether free-ranging or in captivity, may be affected by the intentional or unintentional actions of humans as well as the natural processes within ecosystems and the wider environment;

Concerned that many human activities, including those undertaken for a conservation purpose, may directly or indirectly cause harm to individual wild animals, populations, species, or ecosystems;

Recognising that both conservation and wild animal welfare should implicitly respect the inherent value of wild animals and the natural world, and that both disciplines should try to mitigate harms caused by humans to other species;

Believing that all harms to wild animals should be minimised wherever and to the extent possible, regardless of the human intention and purpose behind them;

Proposing that the principles and actions that underpin Compassionate Conservation, by combining consideration of animal welfare and conservation, will lead to a reduction in harm and in the suffering of individual wild animals, and will improve conservation outcomes;

We undersigned:

Believe that we can accomplish more than could be achieved by applying either animal welfare or conservation practices without consideration of and, where appropriate, application of the other;

And agree that we shall, in our professional lives, seek to: identify, enhance, and promote the commonalities between animal welfare and conservation; pursue, to the extent possible, best practice in these disciplines; and thereby work to achieve shared principles and undertake practical Compassionate Conservation actions.

Compassionate conservation focuses on the quality of life and well-being of *individual* animals. Many conservation biologists and environmentalists are willing to trade off individual lives for the perceived good or benefit of higher levels of organization, such as ecosystems, populations, or a species. How to reconcile the well-being of individuals with these broader concerns is a topic of great interest for those who support compassionate conservation. The differences in the views and agendas of people who call themselves animal welfarists, animal rightists, and conservationists can be rather large and lead to very different outcomes. For example, some might argue that a specific project needs to be put on hold until animal abuse is eliminated, or that a project needs to be terminated if this is not possible. It's also possible, they argue, that some proposed projects must be shelved if they involve abusive treatment that compromises the lives of individual animals.

It's not surprising that some in the compassionate conservation movement want more rapid and radical changes than others. I discuss these topics in more detail in the essay "Animal Emotions, Animal Sentience, Animal Welfare, and Animal Rights" (page 38), and they are also considered in great detail in my new book *Ignoring Nature No More: The Case for Compassionate Conservation*, as well as in Gill Aitken's *A New Approach to Conservation*. The important thing is to have people with different agendas talk with, and not at, one another. There's a lot of work to be done, and I'm personally hopeful that more and more people will come to value the lives of individuals in their work and that compassionate conservation will lead the way. It's difficult for me to imagine that striving for a more compassionate world wouldn't be high on the agenda of everyone who has the opportunity and privilege of working with other animals.

I have been interested in compassionate conservation since long before the field had a name. *Ignoring Nature No More* is an edited volume in which I've gathered twenty-six essays written by colleagues who represent numerous disciplines and work in a number of different countries. They were penned for a general audience as well as for researchers, and they cover many "hot" topics pertaining to conservation biology, conservation behavior (see *A Primer of Conservation Behavior* by Daniel Blumstein and Esteban Fernandez-Juricic), conservation psychology (see Susan Clayton's books *Conservation Psychology*, coauthored with Gene Myers, and the *Oxford Handbook of Environmental and Conservation Psychology*), evolutionary biology, anthrozoology, and animal protection (animal welfare and animal rights).

Compassionate conservation is no longer an oxymoron. Luckily for the animals, there are people working hard to make their lives better and who give us hope and inspiration so that the world our children inherit will be the best possible world. Truly, because of our past activities, it is not the best of all possible worlds yet. We must rewild our hearts and build corridors of compassion and coexistence that include all beings. We need to treat animals better or leave them alone. That is their manifesto.

What animals feel matters to them, and it must matter to us. The lives of *individual* animals must be taken very seriously and researchers must make this a priority. We are responsible for who lives and who dies. We can do anything we want, but this power does not give us the license to ruin a spectacularly beautiful planet, its wondrous webs of nature, and its magnificent nonhuman residents.

Those of us who can do something must do something now, not when it's "more convenient." Time is not on our side, and the animals need all the help they can get. How exciting it is to work in the field of compassionate conservation with colleagues all over the world who come to the table with different and often competing interests, but with a shared goal of working hard to make the world a better place for all beings. This is what striving to create a more compassionate world is all about.

Compassionate conservation is a wonderful "meeting place" — a much-needed paradigm shift and social movement — for everyone concerned with protecting all animals. When we ignore nature, we not only harm other animals but we do so at our own peril.

[ORIGINALLY POSTED ON APRIL 16, 2013]

PART II

REWILDING OUR HEARTS

The Importance of Kindness,
Empathy, and Compassion
for All Beings

HERE IS THE BIG QUESTION: What can we do to make the world a better place for all beings, human and nonhuman, and to protect their homes? There are no easy answers. We need to move out of our comfort zones and think and act outside of the box because what we've been doing in the past hasn't worked very well. We really are decimating our planet at an unprecedented rate, and we need to stop doing this now. We've ignored nature for far too long a time, and we can't continue living as if what we do doesn't really matter, as if we don't need to make changes right now to stop plundering Earth. What we do really does matter in all arenas. Humans are very accomplished denialists. I often think we should be called *Homo denialus* rather than *Homo sapiens*.

I travel a lot, and I meet many wonderful people who are working tirelessly and selflessly for other animals, humans, and the planet as a whole. I'm an unflinching, card-carrying optimist, and that's because I know there are many others doing all they can do. This keeps my hopes and dreams alive. Many people lose faith and burn out because the work is tedious and can be rather depressing. I always say to avoid burnout one should work hard, play hard, rest hard, and be able to step back and laugh at oneself when need be. Also, avoid being sidetracked by people who just want to waste your time as you work to make the world a better, safer, and more peaceful and compassionate place for all beings.

Everyone can be an activist and choose to work for a healthier planet. Every individual counts. One doesn't have to found a movement or have a lot of extra time and money to make a difference. Being an activist isn't being radical. Other animals and Earth need all the help they can get from people who are willing to change their ways. In our activism we need to be proactive, passionate, and polite. The essays that follow show how easy it is to make a difference and that we can never be too kind or too nice, even to those with whom we disagree. Indeed, we'll never run out of compassion because compassion is contagious. As these essays show, compassion begets compassion.

Twelve Millennial Mantras
(with Jane Goodall):
Hope Abounds

EVERY DECEMBER I sit down and reflect on the past year and what's coming up as we enter the New Year, and it came to me that revisiting and updating a short essay I wrote with renowned primatologist and conservationist Jane Goodall in December 1999 as we were heading into a new century could provide a good beginning and some much needed hope. This essay, called the "Twelve Millennial Mantras," which in many ways remains timeless, eventually served as the basis for our book *The Ten Trusts: What We Must Do to Care for the Animals We Love*. Indeed, all animals, human and nonhuman, and their homes and habitats, will benefit from the efforts, no matter how big or small, of those who can do something to make a positive difference in difficult times.

The Twelve Millennial Mantras

ONE: Compassion and empathy for animals begets compassion and empathy for humans. Cruelty toward animals begets cruelty toward humans.

TWO: All life has value and should be respected. Every animal owns her or his own life spark. Animals are not owned as property. All living creatures deserve these basic rights: the right to life, freedom from torture, and liberty to express their individual natures. Many law schools offer courses in animal law. If we agree, we would interact with animals in rather different ways. We shall need compelling reasons for denying these rights and to ask forgiveness for any animal we harm.

THREE: Do unto others as you would have them do unto you. Imagine what it would be like to be caged, trapped, restrained, isolated, mutilated, shocked, starved, socially deprived, hung upside down awaiting death, or watching others slaughtered. Biological data clearly show that many animals suffer physically and psychologically and feel pain.

FOUR: Dominion does not mean domination. We hold dominion over animals only because of our powerful and ubiquitous intellect. Not because we are morally superior. Not because we have a "right" to exploit those who cannot defend themselves. Let us use our brain to move toward compassion and away from cruelty, to feel empathy rather than cold indifference, to feel animals' pain in our hearts.

FIVE: Human beings are a part of the animal kingdom, not apart from it. The separation of "us" from "them" creates a false picture and is responsible for much suffering. It is part of the in-group/out-group mentality that leads to human oppression of the weak by the strong, as in ethnic, religious, political, and social conflicts. Let us open our hearts to two-way relationships with other animals, each giving and receiving. This brings pure and uncomplicated joy.

SIX: Imagine a world without animals. No birdsong, no droning of nectar-searching bees, no coyotes howling, no thundering of hooves on the plains. Rachel Carson chilled our hearts with thoughts of the silent spring. Now we face the prospect of silent summers, falls, and winters.

SEVEN: Tread lightly. Only interfere when it will be in the best interests of the animals. Imagine a world where we truly respect and admire animals and feel heartfelt empathy, compassion, and understanding. Imagine how we should be freed of guilt, conscious or unconscious.

EIGHT: Make ethical choices in what we buy, do, and watch. In a consumer-driven society, our individual choices, used collectively for the good of animals and nature, can change the world faster than laws.

NINE: Have the courage of conviction. Never say never. Act now. Be proactive; prevent animal abuse before it starts. Dare to speak out to save the world's precious and fragile resources. Live as much as possible in harmony with nature, respecting the intrinsic value of all life and the wondrous composition of earth, water, and air.

TEN: Every individual matters and has a role to play. Our actions make a difference. Public pressure has been responsible for much social change, including more humane treatment of animals. "Whistle-blowers" have courageously revealed intolerable conditions in laboratories, circuses, slaughterhouses, and so on, often at the expense of their jobs.

ELEVEN: Be a passionate visionary, a courageous crusader. Combat cruelty and catalyze compassion. Do not fear to express love. Do not fear to be too generous or too kind. Above all, understand that there are many reasons to remain optimistic even when things seem grim. Let us harness the indomitable human spirit. Together we can make this a better world for all living organisms. We must, for our children and for theirs. We must stroll with our kin, not walk away from them.

TWELVE: A millennial mantra: When animals lose, we all lose. Every single loss diminishes us as well as the magnificent world in which we live together.

The Ten Trusts

As I mentioned above, these twelve mantras served as the basis for "The Ten Trusts," as follows:

ONE: Rejoice that we are part of the Animal Kingdom.
TWO: Respect all life.
THREE: Open our minds, in humility, to animals and learn from them.
FOUR: Teach our children to respect and love nature.
FIVE: Be wise stewards of life on earth.
SIX: Value and help preserve the sounds of nature.
SEVEN: Refrain from harming life in order to learn about it.
EIGHT: Have the courage of our convictions.
NINE: Praise and help those who work for animals and the natural world.
TEN: Act knowing we are not alone and live with hope.

Where To from Here?

In so many ways these Mantras and Trusts remain useful guidelines for action today, and while we've made a good deal of progress in many areas of animal protection and animal conservation and in helping humans in need, much more needs to be done. We continue to learn about how our own well-being is tightly linked to the well-being of other animals and their homes, and that we and other animals display a wide range of positive emotions, including kindness, compassion, and empathy. We've learned that it's natural to be good, cooperative, kind, empathic, and compassionate (see "Human-Like Violence Is Extremely Rare in Other Animals," page 201). A relatively new and growing movement called compassionate conservation also stresses how we must tap into our natural goodness and help all animals, nonhuman and human, who need our support (see my book *Ignoring Nature No More*).

We also know that we must work very closely with youngsters all over the world. Jane Goodall's Roots & Shoots (http://rootsandshoots.org) groups are doing just that and much, much more. Dr. Goodall's message that every individual makes a difference rings loudly and clearly, and we must remember this because every person working within a unified community can truly make the world a better place for all beings. A free online book called *Kids & Animals: Drawings from the Hands and Hearts of Children and Youth* shows just how much youngsters care about all animals, human and nonhuman, and their homes and habitats.

In an essay I wrote last year around this time called "Rewilding Our Hearts: Maintaining Hope and Faith in Trying Times" (page 322), I reiterated the message that there really are many reasons for hope and that we must remain positive as we head into the new year. I also focused on animals who had been abused beyond belief and who recovered as models for resilience and faith.

We can learn a lot about being positive from other animals. For instance, there's always Jasper, a recovered Asiatic moon bear, who provides inspirational lessons about remaining positive even in difficult times. After years of horrific suffering, Jasper remains the spokes-bear for forgiveness and hope (see "Animals Can Be Ambassadors for Forgiveness,

Generosity, Peace, Trust, and Hope," page 25). A 2013 kid's book called *Jasper's Story*, which I wrote with Jill Robinson, inspires hope for future generations by telling Jasper's story to youngsters, on whose goodwill we will all depend in the future.

The ideas behind rewilding our hearts stress that the time is right and the time is now for an inspirational, revolutionary, and personal social movement that can save us from gloom and doom and keep us positive while we pursue our hopes and dreams as a unified global community. I remain even more optimistic that we can do much better as we move into the New Year.

The activism engendered by rewilding needs to be proactive, positive, persistent, patient, peaceful, practical, and passionate. I call these the "Seven Ps of Rewilding," and because it will come from deep in our heart, the rewilding movement will be contagious and long-lasting because no one should feel threatened. We know that being positive and hopeful are important for getting people to care and to act and that concentrating on successes, on what works, is important for overcoming hopelessness. We need to be persistent and "stick with" our beliefs and ethical principles with deep passion and follow up with positive actions. Pessimism is a turn-off, and we need to look on the bright side and talk up successes. It's also important to "be nice" to those *with* whom one disagrees and to talk with, not to or at, others.

(Re)connecting with nature and other animals can surely help us along in providing help to all of those individuals who dearly and sorely need our support. So let's join hands and face up to the task at hand as we move into a challenging future. Never say never, ever.

[ORIGINALLY POSTED ON DECEMBER 12, 2012]

Compassion Begets Compassion

A July 2012 essay in the *New York Times* called "Compassion Made Easy" by David DeSteno, a professor of psychology at Northeastern University, made me think about what we know about compassion in nonhuman animals.

As Dr. DeSteno puts it, "As a social psychologist interested in the emotions, I long wondered whether this spiritual understanding of compassion was also scientifically accurate. Empirically speaking, does the experience of compassion toward one person measurably affect our actions and attitudes toward other people? If so, are there practical steps we can take to further cultivate this feeling? Recently, my colleagues and I conducted experiments that answered yes to both questions."

I contacted Dr. DeSteno, and he told me about an exciting meeting taking place this week in Telluride, Colorado, called "The Science of Compassion," run by the Center for Compassion and Altruism Research and Education (http://ccare.stanford.edu). A group of renowned scholars will be talking about various aspects of compassion, and I regret I can't be there because I would like to see more discussion about compassion in nonhuman animals from an ethological/animal behavior perspective. I would also like to see more noninvasive research on animals that speaks to questions about compassion and empathy.

I was very excited to read about his and others' research in this area that focuses on humans because for years I've been suggesting just this, namely, that "compassion begets compassion." I've also written about how we can and must expand our compassion footprint and about an "umbrella of compassion" that reflects how compassion can be contagious and envelop people even without their knowing it. It's also noteworthy that there is research that shows that vegetarians and vegans are empathic than omnivores.

While I didn't have a broad and strong database to support my intuitions, I've experienced this in various venues. In my research on animal emotions, I've written stories about how compassion can spread across a group of individuals — when one animal cares for another group member, other group members join in. As DeSteno notes, "This idea is often articulated by the Dalai Lama, who argues that individual experiences of compassion radiate outward and increase harmony for all." We also know that many different animals display empathy, including mice, rats, and chickens. We also know that animals are far nicer to one another than previously thought and that cooperation and empathy are widespread among a wide variety of species.

I've also seen contagious compassion in my work with inmates in my Roots & Shoots group at the Boulder County, Colorado, jail. Many of the guys over the years (both in jail and when I've seen them after they've

been released) have told me that they've developed more compassion for humans and other animals by talking about it and seeing videos of compassion and empathy in animals.

A discussion about Buddhism and compassion resulted in one of the inmates making the most amazing soap sculptures reflecting the influence of the Buddha (see photo). He began with tiny bars of soap and melted them together with his hands, made paintbrushes using his own hair, and fashioned different colors from the food he was served.

All the inmates were very impressed with his artwork, and when we had discussions, we all agreed that compassion can beget compassion, that simply talking about this and seeing examples from different animals made the guys feel better about themselves and others. Some didn't realize it was happening until we discussed it.

I was really touched by these discussions. Just a few weeks ago I received an email from one of my past students in which he wrote, "I find myself today spending much more time outdoors and reliving my teenage years in the woods and mountains. I feel your class helped me rediscover what it means to love and respect our world, our ecosystems."

I'm sure that as time goes on we'll see more research on how compassion can easily spread among individuals in various species. Indeed, it's this process that is an essential part of my own project on rewilding our hearts and reconnecting with all aspects of nature (see also *Orion* magazine's book *Thirty-Year Plan*, edited by Jennifer Sahn, on what we need to do to build a better future).

It's clear that conflict and war don't work and that the future of all animals, human and nonhuman, depends on the development of a science of peace, or, as ethologist Peter Verbeek calls it, a "peace ethology" that reflects our true nature. This sort of movement inspires me and gives me hope for the future. We really can do much better than we've done, and it's consistent with who we really are.

[Originally posted on July 19, 2012]

Old Brains, New Bottlenecks, and Animals: Solastalgia and Our Relationship with Other Beings

A FEW DAYS AGO one of my colleagues, Philip Tedeschi, founder of the Institute for Human-Animal Connection (www.humananimalconnection .org) at the University of Denver, reminded me of a very interesting and important *New York Times* essay concerning our relationship with nature in which the concept of "solastalgia" was discussed.

While the concept seems to apply more to our relationship with landscapes, describing the pain we feel when we witness and feel their destruction, I had also written about solastalgia in my book *Minding Animals* concerning our relationships with nonhuman animals, who surely are an integral part of natural landscapes. People often forget that the integrity of an ecosystem is inextricably woven in with the well-being of the animals who live there, and that when we "redecorate nature," we can have serious effects on the lives of other animals. When we are removed from the natural world, we often feel alone and alienated because our old brain pulls us back to what is natural and what feels good. This is what E. O. Wilson proposed with his "biophilia hypothesis."

Basically, our old big brains force us to seek nature's wisdom even though we are living in — some might say we're really trapped in — new technological and sociocultural bottlenecks. We become very uncomfortable when we allow ourselves to reflect on how alienated we truly are. It's important to ask why we feel good when we're out in nature. Years ago I discovered the following quotation by the renowned author Henry Miller: "If we don't always start from Nature we certainly come to her in our hour of need." Perhaps there isn't only one reason why nature's wisdom is frequently sought when we feel out of balance, when times are tough. Perhaps we can look to evolution to understand why we do so.

I find I'm never alone and neither do I feel lonely when I'm out in nature. Her wisdom easily captures me, and I feel safe and calm wrapped in her welcoming arms. We converse with one another. Why do we go to nature for guidance? Why do we feel so good, so much at peace, when we see, hear, and smell other animals, when we look at trees and smell the fragrance of flowers, when we watch water in a stream, a lake, or an ocean? We often cannot articulate why, when we are immersed in nature, there are such penetrating calming effects, why we often become breathless, why we sigh, why we place a hand on our heart as we sense and feel nature's beauty, awe, mystery, and generosity. Perhaps the feelings that are evoked are so very deep and primal that there are no words that are rich enough to convey just what we feel — joy when we know that nature is doing well and deep sorrow and pain when we feel that nature is being destroyed, exploited, and devastated. I ache when I feel nature being wounded. I experience solastalgia, as do so many others.

What about our ancestors? Surely, there must have been more significant consequences for them if they "fooled" with nature. They didn't have all of the mechanical and intellectual know-how to undo their intrusions into natural processes. And of course, neither do we, because our rampant intrusions are so devastating, and in many cases irreversible. Indeed, early humans were probably so busy just trying to survive that they could not have had the opportunities to wreak the havoc that we have brought to nature. And the price of their injurious intrusions would likely have been much more serious for them than they are for us, because of their intimate interrelations with, and dependency on, nature.

We can easily fool ourselves into thinking things are "all right" when they're not. Denialism is a great mechanism for allowing us to ignore the effects of what we've done and to continue on the heinous path of destruction. Nonetheless, our psyches, like those of our ancestors, suffer when nature is harmed. Human beings worldwide commonly lament how bad they feel when they sense nature and her complex webs being spoiled, and ecopsychologists argue just this point. It would be invaluable if we could tune in to our old big brains and let them guide us, for our brains are very much like those of our ancestors. However, our sociocultural milieus and technology have changed significantly over time, and we face new and challenging bottlenecks. Cycles of nature are still with us and also within us, although we might not be aware of their presence because we can so easily override just about anything "natural." Much technology and our incessant "busy-ness" cause alienation from nature. This breach in turn leads to our wanton abuse of nature. It's all too easy to harm environs to which we are not attached or to abuse other beings to whom we are not bonded, to whom we don't feel close. But of course, if we carefully listen, animals are constantly asking us to treat them better or leave them alone. Our brains can distance us from nature, but they also can lead us back to her before the rubber band snaps. For when it does, we easily continue on the path of destruction that harms ecosystems, their animal residents, and us. There's an instinctive drive to have close ties with nature, and when these reciprocal interconnections are threatened or ruptured, we seek nature as a remedy. Our old brains still remember the importance of being an integral and cardinal part of innumerable natural processes; they remind us how good these deep interconnections felt.

Perhaps our close ancestral ties with nature offer reasons for hope, reasons for being optimistic about healing a deeply wounded nature. It just does *not* feel good to cause harm to nature. Perhaps the intense joy we feel when nature is healthy, the joy we feel when we are embedded in nature's mysterious ways and webs, is but one measure of the deep love we have for her. This love offers us a chance to change our ways, for this love awakens us from a dangerous and pitiful apathy that amounts to the betrayal of our collective responsibility to act proactively and with passion and compassion to save nature for our and future generations. Calling attention to our destructive ways and doing something to right the wrongs can be healing for us and nature. It is but one way for us to return to nature some of the wisdom and solace she provides, to allow her to continue to exist for all to relish.

So let's all rewild our hearts and build corridors of compassion that connect diverse landscapes and all of the amazing animals who depend on our goodwill. Indifference is deadly and inexcusable. Let's allow our old brains do their job before it's too late.

[ORIGINALLY POSTED ON MAY 3, 2010]

Animal Losses Are Rampant,
but Conservation Efforts Work

WE ARE CONSTANTLY REMINDED that many species are facing extinction, but now we have some hard data on the major problems at hand. At the Conference of the Parties to the Convention on Biological Diversity held in Nagoya, Japan, this week, we've learned that one in five vertebrate species across the world are indeed threatened with extinction. One report on the conference said, "The results reveal that, on average, fifty species of mammal, bird, and amphibian are pushed closer to extinction each year. The situation has been most stark in Southeast Asia where many species are threatened by habitat loss due to the planting of crops like oil palm, deforestation by commercial timber operations, agricultural conversion to rice paddies, and unsustainable hunting." It's not a pretty picture, and humans are surely at the center of the global problems.

But, on the bright side of things, we also are told that "the status of biodiversity would have declined by at least an additional 20 percent if conservation action had not been taken." So, it's important to remain positive even in the grimmest of times and know that our efforts to reduce losses in biodiversity actually work. We really have no choice but to work hard — actually, much harder — to reduce losses or else many species are doomed, including ourselves, for we also suffer when biodiversity is lost.

One field that can surely make a significant difference is the growing discipline of *conservation psychology*, which according to the Conservation Psychology website (www.conservationpsychology.org) is concerned with "the scientific study of the reciprocal relationships between humans and the rest of nature, with a particular focus on how to encourage conservation of the natural world" (see also *Conservation Psychology* by Susan Clayton and Gene Myers). Coexistence is mandatory, as we also suffer the indignities we impose on other animals.

Biodiversity enables human life; it is imperative that all of humanity reconnects with what sustains the ability of our species to persist. When animals die, we die, too. Animals are needed for our own psychological well-being, and we can learn a lot from them. We are *that* connected to other beings; that's why so many of us seek comfort from our companion animals or refuge in nature when times are tough.

Conservation psychology, the social sciences, and humane education will surely help figure out the best ways to move forward and to give animals the respect, compassion, and love they deserve. Let's all work together to make this the century of compassion and expand our compassion footprint because we truly do live in a troubled world that is in dire need of healing. Time is not on our side.

[ORIGINALLY POSTED ON OCTOBER 27, 2010]

Rewilding Our Hearts:
Maintaining Hope and Faith
in Trying Times

HUMANS ARE A FORCE IN NATURE. "Tell me something I don't know," I hear you lament. We're all over the place, big-brained, big-footed, arrogant, invasive, menacing, and marauding mammals. No need to look for mythical Bigfoot: we're here! We leave huge footprints all over the place and have been rather unsuccessful at solving urgent problems. Robert Berry fears we're simply "running out of world." Perhaps we've already "run out of world," including wildness. Some go so far as to argue we've created a world that's so technologically and socially complex we can't control it.

I'm always looking for ways to remain positive and hopeful in challenging times. I know how difficult it can be when it seems that so many things are going wrong. Mass media constantly begins with horror stories about death and destruction, and then at the end of a TV news show, for example, we hear about the good people who are working to make the world a better place for all beings. They sometimes get a minute or two after almost thirty minutes of negativity. I've often suggested that TV and radio news shows should begin with two positive stories, talk about other news, and then end with at least two positive messages.

In fact, in my writing, I've been thinking of ways to keep that loving feeling in times when many people are suffering and can't seem to see the light. Because of what I do for a living, I look to other animals for guidance. And I found just what I was looking for when I began to read about what are called rewilding projects.

The word "rewilding" became an essential part of talk among conservationists in the late 1990s when two well-known conservation biologists, Michael Soulé and Reed Noss, wrote a now-classic paper called "Rewilding and Biodiversity: Complementary Goals for Continental Conservation" that appeared in the magazine *Wild Earth*.

In her book *Rewilding the World*, conservationist Caroline Fraser noted that rewilding basically could be boiled down to three words: cores, corridors, and carnivores. In his book *Rewilding North America*, Dave Foreman, director of the Rewilding Institute (http://rewilding.org/rewild it/) in Albuquerque, New Mexico, a true visionary, sees rewilding as a conservation strategy based on three premises: "(1) healthy ecosystems need large carnivores, (2) large carnivores need big, wild roadless areas, and (3) most roadless areas are small and thus need to be linked." Conservation biologists and others who write about rewilding or work on rewilding projects see it as a large-scale process involving projects of different sizes that go beyond carnivores, such as the ambitious, courageous, and forward-looking Yellowstone to Yukon Conservation Initiative, well known as the Y2Y project (http://y2y.net). Of course, rewilding goes beyond carnivores, as it must.

The core words associated with large-scale rewilding projects are connection and connectivity, the establishment of links among geographical areas so that animals can roam as freely as possible with few if any disruptions to their movements. For this to happen, ecosystems must be connected so that their integrity and wholeness are maintained or reestablished.

Regardless of scale — ranging from huge areas encompassing a wide variety of habitats that need to be reconnected or that need to be protected to personal interactions with animals and habitats — the need to rewild and reconnect and to build or maintain links centers on the fact that there has been extensive isolation and fragmentation "out there" in nature, between ourselves and nature, and within ourselves. Many, perhaps most, human animals are isolated and fragmented internally concerning their relationships with nonhuman animals, so much so that we're alienated from them. We don't connect with other animals, including other humans, because we can't or don't empathize with them. The same goes for our lack of connection with various landscapes. We don't understand they're alive, vibrant, dynamic, magical, and magnificent. Alienation often results in different forms of domination and destruction, but domination is not what it means "to be human." Power does not mean license to do whatever we want to do because we can.

Rewilding projects often involve building wildlife bridges and under-passes so that animals can freely move about. These corridors, as they're called, can also be more personalized. I see rewilding our hearts as a dynamic process that will not only foster the development of corridors of coexistence and compassion for wild animals but also facilitate the forma-tion of corridors in our bodies that connect our heart and brain. In turn, these connections, or reconnections, will result in feelings that will facili-tate heartfelt actions to make the lives of animals better. These are the sorts of processes that will help further develop the new field of compassionate conservation. When I think about what can be done to help others, a warm feeling engulfs me, and I'm sure it's part of that feeling of being rewilded. To want to help others in need is natural, so that glow is to be expected.

Erle Ellis, who works in the Department of Geography and Environ-mental Systems at the University of Maryland, Baltimore County, notes that while it's true that we've transformed Earth beyond recovery, rather than looking back in despair, we should look ahead to what we can achieve. He writes:

> There will be no returning to our comfortable cradle. The global patterns of the Holocene have receded and their return is no lon-ger possible, sustainable, or even desirable. It is no longer Mother Nature who will care for us, but us who must care for her. This raises an important but often neglected question: can we create a good Anthropocene? In the future will we be able to look back with pride? ... Clearly it is possible to look at all we have created and see only what we have destroyed. But that, in my view, would be our mistake. We most certainly can create a better Anthropo-cene. We have really only just begun, and our knowledge and power have never been greater. We will need to work together with each other and the planet in novel ways. The first step will be in our own minds. The Holocene is gone. In the Anthropocene

we are the creators, engineers, and permanent global stewards of a sustainable human nature.

In addition to being proactive, we need to be positive and exit the stifling vortex of negativity once and for all. Negativity is a time and energy bandit, and it depletes us of the energy we need to move on. We don't get anywhere dwelling in anguish, sorrow, and despair. In a taxicab in Vancouver, British Columbia, on my way to a meeting about animals in art, I saw a sign in front of a church that really resonated with me: "Make the most of the best and the least of the worst." Amen.

Compassion begets compassion, and there's actually a synergistic relationship, not a trade-off, when we show compassion for animals and their homes. There are indeed many reasons for hope. There's also compelling evidence that we're born to be good and that we're natural-born optimists. Therein lie many reasons for hope that in the future we will harness our basic goodness and optimism and all work together as a united community. We can look to the animals for inspiration. So, let's tap into our empathic, compassionate, and moral inclinations to make the world a better place for all beings. We need to build a culture of empathy (http://cultureofempathy.com).

People who care about animals and nature should not be considered "the radicals" or "bad guys" who are trying to impede "human progress"; in fact, they could be seen as heroes who are fighting not only for animals but also for humanity. Biodiversity is what enables human life as well as enriches it. It is imperative that all of humanity reconnects with what sustains the ability of our species to persist and that we act as a unified collective while coexisting with other species and retaining the integrity of ecosystems. There are no quick fixes, and we need to realize that when animals die, we die, too.

We need to retain hope and try as hard as we can to realize our dreams for a better future for all animals and our planet as a whole. If we present a negative picture to youngsters and those working to make the planet a better place for all beings, then we can hardly expect them to do much at all. As we learn more about what we can and cannot do, I truly believe that we will be able to succeed in many of our attempts to right the numerous wrongs and bring more compassion, peace, and harmony to our world. In the movie *Invictus*, Nelson Mandela (played by Morgan Freeman) tells the South African soccer team, "We must exceed our own expectations." When I need an "upper," I find myself revisiting another essay I wrote on remaining hopeful and keeping our dreams alive. Some guidelines included:

- Be proactive. We need to look at what's happening and prevent further abuse and not always be "putting out the fires" that have started.

- Be nice and kind to those with whom you disagree and move on. Sometimes it's just better to let something go, so pick your "battles" carefully and don't waste time and energy. Don't waste time "fighting" people who won't change and don't let them deflect attention from the important work that needs to be done. Don't get in "pissing matches" with people who want you to waste precious time and energy fighting them, time and energy that must go into working for animals and Earth and peace and justice.

- If we let those who do horrible things get us down or deflect us from the work we must do, they "win" and animals, Earth, and we lose. While this may be obvious, I thought it worth saying again because it's a common ploy to get people into tangential discussions and arguments that take them away from the important work that must be done.

- Teach the children well, for they are the ambassadors for a more harmonious, peaceful, compassionate, and gentle world.

We can all make more humane and compassionate choices to expand our compassion footprint, and we can all do better. We must all try as hard as we can to keep thinking positively and proactively. Never say never, ever. Perhaps a good resolution as we welcome a new year is that we will all try to do better for animals — both nonhuman and human — and Earth, and we will work for more peace and justice for all. We can and must keep our hopes and dreams alive.

When all is said and done, and more is usually said than done, we need a heartfelt revolution in how we think, what we do with what we know, and how we act. Rewilding can be a very good guide. The revolution has to come from deep within us and begin at home, in our hearts and wherever we live. I want to make the process of rewilding a more personal journey and exploration that centers on bringing other animals and their homes, ecosystems of many different types, back into our heart. For some they're already there or nearly so, whereas for others it will take some work to have this happen. Nonetheless, it's inarguable that if we're going to make the world a better place now and for future generations, personal rewilding is central to the process and will entail a major paradigm shift in how we view and live in the world and how we behave. It's not that hard to expand our compassion footprint, and if each of us does something, the movement will grow rapidly.

The time is right, the time is now, for an inspirational, revolutionary, and personal social movement that can save us from doom and keep us positive while we pursue our hopes and dreams.

Rewild now. Perhaps make it one of your New Year's resolutions. Take the leap. Leap and the net will appear. It'll feel good because compassion and empathy are extremely contagious.

[Originally posted on December 19, 2011]

ENDNOTES

Part 1. Animals and Us: Reflections on Our Challenging, Frustrating, Confusing, and Deep Interrelationships with Other Animals

7   *An article about the 2011 California Institute of Technology and UCLA study*: Katie Neith, "Captivated by Critters: Humans Are Wired to Respond to Animals," California Institute of Technology press release, February 9, 2011, www.caltech .edu/article/13449.

7   *Renowned and eclectic scientist Stephen Jay Gould wrote a fascinating essay*: Stephen Jay Gould, "Mickey Mouse Meets Konrad Lorenz," *Natural History* 88, no. 5 (1979): 30–36.

8   *Researchers Robert Hinde and L. A. Barden likewise discovered that during the twentieth century*: Robert Hinde and L. A. Barden, "The Evolution of the Teddy Bear," *Animal Behaviour* 33 (1985): 1,371–73.

10 *As an excellent opinion piece in* New Scientist *said*: "We Need Another Kind of Scientist to Save the World," op-ed, *New Scientist*, no. 2700 (March 19, 2009), www .newscientist.com/article/mg20127003.000we-need-another-kind-of-scientist -to-save-the-world.html.

12 *Here are a few tidbits from a July 2010* USA Weekend *article*: Steve Dale, "Why Pets Are Good for Us," *USA Weekend*, July 22, 2010, www.usaweekend.com/article /20100723/HOME05/7250320/Why-pets-are-good-for-us.

17 *According to a* USA Today *article on the study:* Nanci Hellmich, "Study: New Children's Books Lack Reference to Nature, Animals," *USA Today*, February 28, 2012.

18 *A free online book I published last year called* Kids & Animals: Marc Bekoff, *Kids & Animals: Drawings from the Hands and Hearts of Children and Youth* (Boulder, CO: Children, Youth & Environments Center, University of Colorado, 2011); download a copy of this book at www.ucdenver.edu/academics/colleges/Architecture Planning/discover/centers/CYE/Publications/Pages/Books.aspx.

21 *She notes that what is generally called "the Link" refers to*: Eleonora Gullone, *Animal Cruelty, Antisocial Behaviour, and Aggression: More than a Link* (Hampshire, England: Palgrave Macmillan, 2012), ix.

21 *"the conceptualization of animal cruelty as deviant...will have varying validity"*: Gullone, *Animal Cruelty*, 131.

21   *it is essential to remove the property status of animals in legal systems*: For more information on this topic, see Gary L. Francione, "Animals as Property," Animal Legal & Historical Center, 1996, www.animallaw.info/articles/arusgfrancione1996.htm.

22   *"By positioning acts of animal abuse within the continuum of other antisocial behaviours"*: Gullone, *Animal Cruelty*, x.

22   *"many crimes against humans may well have been prevented"*: Gullone, *Animal Cruelty*, 135–36.

22   *"laws should punish criminals according to the severity of the acts they perpetrate"*: Gullone, *Animal Cruelty*, 139.

23   *Since I hadn't, Katherine sent me a copy of a 2010 paper*: Kimberly Costello and Gordon Hodson, "Exploring the Roots of Dehumanization: The Role of Animal–Human Similarity in Promoting Immigrant Humanization," *Group Processes Intergroup Relations* 13, no. 1 (January 2010): 3–22, http://gpi.sagepub.com/content/13/1/3.abstract?rss=1.

23   *A later essay published by Costello, Hodson, and their colleagues*: Brock Bastian, Kimberly Costello, Steve Laughan, and Gordon Hodson, "When Closing the Human-Animal Divide Expands Moral Concern: The Importance of Framing," *Social Psychology and Personality Science* (November 1, 2011), doi: 10.1177/1948550611425106.

23   *In the 2010 paper, Costello and Hodson also write*: *"Recognizing that heightened"*: Costello and Hodson, "Exploring the Roots," 19.

25   *Jasper is a moon bear. I try to practice what he teaches*: For more on bile farms and bear rescue, see the website of Animals Asia, www.animalsasia.org, and Marc Bekoff, "Bear Tapping: A Bile Business," *New Scientist*, no. 2706 (May 4, 2009), www.newscientist.com/article/mg20227061.400-bear-tapping-a-bile-business.html.

27   *Jill told me that at a social function to celebrate their 2008 book* Freedom Moon: To get a copy of *Freedom Moon*, order from the Animals Asia website, www.animalsasia.org/index.php?UID=95YUO1F9LS0.

Part 2. Against Speciesism: Why All Individuals Are Unique and Special

43   *A July 2011 essay by philosopher Steven Best provides*: Steven Best, "Minding the Animals: Ethology and the Obsolescence of Left Humanism," blog, Canadians for Emergency Action on Climate Change, July 28, 2011, http://climatesoscanada.org/blog/2011/07/28/minding-the-animals-ethology-and-the-obsolescence-of-left-humanism/.

45   *This weekend I received a few emails about a recent essay written for* Psychology Today: Neel Burton, "The Seven Things That Only Human Beings Can Do," *Psychology Today*, August 27, 2012; www.psychologytoday.com/blog/hide-and-seek/201208/the-seven-things-only-human-beings-can-do.

48   *Based on her observations of waterfall dances in chimpanzees, Jane Goodall wonders*: Jane Goodall, "Primate Spirituality," in *The Encyclopedia of Religion and Nature*, ed. Bron Taylor (London & New York: Thoemmes Continuum, 2005), 1,303–6.

49   *In an excellent review of Corballis's book, anthropologist Barbara J. King*: Barbara J. King,

"Is Mental Time Travel What Makes Us Human?" review of *The Recursive Mind*, by Michael Corballis, *Times Literary Supplement*, October 26, 2011, www.the-tls .co.uk/tls/public/article807136.ece.

50 *As an example she writes about the hunting behavior of wild chimpanzees described by prominent primatologists*: Christophe and Hedwige Boesch-Ackerman, *The Chimpanzees of the Taï Forest* (New York: Oxford University Press, 2000).

Part 3. Media and the (Mis)representation of Animals

55 *In a 2009 Communication Review journal article*: Carrie Packwood Freeman, "This Little Piggie Went to Press: The American News Media's Construction of Agricultural Animals," *Communication Review* 12, no. 1 (February 2009): 78–103, doi: 10.1080/10714420902717764.

55 *I also heard a recent National Public Radio (NPR) report*: Robert Krulwich, "Ants That Count!" blog, National Public Radio, November 25, 2009, www.npr.org/blogs /krulwich/2011/06/01/120587095/ants-that-count.

56 *They are often depicted as human caricatures, doing silly tricks, wearing clothes*: S. R. Ross et al., "Inappropriate Use and Portrayal of Chimpanzees," *Science* 319, no. 5869 (March 14, 2008): 1487, www.sciencemag.org/content/319/5869/1487.short.

56 *The author of a 2008 Connect magazine report noted, "In addition to media-created misperceptions"*: Steve Ross, "Not a Laughing Matter: Conservation Effects of Media Portrayals," *Connect*, September 2008.

56 *Also, it's a little-known fact, but animals are misrepresented in still photography and in wildlife films*: For more on this topic, see Chris Palmer, *Shooting in the Wild: An Insider's Account of Making Movies in the Animal Kingdom* (San Francisco: Sierra Club Books, 2010).

56 *In 2010, a wildlife photographer was stripped of his*: Robert Booth, "Wildlife Photographer of the Year Stripped of His Award," *The Guardian*, January 20, 2010, www.guardian.co.uk/environment/2010/jan/20/wolf-wildlife-photographer -award-stripped.

58 *In a 2011 review of a new and extremely interesting book on African apes*: Rowan Hooper, "Going Ape: Ultraviolence and Our Primate Cousins," review of *Among African Apes* by Martha Robbins and Christophe Boesch, *New Scientist*, no. 2815 (June 1, 2011).

58 *Jane Goodall noted in her book* The Chimpanzees of Gombe, *"It is easy to get the impression"*: Jane Goodall, *The Chimpanzees of Gombe* (Cambridge, MA: Belknap Press, 1986), 357.

58 *In* Scientific American *in 2010, John Horgan noted the evidence*: John Horgan, "Quitting the Hominid Fight Club: The Evidence Is Flimsy for Innate Chimpanzee — Let Alone Human — Warfare," *Scientific American*, June 29, 2010, www.scientificamerican .com/blog/post.cfm?id=quitting-the-hominid-fight-club-the-2010-06-29.

58 *Similarly, Robert Sussman, an anthropologist at Washington University*: Robert Sussman, Paul A. Garber, and Jim Cheverud, "Importance of Cooperation and Affiliation in the Evolution of Primate Sociality," *The American Journal of Physical Anthropology* 128, no. 1 (2005): 84–97.

59   *Humans, too, are highly cooperative and egalitarian, even among strangers*: For more on this, see Jessica Pierce and Marc Bekoff, "Moral in Tooth and Claw," *Chronicle of Higher Education* (October 18, 2009), http://chronicle.com/article/Moral-in -ToothClaw/48800/. See also: Michael Marshall, "It Is Human Nature to Cooperate with Strangers," *New Scientist* (June 13, 2011).

60   *The first, by Stephen Ross and his colleagues, shows*: Stephen R. Ross, Vivian M. Vreeman, and Elizabeth V. Lonsdorf, "Specific Image Characteristics Influence Attitudes about Chimpanzees Conservation and Use as Pets," PLOS ONE (July 13, 2011), www.plosone.org/article/info%3Adoi%2F10.1371%2Fjournal.pone.0022050.

60   *Another study, conducted by Kara Schroepfer and her colleagues*: Kara K. Schroepfer et al., "The Use of 'Entertainment' Chimpanzees in Commercials Distorts Public Perception Regarding Their Conservation Status," PLOS ONE (October 12, 2011), www.plosone.org/article/info%3Adoi%2F10.1371%2Fjournal.pone.0026048.

61   *Simon Townsend and his colleagues have recently demonstrated*: Brandon Keim, "Clever Test Shows Meerkat Voices Are Personal," *Wired*, October 12, 2011, www.wired .com/wiredscience/2011/10/meerkat-voices/.

Part 4. Why Dogs Hump: Or, What We Can Learn from Our Special Friends

74   *On any given night there are about 640,000 homeless people*: James Eng, "Homeless Numbers Down, But Risks Rise," NBC News, January 18, 2012, http://usnews .nbcnews.com/_news/2012/01/18/10177017-homeless-numbers-down-but-risks -rise?lite.

74   *It's also been estimated that 5 to 10 percent of homeless*: see Pets of the Homeless, FAQ, www.petsofthehomeless.org/what-we-do/faqs.html.

76   *there were a few requests for me to alert readers to a heartwarming story in the* New York Times: Melissa Fay Greene, "Wonder Dog," *New York Times Magazine*, February 2, 2012, www.nytimes.com/2012/02/05/magazine/wonder-dog.html.

79   *In the United States, about 40 percent of households have*: For pet ownership statistics, see "U.S. Pet Ownership Statistics," Humane Society of the United States, last modified August 12, 2011, www.humanesociety.org/issues/pet_overpopulation/facts/pet _ownership_statistics.html.

79   *In a September 1, 2009,* Psychology Today *blog*: Alexandra Horowitz, "Minds of Animals," *Psychology Today*, September 1, 2009, www.psychologytoday.com/blog /minds-animals/200909/why-do-we-treat-dogs-so-much-better-we-treat-wolves.

79   *some recent discoveries based on an August 2009 essay titled "Going to the Dogs"*: Virginia Morell, "Going to the Dogs," *Science* 325, no. 5944 (August 28, 2009): 1,062–65, www.sciencemag.org/content/325/5944/1062.summary.

80   *Much of what is currently known about the cognitive abilities of dogs*: Márta Gácsi et al., "Explaining Dog Wolf Differences in Utilizing Human Pointing Gestures: Selection for Synergistic Shifts in the Development of Some Social Skills," PLOS ONE (2009), doi: 10.1371/journal.pone.0006584.

83   *A number of people have asked me to write something*: One news story at the time with event details is: "Pittsburgh Zoo Official: Child, 2, Killed by African Painted Dog

Mauling, Not Fall," WPXI, November 5, 2012, www.wpxi.com/news/news/local /crews-probe-report-childs-death-pittsburgh-zoo/nSxFp/.

83 *An interesting essay I just read about this incident titled*: Kathleen Stachowski, " 'Well-Mannered Predators' and Other Speciesist Notions about Animal Captivity," Animal Blawg, November 10, 2012, http://animalblawg.wordpress.com/2012/11/10 /5283/.

84 *Christine Dell'Amore, writing for* National Geographic News, *wonders*: Christine Dell'Amore, "Pittsburgh Zoo Tragedy: Why Did African Wild Dogs Attack Boy?" *National Geographic News*, November 5, 2012, news.nationalgeographic.com/news /2012/11/121105-african-wild-dogs-pittsburgh-zoo-animals-science/.

86 *Just today Dr. Stanley Coren published a very interesting essay on the* Psychology Today *website*: Stanley Coren, "Which Emotions Do Dogs Actually Experience?" *Psychology Today*, March 14, 2013, www.psychologytoday.com/blog/canine-corner /201303/which-emotions-do-dogs-actually-experience.

86 *However, because it's been claimed that other mammals with whom dogs share the same neural*: For evidence of complex emotions in mammals, see my previous books *The Emotional Lives of Animals* and *The Smile of a Dolphin*, as well as *When Elephants Weep* by Jeffrey Moussaieff Masson and Susan McCarthy and *Second Nature: The Inner Lives of Animals* by Jonathan Balcombe.

87 *Brian Hare and Vanessa Woods consider Dr. Horowitz's research on doggy guilt*: Brian Hare and Vanessa Woods, *The Genius of Dogs: How Dogs Are Smarter than You Think* (New York: Dutton, 2013), 183ff.

87 *I frequently hear people say that Dr. Horowitz's project showed dogs* cannot *feel guilt and this is not so*: For a correct description of Dr. Horowitz's research findings, see David Braun, "Dog 'Guilt' Is All in the Mind of Human Owner, Study Suggests," *National Geographic*, June 11, 2009, http://newswatch.nationalgeographic .com/2009/06/11/dog_guilt_is_all_in_the_mind/. For Dr. Horowitz's response to my "The Genius of Dogs" essay, where I first raised this issue, see Alexandra Horowitz, February 4, 2013, comment on Marc Bekoff, "The Genius of Dogs and the Hidden Life of Wolves," *Psychology Today*, February 4, 2013, www.psychology today.com/blog/animal-emotions/201302/the-genius-dogs-and-the-hidden-life -wolves/comments#comment-507763. For Horowitz's original 2009 study, see the second endnote for page 95, below.

90 *According to a* Scientific American *report on a 2012 study*: Sophie Bushwick, "Your Dog Wants Your Food," podcast, *Scientific American*, 2012. The original study is Sarah Marshall-Pescini et al., "Do Dogs (*Canis lupus familiaris*) Make Counterproductive Choices Because They Are Sensitive to Human Ostensive Cues?" PLOS ONE (2012), doi: 10.1371/journal.pone.0035437.

91 *In one 2010 study, we learn that when young dogs are exposed to videos*: Jolanda Pluijmakers, David Appleby, and John Bradshaw, "Exposure to Video Images Between 3 and 5 weeks of Age Decreases Neophobia in Domestic Dogs," *Applied Animal Behaviour Science* 126, no. 1 (August 2010): 51–58, www.appliedanimalbehaviour.com/article /S0168-1591(10)00160-7/abstract.

91 *Meanwhile, another 2010 study shows that dogs know what others can and cannot hear*: Shannon Kundey et al., "Domesticate Dogs (*Canis familiaris*) React to What Others

Can and Cannot Hear," *Applied Animal Behaviour Science* 126, no. 1 (August 2010): 45–50, www.appliedanimalbehaviour.com/article/S0168-1591(10)00177-2/abstract.

93 *In the first project, aptly titled "Dogs Steal in the Dark"*: Julian Kaminski, Andrea Pitsch, and Michael Tomasello, "Dogs Steal in the Dark," *Animal Cognition* 16, no. 3 (May 2013): 385–94, http://link.springer.com/article/10.1007/s10071-012-0579-6.

93 *In the second study, titled "Domestic Dogs Conceal Auditory But Not Visual Information from Others"*: Juliane Bräuer et al., "Domestic Dogs Conceal Auditory but Not Visual Information from Others," *Animal Cognition* 16, no. 3 (May 2013): 351–59, http://link.springer.com/article/10.1007/s10071-012-0576-9.

95 *These features correspond with neoteny, or juvenilization, and could include, Lorenz wrote*: Konrad Lorenz, *Ganzheit und Teil in der tierischen und menschlichen Gemeinschaft* (1950), reprinted in *Studies in Animal and Human Behaviour*, vol. 2, ed. R. Martin (Cambridge, MA: Harvard University Press, 1971), 115–95.

95 *See Alexandra Horowitz's 2009 study "Disambiguating the 'Guilty Look'"*: Alexandra Horowitz, "Disambiguating the 'Guilty Look': Salient Prompts to a Familiar Dog Behavior," *Behavioural Processes* 81 (2009): 447–52, www.ncbi.nlm.nih .gov/pubmed/19520245; see also, Alexandra Horowitz and Marc Bekoff, "Naturalizing Anthropomorphism: Behavioral Prompts to Our Humanizing of Animals," *Anthrozoös* 20 (2007): 23–35.

96 *I had the pleasure of hearing Julie Hecht recently present her and Alexandra Horowitz's research*: Julie Hecht and Alexandra Horowitz, "Physical Prompts to Anthropomorphism of the Domestic Dog," Third Canine Science Forum, Barcelona, Spain (July 2012), www.columbia.edu/~ah2240/. For more on Julie Hecht, visit http://dogspies .com.

97 *So wrote Julie Hecht in her excellent review in August 2012 of humping by dogs*: Julie Hecht, "H*mping: Why Do They Do It?" *The Bark*, June–August 2012, 70, 56–60, http://thebark.com/content/hmping.

98 *In my own studies of the development of social behavior in young dogs, coyotes, and wolves*: Marc Bekoff and Michael Wells, "Social Ecology and Behavior of Coyotes," *Advances in the Study of Behavior* 16 (1986): 251–338.

98 *Years ago in a detailed study of urination patterns in dogs I could easily follow:* Marc Bekoff, "Scent-marking by Domestic Dogs. Olfactory and Visual Components," *Biology of Behaviour* 4 (1979): 123–39.

98 *Mounting, including humping and masturbation, are normal behaviors*: For more information, see ASPCA Virtual Pet Behaviorist, "Mounting and Masturbation," www .aspca.org/Pet-care/virtual-pet-behaviorist/dog-articles/mounting-and-mastur bation," as well as Laurie Bergman, "Canine Mounting: An Overview," North American Veterinary Conference *Clinician's Brief* (January 2012): 61–63, www.clinicians brief.com/column/applied-behavior/canine-mounting-overview?9RfscGvCZp. See also Julie Hecht, Dog Spies blog, "Resources on Humping," http://dogspies .blogspot.com/2012/09/humping-resources.html.

102 *In 1981 renowned primatologist Irwin Bernstein published a most important essay on dominance*: Irwin Bernstein, "Dominance: The Baby and the Bathwater," *Behavioral and Brain Sciences* 4, no. 3 (September 1981): 419–29, doi: 10.1017/S0140525X00009614.

103 *Note: This essay was originally written as a critical response*: Lee Charles Kelley's

original *Psychology Today* blog posts are no longer available online through the magazine website (since Kelley no longer writes a blog for the magazine). However, a very good overview of this incident, with generous quotes from Kelley's blog, can be found on the blog Terrierman's Daily Dose by Patrick Burns, "Oops. There Really IS Dominance in Wolves," February 24, 2012, http://terriermandotcom.blogspot .com/2012/02/oops-there-really-is-dominance-in.html. For more information on Lee Charles Kelley and his views on dog training, visit www.leecharleskelley.com.

103 *I questioned some misrepresentations of current research, particularly by Dr. David Mech*: In his blog, Kelley references the following journal article: L. David Mech, "Alpha Status, Dominance, and Division of Labor in Wolf Packs," *Canadian Journal of Zoology* 77 (1999): 1,196–1,203. In this, Dr. Mech does not reject the notion of dominance. Indeed, in it he wrote: "Similarly, pups are subordinate to both parents and to older siblings, yet they are fed preferentially by the parents, and even by their older (*dominant*) siblings (Mech et al. 1999). On the other hand, parents both dominate older offspring and restrict their food intake when food is scarce, feeding pups instead. Thus, the most practical effect of social *dominance* is to allow the dominant individual the choice of to whom to allot food."

Clearly, there's lots of confusion on this matter, as well as about Mech's research and conclusions. He does argue, as do others, that the notion of social dominance is not as ubiquitous as some claim it to be, but he doesn't reject it across the board. Another paper by Dr. Mech that describes his views on dominance is L. David Mech, "Prolonged Intensive Dominance Behavior Between Gray Wolves, *Canis lupus*," *Canadian Field-Naturalist* 124, no. 3 (2010).

Finally, in response to my essay, David Mech wrote to me: "I probably won't have time to read this right now, for I'm preparing for a trip out of the country early next week. However, a quick scan of the Kelley article reveals much misinformation attributed to me. This misinterpretation and total misinformation like Kelley's has plagued me for years now. I do not in any way reject the notion of dominance."

104 *Last year I received a video showing Cesar Millan (a.k.a. the "dog whisperer") hanging a husky*: "Shadow turns blue" on YouTube, uploaded December 19, 2009; www.you tube.com/watch?v=Qh9YOyM2TAk.

104 *For further discussion of Millan's methods, please see Mark Derr's* New York Times *editorial*: Mark Derr, "Pack of Lies," op-ed, *New York Times*, August 31, 2006, www .nytimes.com/2006/08/31/opinion/31derr.html.

105 *Many people who work with domestic and wild animals are using*: To learn more about positive reinforcement, see the Humane Society website, www.humanesociety.org /animals/dogs/tips/dog_training_positive_reinforcement.html.

Part 5. Consciousness, Sentience, and Cognition:
A Potpourri of Current Research on Flies, Fish, and Other Animals

108 *For instance, see "Anthropomorphic Double-Talk" in my book* The Emotional Lives of Animals: Marc Bekoff, *The Emotional Lives of Animals* (Novato, CA: New World Library, 2007), 126–31. On June 24, 2009, I also revised and presented this material in the *Psychology Today* essay "Anthropomorphic Double-Talk: Can Animals Be Happy

but Not Unhappy? No!" www.psychologytoday.com/blog/animal-emotions/200906 /anthropomorphic-double-talk-can-animals-be-happy-not-unhappy-no.

111 *And in 2012 another book called* Why Animals Matter *was published*: all quotes by Marian Dawkins are from Marian Dawkins, *Why Animals Matter: Animal Consciousness, Animal Welfare, and Human Well-being* (New York: Oxford University Press, 2012).

111 *Dawkins follows, "It began to look as though no further thought"*: Dawkins, *Why Animals*, 26.

112 *I published an essay in* BioScience *about what I called* biocentric anthropomorphism: Marc Bekoff, "Animal Emotions: Exploring Passionate Natures," *BioScience* 50, no. 10 (2000): 861–70, doi: 10.1641/0006-3568(2000)050[0861:AEEPN]2.0.CO;2.

112 *Dawkins also writes, "Rampant anthropomorphism threatens"*: Dawkins, *Why Animals*, 33.

113 *Later in her book Dawkins notes, "Animal welfare needs new arguments"*: Dawkins, *Why Animals*, 175.

113 *Dawkins goes on to discuss different areas of animal consciousness*: Dawkins, *Why Animals*, 111–12.

113 *She goes on to write, "The mystery of consciousness remains"*: Dawkins, *Why Animals*, 171–72.

113 *Along these lines it's important to note that the Lisbon Treaty*: for more on the Lisbon Treaty, see John Webster, "The Lisbon Treaty: Recognising Animal Sentience," *Compassion in World Farming News*, December 1, 2009, www.ciwf.org.uk/news /compassion_news/the_lisbon_treaty_recognising_animal_sentience.aspx.

114 *She claims, "[I]it is much, much better for* animals *if we remain skeptical"*: Dawkins, *Why Animals*, 177.

114 *I am not a science-basher, nor do I ridicule scientists for "pointing out how hard it is"*: Dawkins, *Why Animals*, 184.

116 *The email was about a story published by my colleague Michael Mountain*: Michael Mountain, "Scientists Declare: Nonhuman Animals Are Conscious," *Earth in Transition*, July 30, 2012, www.earthintransition.org/2012/07/scientists-declare-non human-animals-are-conscious.

117 *The scientists went so far as to write up what's called "The Cambridge Declaration on Consciousness"*: For an online version of this document, visit http://fcmconference .org/img/CambridgeDeclarationOnConsciousness.pdf.

122 *New York University philosopher Dale Jamieson and I wrote about the idea of nonconscious pain*: Dale Jamieson and Marc Bekoff, "Carruthers on Nonconscious Experience," *Analysis* 52, no. 1 (January 1992): 23–28, http://as.nyu.edu/docs/IO/1192 /JamiesonBekoff-carruthers1992.pdf

122 *Following up on what I call "Dawkins's Dangerous Idea"*: Marian Stamp Dawkins, "Convincing the Unconvinced that Animal Welfare Matters," *Huffington Post Science*, June 8, 2012, www.huffingtonpost.com/marian-stamp-dawkins/animal-welfare _b_1581615.html.

122 *Two quotations from a 2012 essay by Jeff Warren about personhood in whales*: Jeff Warren, "Why Whales Are People Too," *Reader's Digest Canada*, July 2012, www.readers digest.ca/magazine/true-stories/why-whales-are-people-too.

124 *In Bruce Friedrich's review of the 2012 documentary* Speciesism: The Movie: Bruce Friedrich, " 'Speciesism: The Movie May Change Your Worldview,' " *Huffington Post*

Green, March 21, 2012, www.huffingtonpost.com/bruce-friedrich/speciesism-the -movie-may-_b_1347514.html.

126 *It's long been known that matriarchs are the "social glue"*: For more on this, see www .andrews-elephants.com/matriarch-elephant.html.

126 *Now we've just learned that matriarchs over sixty years of age assess threats*: Sindya N. Bhanoo, "Older Elephant Matriarchs Keep the Lions at Bay," *New York Times*, March 16, 2011, www.nytimes.com/2011/03/22/science/22obelephant.html.

126 *According to elephant expert Karen McComb*: Susan Milius, "Don't Trust Any Elephant Under 60," *Science News*, April 9, 2011, www.sciencenews.org/view/generic /id/71249/description/Dont_trust_any_elephant_under_60.

127 *Earlier today I wrote about Natasha, the valedictorian of captive chimpanzees*: Marc Bekoff, "'Natasha Einstein' the Chimpanzee Valedictorian," *Psychology Today*, August 29, 2012, www.psychologytoday.com/blog/animal-emotions/201208/nata sha-einstein-the-chimpanzee-valedictorian.

127 *An essay in* New Scientist *titled "Bonobo Genius Makes Stone Tools Like Early Humans Did"*: Hannah Krakauer, "Bonobo Genius Makes Stone Tools Like Early Humans Did," *New Scientist* (August 21, 2012), www.newscientist.com/article/dn22197 -bonobo-genius-makes-stone-tools-like-early-humans-did.html.

127 *The abstract of the original research paper reads as follows*: Itai Roffman et al., "Stone Tool Production and Utilization by Bonobo-Chimpanzees (*Pan paniscus*)," *Proceedings of the National Academy of Sciences* (PNAS) (August 21, 2012), doi: 10.1073/ pnas.1212855109.

128 *This essay, titled "Cultured Killer Whales Learn by Copying"*: Michael Marshall, "Zoologger: Cultured Killer Whales Learn by Copying," *New Scientist* (August 16, 2012).

131 *Recently I wrote about a rare and endangered spider called the Braken Bat Cave meshweaver*: Marc Bekoff, "Along Came a Spider Who Stopped a Highway Project," *Psychology Today*, October 7, 2012; www.psychologytoday.com/blog/animal-emotions /201210/along-came-spider-who-stopped-highway-project.

131 *These spiders show complex predatory strategies that involve problem solving*: Duane P. Harland and Robert R. Jackson, "'Eight-legged Cats' and How They See — a Review of Recent Research on Jumping Spiders (*Araneae: Salticidae*)," *Cimbebasia* 16 (2000): 231–40.

131 *Now we've learned there is a spider who is a member of the genus* Cyclosa: Chris Gayomali, "The Spider That Builds Its Own Lifelike Decoys," *Yahoo! News*, December 19, 2012. See also Nadia Drake, "Spider That Builds Its Own Spider Decoys Discovered," *Wired*, December 18, 2012, www.wired.com/wiredscience/2012/12/spider -building-spider/.

133 *we know now that flies will self-medicate by drinking alcohol*: "Parasite-plagued Flies Self-medicate on Booze," *New Scientist*, no. 2853 (February 22, 2012), www .newscientist.com/article/mg21328536.300-parasiteplagued-flies-selfmedicate-on -booze.html.

133 *A PBS story about this phenomenon reports*: Rebecca Jacobson, "To Kill Parasites, Fruit Flies Self-medicate with Alcohol," *PBS Newshour*, February 22, 2012, www.pbs.org/newshour/rundown/2012/02/to-kill-parasites-fruit-flies-self -medicate-with-alcohol.html.

133 *orangutans are being trained to use iPads to paint and to video chat with other orangutans*: Eric Pfeiffer, "Apps for Apes: Orangutans Using iPads to Paint and Video Chat with Other Apes," *Yahoo! News*, February 28, 2012, http://news.yahoo.com/blogs/side show/apps-apes-orangutans-using-ipads-paint-video-chat-174457692.html.

135 *Now, we've just learned that they, like other animals, show changes in behavior*: Janet Raloff, "Acidification Alters Fish Behavior," *Science News*, February 25, 2012, www .sciencenewsdigital.org/sciencenews/20120225/?pg=16#pg16. See also G. E. Nilsson et al., "Near-future Carbon Dioxide Levels Alter Fish Behaviour by Interfering with Neurotransmitter Function," *Nature Climate Change* (January 16, 2012), doi:10.1038/nclimate1352.

135 *Lizards are also affected by climate change*: Alasdair Wilkins, "Global Warming Might Make Lizards Super-Intelligent," *io9*, January 12, 2012, http://io9.com/5875545 /global-warming-might-make-lizards-super+intelligent.

137 *Bradley Smith of the University of South Australia and his colleagues*: Paul F. Norris, "Setting His Own Dinner Table: Spontaneous Tool Use by a Dingo," *AnimalWise*, December 7, 2011, http://animalwise.org/2011/12/07/setting-his-own -dinner-table-spontaneous-tool-use-by-a-dingo. The original study can be found at Bradley Smith et al., "Spontaneous Tool-use: An Observation of a Dingo (*Canis dingo*) Using a Table to Access an Out-of-reach Food Reward," *Behavioural Processes* (2011), doi: 10.1016/j.beproc.2011.11.004.

139 *This was among the wide variety of topics discussed at a 2011 meeting I attended*: For a description of this meeting, see Marc Bekoff, "Animal and Humans: Meaningful Meetings of Common Minds," *Psychology Today*, August 15, 2011, www .psychologytoday.com/blog/animal-emotions/201108/animal-and-humans -meaningful-meetings-common-minds.

139 *A newspaper article reporting on comparisons in performance*: Michael Hanlon, "The Disturbing Question Posed by IQ Tests — Are Chimps Cleverer than Us?" *Daily Mail*, December 5, 2007, www.dailymail.co.uk/news/article-499989/The-disturb ing-question-posed-IQ-tests--chimps-cleverer-us.html.

141 *Recently, bonobos, also known as a pygmy chimpanzees, were filmed saying "no"*: Jody Bourton, "Bonobo Chimps Filmed Shaking Their Head to 'Say No,'" *BBC Earth News*, May 5, 2010, http://news.bbc.co.uk/earth/hi/earth_news/newsid _8659000/8659411.stm.

141 *Another very interesting finding is that animals show a preference*: Nora Schultz, "Southpaws: The Evolution of Handedness," *New Scientist*, no. 2758 (April 30, 2010), www.newscientist.com/article/mg20627581.600-southpaws-the-evolution-of -handedness.html.

142 *Finally, something we "know" has been verified: "Just five minutes"*: "'Green' Exercise Quickly 'Boosts Mental Health,'" *BBC News*, May 1, 2010, http://news.bbc .co.uk/2/hi/health/8654350.stm.

144 *Jane Goodall wonders whether these dances are indicative of religious behavior*: Jane Goodall, "Primate Spirituality," in *The Encyclopedia of Religion and Nature*, ed. Bron Taylor (New York: Thoemmes Continuum, 2005), 1,303–6.

147 *Bees also use their right antenna*: www.sciencenews.org/view/generic/id/351355 /description/Honeybees_use_right_antennae_to_tell_friend_from_foe.

Part 6. The Emotional Lives of Animals: The Ever-Expanding Circle of Sentience Includes Depressed Bees and Empathic Chickens

149 *In the first study, Melissa Bateson and her colleagues at Newcastle University*: Brandon Keim, "Honeybees Might Have Emotions," *Wired*, June 17, 2011, www.wired.com /wiredscience/2011/06/honeybee-pessimism/.

149 *According to one report, "Bateson says the results can be interpreted to mean"*: Branwen Morgan, "Pessimistic Bees Forgo Life's Pleasures," *ABC Science*, June 3, 2011, www .abc.net.au/science/articles/2011/06/03/3234845.htm.

149 *Another study showed that bees also outperform computers in solving what is called "the traveling salesman problem"*: For a full description of this study, see Marc Bekoff, "Bees Versus Computers: Pea-brained Bees Win the 'Traveling Salesman Problem,'" *Psychology Today*, October 25, 2010, www.psychologytoday.com/blog /animal-emotions/201010/bees-versus-computers-pea-brained-bees-win-the -traveling-salesman-problem.

150 *Jellyfish also have been in the news*: Natalie Angier, "So Much More Than Plasma and Poison," *New York Times*, June 6, 2011, www.nytimes.com/2011/06/07/science /07jellyfish.html.

151 *See the Wikipedia entry for "encephalization quotient" for a chart*: "Encephalization quotient," Wikipedia, http://en.wikipedia.org/wiki/Encephalization_quotient.

151 *Finches use strict rules of syntax*: Jennifer Barone, "When Good Tweets Go Bad," *Discover*, November 7, 2011, http://discovermagazine.com/2011/nov/06-when-good -tweets-go-bad.

151 *New Caledonian crows show the advanced capability of metacognition*: See Marc Bekoff, "Crows and Tools: Calling Someone a Birdbrain Can Be a Compliment," *Psychology Today*, October 26, 2010, www.psychologytoday.com/blog/animal-emotions /201010/crows-and-tools-calling-someone-birdbrain-can-be-compliment.

152 *Alex, the world-renowned African gray parrot*: Ewen Callaway, "Alex the Parrot's Last Experiment Shows His Mathematical Genius," *Nature News Blog*, February 20, 2012, http://blogs.nature.com/news/2012/02/alex-the-parrots-last-experiment-shows -his-mathematical-genius.html.

152 *Most remarkably, bees with tiny brains use abstract thought and symbolic language*: The details about bees in this paragraph come from the following sources: "Insects Master Abstract Concepts," Phys.org, May 3, 2012, http://phys.org/news/2012 -05-insects-master-abstract-concepts.html; Virginia Morell, "Flying Math: Bees Solve Traveling Salesman Problem," *Wired*, September 21, 2012, www.wired.com /wiredscience/2012/09/bumblebee-traveling-salesman; Michael Simone-Finstrom and Marla Spivak, "Increased Resin Collection after Parasite Challenge: A Case of Self-Medication in Honey Bees?" PLOS ONE, March 29, 2012, doi: 10.1371 /journal.pone.0034601; W. Wu et al., "Honeybees Can Discriminate Between Monet and Picasso Paintings," *Journal of Comparative Physiology* 199, no. 1 (January 2013): 45–55, doi: 10.1007/s00359-012-0767-5.

152 *When songbirds learn their songs from mentors, specific neurons*: Sarah Bottjer, "Neural Circuit in the Songbird Brain That Encodes Representation of Learned Vocal Sounds

Located," *Neuroscience*, November 12, 2012, http://medicalxpress.com/news/2012 -11-neural-circuit-songbird-brain-encodes.html.

152 *An example is a specialized region for vocalization*: "Homolog of Mammalian Neo- cortex Found in Bird Brain," *Science Daily*, October 1, 2012, www.sciencedaily.com /releases/2012/10/121001151953.htm.

153 *The tiny honeybee brain has only around one million neurons, and according to one report*: Randolf Menzel, "The Honeybee as a Model for Understanding the Basis of Cogni- tion," *Nature Reviews Neuroscience* 13 (November 2012): 758–68, doi: 10.1038/nrn3357.

153 *Now we've learned that thrill-seeking individuals, known as scouts — who, according to a* New York Times *article*: Sindya Bhando, "Brains of Bee Scouts Are Wired for Ad- venture," *New York Times*, March 9, 2012, www.nytimes.com/2012/03/13/science /brains-of-honeybee-scouts-are-wired-for-adventure.html.

153 *Honeybees have forty different kinds of neurons*: Jon Lieff, "The Remarkable Bee Brain," Searching for the Mind blog, November 12, 2012, http://jonlieffmd.com /blog/the-remarkable-bee-brain-2.

154 *In an essay titled "Are Bigger Brains Better?"*: Lars Chittka and Jeremy Niven, "Are Bigger Brains Better?" *Current Biology* 19, no. 21 (November 17, 2009), doi: 10.1016 /j.cub.2009.08.023.

155 *Note: This essay was cowritten with Jon Lieff, MD*: Dr. Jon Lieff has spent three decades exploring the mind and how it functions in humans, animals, and nature. He is a graduate of Yale College and Harvard Medical School, and a past president of the American Association for Geriatric Psychiatry. His blog is Searching for the Mind (http://jonlieffmd.com), twitter @jonlieffmd, and Facebook, "Searching for the Mind."

156 *In a 2013 study by Barry Magee and Robert W. Elwood published*: Barry Magee and Robert W. Elwood, "Shock Avoidance by Discrimination Learning in the Shore Crab (*Carcinus maenas*) Is Consistent with a Key Criterion for Pain," *Journal of Experi- mental Biology* 216 (February 1, 2013), doi: 10.1242/ jeb.072041. The quote is from Joseph Castro, "Crabs Really Do Feel Pain: Study," *LiveScience*, January 16, 2013, www.livescience.com/26338-crabs-feel-pain.html.

156 *At the beginning of her chapter titled "Looking to the Future," she writes*: Victoria Braith- waite, *Do Fish Feel Pain?* (New York: Oxford University Press, 2010), 153.

157 *see the Endnotes for a study on mortality and catch-and-release methods*: Paul Reiss et al., "Catch and Release Fishing Effectiveness and Mortality," *Acute Angling*, last updated 2011, www.acuteangling.com/Reference/C&RMortality.html.

158 *In 2013, a fascinating essay was published by the British Veterinary Association*: Clifford Warwick et al., "Assessing Reptile Welfare Using Behavioural Criteria," in *Practice: Journal of the British Veterinary Association* 35 (May 10, 2013), doi: 10.1136/inp.f1197.

159 *Note: In a very interesting essay in* New Scientist *magazine called*: Adrian Bar- nett, "Tender Turtles: Their Mums Do Care After All," *New Scientist*, no. 2909 (March 28, 2013), www.newscientist.com/article/mg21729092.300-tender-turtles -their-mums-do-care-after-all.html.

160 *In her wonderful story about Kesho and Alf*: Charlotte Uhlenbroek, "The Hug That Says They're Just Like Us: As Two Gorilla Brothers Greet Each Other Like Old Friends, a Zoologist Says They Share Almost Every Human Emotion," *Daily*

Mail, August 16, 2012, www.dailymail.co.uk/news/article-2189591/The-hug-says -theyre-just-like-As-gorilla-brothers-greet-like-old-friends-zoologist-says-share -EVERY-human-emotion.html. For a slide show of photos of the meeting, see "Gorilla Brothers Kesho and Alf 'Joy' at Longleat Reunion," *BBC News,* August 16, 2012, www.bbc.co.uk/news/uk-england-wiltshire-19281347.

160 *researchers at the Max Planck Institute for Psycholinguistics have observed a chimpanzee mother:* Katherine Cronin and Edwin van Leeuwen, "Do Chimpanzees Mourn Their Dead Infants?" Max Planck Institute for Psycholinguistics, January 26, 2011, www .mpi.nl/news/news-archive/chimpanzee-mother-mourns-dead-infant.

162 *now there are some solid observations that they know what a trap means:* Bazi Kanani, "Gorillas Seen Dismantling Deadly Poacher Traps," *ABC News,* July 25, 2012, http://abcnews.go.com/blogs/headlines/2012/07/gorillas-seen-dismantling -deadly-poacher-traps.

164 *Here's what I wrote in 2007 in my book* The Emotional Lives of Animals: Marc Bekoff, *The Emotional Lives of Animals* (Novato, CA: New World Library, 2007), 82–83.

165 *Research by Dr. Hope Ferdowsian and her colleagues has clearly shown:* Hope Ferdowsian et al., "Signs of Mood and Anxiety Disorders in Chimpanzees," PLOS ONE, (June 16, 2011), doi: 10.1371/journal.pone.0019855.

165 *Nor is it surprising that dogs used in war, like humans who survive violent combat:* This example of PTSD in dogs comes from the essay by Marc Bekoff, "PTSD in War Dogs Finally Getting the Attention It Deserves," *Psychology Today,* December 2, 2011, www.psychologytoday.com/blog/animal-emotions/201112/ptsd-in-war-dogs -finally-getting-the-attention-it-deserves.

165 *A 2011 article in the* New York Times *notes:* James Dao, "After Duty, Dogs Suffer Like Soldiers," *New York Times,* December 1, 2011, www.nytimes.com/2011/12/02/us /more-military-dogs-show-signs-of-combat-stress.html.

168 *For example, it's been suggested that whales intentionally beach themselves:* For descriptions of these examples of animal suicides, see these resources: Brian Palmer, "Hairy-Kiri: Do Animals Commit Suicide?" *Slate,* November 16, 2011, www.slate.com /articles/news_and_politics/explainer/2011/11/beached_whales_in_new _zealand_do_animals_commit_suicide_.html; Kristal Parks, Re-Enchanting the World blog, The Elephant Conservationist: Working in Asia page, www.kristalparks .com/pachyderm/workinginasia.htm; Animal Liberation Front blog, David Neff, "Yes, Elephants Commit Suicide, February 1, 2006, www.animalliberationfront .com/Philosophy/Morality/Speciesism/ElephantsSuicide.htm; Neetzan Zimmerman, "Professor Claims Turkish Quake Made Cats Depressed, Suicidal," Gawker, May 22, 2012, http://gawker.com/5912287/professor-claims-turkish-quake-made -cats-depressed-suicidal.

170 *The authors "base every thesis about their human-like behavior":* John Marzluff and Tony Angell, *Gifts of the Crow: How Perception, Emotion, and Thought Allow Smart Birds to Behave Like Humans* (New York: Free Press, 2012), xiii.

170 *some researchers dismiss stories about animal behavior "because of ":* Marzluff and Angell, *Gifts of the Crow,* xii, xiii.

171 *"science teaches us to be skeptical, especially of the fantastic":* Marzluff and Angell, *Gifts of the Crow,* 43.

171   *Marzluff and Angell note that "crows and ravens routinely"*: Marzluff and Angell, *Gifts of the Crow*, 138.

172   *I ended a previous essay as follows*: Marc Bekoff, "Grief in Animals: It's Arrogant to Think We're the Only Animals Who Mourn," *Psychology Today*, October 29, 2009, www.psychologytoday.com/blog/animal-emotions/200910/grief-in-animals-its-arrogant-think-were-the-only-animals-who-mourn.

174   *I'm incredibly fortunate to live among wild animals*: I tell another version of this story, of the fox funeral in my book *The Emotional Lives of Animals*, 63–64.

176   *In the first, three different species of whales were involved*: Candace Calloway Whiting, "Humpback Whales Intervene in Orca Attack on Gray Whale Calf," *Digital Journal Reports*, May 8, 2012, www.digitaljournal.com/article/324348.

177   *In another example of an animal of one species helping a member of another species*: "Dog Pulls Unconscious Owner from Train's Path," WCVB.com, Boston May 8, 2012.

178   *a research group at the University of Bristol, using noninvasive methods*: J. L. Edgar, et al., "Avian Maternal Response to Chick Distress," *Proceedings of the Royal Society of Biological Sciences* 278, no. 1721 (October 2011), doi: 10.1098/rspb.2010.2701. See also David Derbyshire, "Chickens May Be Birdbrained, But They Can Still 'Feel' Each Other's Pain," *Daily Mail*, March 9, 2011, www.dailymail.co.uk/sciencetech/article-1364383/Scientists-say-chickens-empathy-feel-pain.html.

178   *Elephants also are making news once again*: Peter Aldhous, "Elephants Know When They Need a Helping Trunk," *New Scientist* (March 7, 2011), www.newscientist.com/article/dn20212-elephants-know-when-they-need-a-helping-trunk.html.

180   *a study published today conducted by Inbal Ben-Ami Bartal*: Inbal Ben-Ami Bartal, Jean Decety, and Peggy Mason, "Empathy and Pro-Social Behavior in Rats." *Science* 334, no. 6061 (December 9, 2011): 1,427–30, doi: 10.1126/science.1210789. See also Virginia Gewin, "Rats Free Each Other from Cages," *Nature*, December 8, 2011, www.nature.com/news/rats-free-each-other-from-cages-1.9603.

180   *A press release from the University of Chicago*: "Helping Your Fellow Rat: Rodents Show Empathy-Driven Behavior," press release, University of Chicago School of Medicine, December 8, 2011, www.uchospitals.edu/news/2011/20111208-empathy.html.

181   *In an earlier study in mice, researchers caused a lot of excruciating pain*: Ishani Ganguli, "Mice Show Evidence of Empathy," *The Scientist*, June 30, 2006, www.the-scientist.com/?articles.view/articleNo/24101/title/Mice-show-evidence-of-empathy/.

181   *As Jean Decety concludes in a very important paper on the evolution of empathy*: Jean Decety, "The Neuroevolution of Empathy," *Annals of the New York Academy of Sciences* 1231 (August 2011), doi: 10.1111/j.1749-6632.2011.06027.x.

182   *Now, according to an article about a new study, we know that wild ravens in the Austrian Alps use "their beaks and body language"*: Doug O'Harra, "Study: Ravens Communicate Better Than Most of Animal Kingdom," *Alaska Dispatch*, November 29, 2011, www.alaskadispatch.com/article/study-ravens-communicate-better-most-animal-kingdom. See also Linda Geddes, "Ravens Use Gestures to Grab Each Other's Attention," *New Scientist* (November 29, 2011), www.newscientist.com/article/dn21222-ravens-use-gestures-to-grab-each-others-attention.html.

182   *Thomas Bugnyar, a coauthor on this study, wrote on his project website*: Thomas Bugnyar,

"Raven Politics: Understanding and Use of Social Relationships," Konrad Lorenz Research Station, www.klf.ac.at/Research/raven_politics.htm.

183 *The first research paper describes an incident in which a group of bonobos*: Jessica Hamzelou, "Bonobos Are Caring Because They Are Led by Females," *New Scientist* (March 8, 2012), www.newscientist.com/article/mg21328553.800-bonobos-are -caring-because-they-are-led-by-females.html.

183 *A more detailed description of this remarkable event is given in the abstract for the original research paper*: Nahoko Tokuyama et al., "Bonobos Apparently Search for a Lost Member Injured by a Snare," *Primates* 53, no. 3 (July 2012): 215–19, http://link .springer.com/article/10.1007%2Fs10329-012-0298-2.

184 *Then, another study — this one conducted by Duke University researchers Jingzhi Tan and Brian Hare*: Sindya N. Bhanoo, "Milk of Human Kindness Also Found in Bonobos," *New York Times*, January 7, 2013, www.nytimes.com/2013/01/08 /science/the-unexpected-altruism-of-bonobos.html. See also Jingzhi Tan and Brian Hare, "Bonobos Share with Strangers," PLOS ONE, January 2, 2013, doi: 10.1371 /journal.pone.0051922.

185 *However, they do caution, following up on the work of Arizona State University's Kim Hill and his colleagues*: Kim Hill et al., "The Emergence of Human Uniqueness: Characters Underlying Behavioral Modernity," *Evolutionary Anthropology* 18, no. 5 (September/October 2009): 187–200, doi: 10.1002/evan.20224.

186 *Thus, concerning the utility of animal models, Mark Davis*: "We're Too Fixated on Mice, Says Leading Researcher," newsletter, Humane Society of the United States, February 29, 2009, www.humanesociety.org/news/news/2009/02/too_fixated _on_mice_022009.html.

186 *In 1994 I published an essay titled "Cognitive Ethology"*: Marc Bekoff, "Cognitive Ethology and the Treatment of Nonhuman Animals: How Matters of Mind Inform Matters of Welfare," *Animal Welfare* 3, no. 2 (May 1994): 75–96, www.ingenta connect.com/content/ufaw/aw/1994/00000003/00000002/art00002.

188 *When individual cognitive capacities are used for drawing lines along some arbitrary scale*: References for the source notes in the excerpted text for "Cognitive Ethology and the Treatment of Nonhuman Animals" follow in alphabetical order:

Bateson, P. P. G., "Assessment of Pain in Animals," *Animal Behaviour* 42 (1991): 827–39.

Callicott, J. B., "Animal Liberation: A Triangular Affair," in *In Defense of the Land Ethic: Essays in Environmental Philosophy*, J. Callicott (Albany, NY: State University of New York Press, 1980/1989), 15–38.

Cheney, D. L., and R. M. Seyfarth, "Dogs that Don't Bark in the Night: How to Investigate the Lack of a Domain of Expertise?" *Philosophy of Science Association* 2 (1993): 92–109.

DeGrazia, D., "The Moral Status of Animals and Their Use in Research: A Philosophical Review," *Kennedy Institute of Ethics Journal* (March 1991): 48–70.

Dresser, R., "Culpability and Other Minds," *Southern California Interdisciplinary Law Journal* 2 (1993): 41–88.

Duncan, I. J. H., "Measuring Preferences and the Strength of Preferences," *Poultry Science* 71 (1992): 658–63.

Duncan, I. J. H., "The Science of Animal Well-being," *Animal Welfare Information Center Newsletter* 4 (1993a): 1–7.

Duncan, I. J. H., and J. C. Petherick, "The Implications of Cognitive Processes for Animal Welfare," *Journal of Animal Science* 69 (1991): 5,017–22.

Gruen, L., "Animals," in *A Companion to Ethics*, ed. P. Singer (Cambridge, MA: Basil Blackwell, 1992), 343–53.

Hannay, A., *Human Consciousness* (New York: Routledge, 1990).

Kaufman, F., "Machines, Sentience, and the Scope of Morality," *Environmental Ethics* 16 (1994): 57–70.

Lewis, D., "Mad Pain and Martian Pain," in *Readings in Philosophy of Psychology*, vol. 1, ed. N. Block (Cambridge, MA: Harvard University Press, 1980), 216–22.

Mason, G. J., "Review of Wemelsfelder 1993," *Animal Welfare* 3 (1994): 57–60.

Orlans, F. B., In the *Name of Science: Issues in Responsible Animal Experimentation* (New York: Oxford University Press, 1993).

Rozin, P., "The Evolution of Intelligence and Access to the Cognitive Unconscious," in *Progress in Psychobiology and Physiological Psychology*, vol. 6, eds. J. N. Sprague and A. N. Epstein (New York Academic Press, 1976), 245–80.

Szentagothai, J., "The 'Mind-Brain' Relation: a Pseudoproblem?" in *Mindwaves: Thoughts on Intelligence, Identity, and Consciousness*, eds. C. Blakemore and S. Greenfield (New York: Basil Blackwell, 1987), 323–36.

Part 7. Wild Justice and Moral Intelligence: Don't Blame Other Animals for Our Destructive Ways

195   *In our forthcoming book,* Wild Justice: The Moral Lives of Animals, *philosopher Jessica Pierce and I*: Note that much of the material in this essay was taken from the book *Wild Justice*.

199   *Horgan argues, "I believe war will end for scientific reasons"*: John Horgan, *The End of War* (San Francisco: McSweeney's, 2012), 19.

199   *In another essay called "Quitting the Hominid Fight Club"*: John Horgan, "Quitting the Hominid Fight Club," *Scientific American*, June 29, 2010, www.scientificamerican .com/blog/post.cfm?id=quitting-the-hominid-fight-club-the-2010-06-29.

200   *The quotation in the title of this essay is taken from Horgan's book*: Horgan, *End of War*, 182.

201   *Along these lines, Robert W. Sussman, an anthropologist at Washington University*: Robert Sussman, Paul Garber, and Jim Cheverud, "Importance of Cooperation and Affiliation in the Evolution of Primate Sociality," *American Journal of Physical Anthropology* 128, no. 1 (2005): 84–97, doi: 10.1002/ajpa.20196. See also Robert Sussman, Paul Garber, and Jim Cheverud, "Reply to Lawler: Feeding Competition, Cooperation, and the Causes of Primate Sociality," *American Journal of Primatology* 73, no. 1 (January 2011): 91–95, doi: 10.1002/ajp.20889.

202   *Research has also shown that six-month-old babies know right from wrong*: Lin Edwards,

"Psychologists Say Babies Know Right from Wrong Even at Six Months," PhysOrg .com, May 10, 2010, http://phys.org/news192693376.html.

204 *Peterson offers a simple practical definition of morality*: Dale Peterson, *Elephant Reflections* (Berkeley: University of California Press, 2009), 51.

205 *He hopes that in the future we will move toward "greater tolerance"*: Peterson, *Elephant Reflections*, 22.

205 *Peterson's diverse background leads him to take a refreshingly novel and wide-ranging view*: Peterson, *Elephant Reflections*, 13–15.

205 *Alien does not mean lesser, just "imperfectly comprehensible"*: Peterson, *Elephant Reflections*, 285.

205 *He notes of the relationship between himself and his dogs, "we are friends"*: Peterson, *Elephant Reflections*, 19.

207 *an interdisciplinary meeting called "Obstacles and Catalysts of Peaceful Behavior"*: "Obstacles and Catalysts of Peaceful Behavior" was held from March 18 to 22, 2013, at the Lorentz Center in Leiden, The Netherlands, www.lorentzcenter.nl/lc /web/2013/527/info.php3?wsid=527&venue=Oort.

208 *In a recent interview, in response to the question "How does chimp behavior help us"*: Joseph Stromberg, "Interview: Jane Goodall on the Future of Plants and Chimps," *Smithsonian*, February 21, 2013.

209 *How to overcome the challenge of a human society built to wage war is the subject of ex-US Army Captain Paul Chappell's excellent book*: Paul K. Chappell, *Peaceful Revolution: How We can Create the Future Needed for Humanity's Survival* (Westport, CT: Easton Studio Press, 2012), xii, xiii.

Part 8. The Lives of Captive Creatures: Why Are They Even There?

213 *While there are "better" and "worse" zoos, animals residing in captivity live highly compromised lives*: For more on the living conditions of zoo animals, see Dale Jamieson, "Against Zoos," in *In Defense of Animals*, ed. Peter Singer (New York: Basil Blackwell, 1985), 108–17, www.animal-rights-library.com/texts-m/jamieson01.htm. See also my book *The Animal Manifesto*.

213 *some, like African elephants, die at a significantly younger age than their wild relatives*: "Elephants 'Die Earlier in Zoos,'" *BBC News*, December 11, 2008, http://news.bbc .co.uk/2/hi/science/nature/7777413.stm.

213 *No, according to a detailed 2010 study published in a peer-reviewed professional journal*: Lori Marino et al., "Do Zoos and Aquariums Promote Attitude Change in Visitors? A Critical Evaluation of the American Zoo and Aquarium Study," *Society and Animals* 19, no. 2 (2010): 126–38, doi: 10.1163/156853010X491980. For the AZA study, see www.aza.org/visitor-and-public-research.

215 *I just read an interesting interview in* National Geographic *with zoo expert David Hancocks*: Jordan Carlton Schaul, "A Critical Look at the Future of Zoos — An Interview with David Hancocks," *National Geographic*, March 13, 2012, http:// newswatch.nationalgeographic.com/2012/03/13/39842/.

218 *A recent essay in the* New York Times *has made me rethink why zoos exist*: Leslie Kaufman, "When Babies Don't Fit Plan, Question for Zoos Is, Now What?"

New York Times, August 2, 2012, www.nytimes.com/2012/08/03/science/zoos -divide-over-contraception-and-euthanasia-for-animals.html.

218   *My colleague Jessica Pierce also wrote about this essay*: Jessica Pierce, "Dilemma for Zoos: Contraception Before or Euthanasia After?" *Psychology Today*, August 3, 2012, www.psychologytoday.com/blog/all-dogs-go-heaven/201208/dilemma-zoos -contraception-or-euthanasia-after-o.

218   *I also was sickened to see an abstract of a paper by Paul Andrew, curator of the Taronga Zoo*: Animal Death Symposium, held on June 12 and 13, 2012, University of Sydney. Abstract of presentations, Paul Andrew, "Ethics and Intuition in Zoo Population Man-agement," http://sydney.edu.au/arts/research/harn/documents/Abstracts42012.pdf.

220   *For further discussion about why zoos must go, please see Dale Jamieson's essay "Against Zoos"*: Dale Jamieson, "Against Zoos," in *In Defense of Animals*, ed. Peter Singer (New York: Basil Blackwell, 1985), 108–17, www.animal-rights-library.com/texts-m /jamieson01.htm.

221   *As Michael Mountain reports on his Earth in Transition blog*: Michael Mountain, "Judge Rules for Elephants Against L.A. Zoo," Earth in Transition blog, July 25, 2012, www .earthintransition.org/2012/07/judge-rules-for-elephants-against-l-a-zoo/.

224   *Indeed, in 2010, SeaWorld was fined seventy-five thousand dollars by the Occupational Safety and Health Administration*: Dugald McConnell, "SeaWorld Fined $75,000 for Safety Violations," *CNN*, August 23, 2010, www.cnn.com/2010/US/08/23 /seaworld.fine/index.html.

225   *This wasn't the first time Tilly had killed a human*: For an overview of Tilly and the three human deaths he has been connected to, see Wikipedia, "Tilikum," http://en .wikipedia.org/wiki/Tilikum_(orca).

225   *I just learned that humans go into the water to play with Tilly's willy so that he pro-duces semen*: Karin Bennett, "Tommy Lee: Stop SeaWorld's Jerk-Offs," PETA Files, December 7, 2010, www.peta.org/b/thepetafiles/archive/tags/Tilikum" /default.aspx.

225   *One article about this includes a video of this process*: "How Does SeaWorld Mas-turbate Their Stud Killer Whales? Rocker Tommy Lee Says 'Cow Vaginas' and He Is Almost Right," The Orca Project blog, December 9, 2010, http://the orcaproject.wordpress.com/2010/12/09/how-does-seaworld-masturbate-their -stud-killer-whales-rocker-tommy-lee-says-"cow-vaginas"-and-he-is-almost-right. The webpage includes a video of this process, which can also be accessed on You-Tube at www.youtube.com/watch?v=TIU2-m_Vc7U.

227   *Damian Aspinall, who has taken over two wildlife parks founded by his father*: David Jones, "Why I'm Letting the Gorillas I Love Go Free: Son of Legendary Gambler John Aspinall Reveals He's Releasing the Animals from His Family Zoo Back to the Wild," *Daily Mail*, June 15, 2012, www.dailymail.co.uk/news/article-2160127 /John-Aspinalls-son-Damian-reveals-hes-releasing-animals-family-zoo-wild.html.

229   *I recently learned about a success story that is unfolding concerning*: Ivan Watson, "After Years in Captivity, Dolphins Released," *CNN*, May 12, 2012, www.cnn .com/2012/05/11/world/europe/turkey-dolphin-release/index.html. For a video story about their release, see "Dolphin Rescue — Tom and Misha," YouTube, posted September 9, 2010, www.youtube.com/watch?v=RNiNCWswQCI.

230 *However, serious injuries often occur when these animals are pushed beyond*: "The Jockey Club Releases Fatality Rate Data for Thoroughbred Racehorses," *Equine Chronicle*, March 24, 2010, www.equinechronicle.com/health/the-jockey-club-releases -fatality-rate-data-for-thoroughbred-racehorses.html.

230 *In May 2008, people around the world were horrified when Eight Belles*: "Eight Belles, Kentucky Derby Horse, Dies on Track," *Huffington Post*, May 11, 2008, www.huffing tonpost.com/2008/05/03/kentucky-derby-horse-eigh_n_99987.html.

230 *new research from the University of Sydney shows that "whipping horses is pointless"*: "Study Reveals Futility of Whipping Racehorses," RSPCA press release, January 27, 2011, www.rspca.org.au/media-centre/study-reveals-futility-of-whipping -racehorses.html. For an interview on the topic, see "Whipping Race Horses — Can It Be Justified?" *RN The Science Show*, January 29, 2011, www.abc.net.au /radionational/programs/scienceshow/whipping-race-horses---can-it-be-justified /3006250.

230 *The summary from the peer-reviewed published paper reads as follows*: David Evans and Paul McGreevy, "An Investigation of Racing Performance and Whip Use by Jockeys in *Thoroughbred Races*," PLOS ONE (January 27, 2011), doi: 10.1371/journal .pone.0015622.

232 *Some even died as a result of their mistreatment*: Rachel Abramowitz, "Animals Were Harmed in the Making of These Films," *The Age*, September 7, 2008, www.theage.com.au/news/entertainment/film/animals-were-harmed-in-the -making-of-these-films/2008/09/06/1220121589724.html. I also address this issue in the book *The Ten Trusts*, which I coauthored with Jane Goodall.

233 *CJ and Buddy, the two chimpanzees who escaped from a residential Clark County neighborhood in July 2012*: Many newspapers at the time covered this story. An interesting overview at the time was provided by George Knapp, "George Knapp: More on Chimps Buddy and C.J.," *Las Vegas CityLife*, July 25, 2012, http://lasvegascity life.com/sections/opinion/knappster/george-knapp-more-chimps-buddy-and -cj.html.

233 *We know that captive chimpanzees and other animals suffer from a wide variety*: For more on this, see the following resources: H. R. Ferdowsian et al., "Signs of Mood and Anxiety Disorders in Chimpanzees," PLOS ONE (2011), doi: 10.1371/journal .pone.0019855; "Chimpanzees Suffer PTSD Like Humans," *Project R&R News*, April 24, 2008, www.releasechimps.org/resources/article/chimpanzees-suffer-ptsd -like-humans; and Gay Bradshaw, *Elephants on the Edge* (New Haven, CT: Yale University Press, 2010).

234 *Then, consider the tragic story of the Connecticut woman whose face*: For an overview of this incident, see Wikipedia, "Travis (chimpanzee)," http://en.wikipedia.org/wiki /Travis_(chimpanzee).

235 *Let's also not forget the massacre of exotic animals in Ohio*: For information on this incident, see Greg Bishop and Timothy Williams, "Police Kill Dozens of Animals Freed on Ohio Reserve," *New York Times*, October 19, 2011, www.nytimes .com/2011/10/20/us/police-kill-dozens-of-animals-freed-from-ohio-preserve .html; and Marc Bekoff, "Bloodbath in Ohio: Numerous Exotic Animals Killed After Being Freed," *Psychology Today*, October 19, 2011, www.psychologytoday.com

/blog/animal-emotions/201110/bloodbath-in-ohio-numerous-exotic-animals
-killed-after-being-freed.

235 *Ohio had no regulations concerning the keeping of exotic animals as pets, but now they
     do*: "Ohio Gets an Overdue Law to Oversee Wild-Animal Ownership," Vindy.com,
     June 8, 2012, www.vindy.com/news/2012/jun/08/ohio-gets-an-overdue-law-to
     -oversee-wild/?newswatch.

Part 9. *Who* We Eat Is a Moral Question

241 *According to a 2009 essay in the* New York Times: Jane Brody, "Paying a Price for
     Loving Red Meat," *New York Times*, April 27, 2009, www.nytimes.com/2009/04/28
     /health/28brod.html.

241 *As Barbara Cook Spencer notes, when we abuse animals*: Barbara Cook Spencer, "When
     We Abuse Animals We Debase Ourselves," *Christian Science Monitor*, April 11, 2008,
     www.csmonitor.com/Commentary/Opinion/2008/0411/p09s01-coop.html.

242 *A December 2009 column in the* New York Times, *"Sorry, Vegans: Brussels Sprouts"*:
     Natalie Angier, "Sorry, Vegans: Brussels Sprouts Like to Live, Too," *New York
     Times*, December 21, 2009, www.nytimes.com/2009/12/22/science/22angi.html.

242 *federal legislation protecting "downer" cows and banning their use in food*: "Government
     Bans 'Downer' Cows from Food Supply," *Associated Press*, March 14, 2009, www
     .newsvine.com/_news/2009/03/14/2546655-government-bans-downer-cows-from
     -food-supply.

243 *In New Zealand, 34.2 million sheep, 9.7 million cattle, 1.4 million deer*: Bijal Trivedi,
     "How Kangaroo Burgers Could Save the Planet," *New Scientist*, no. 2687 (December
     25, 2008), www.newscientist.com/article/mg20026873.100-how-kangaroo-burgers
     -could-save-the-planet.html.

243 *As a* New York Times *story reported, "Producing a pound of beef"*: Elisabeth Rosenthal,
     "As More Eat Meat, a Bid to Cut Emissions," *New York Times*, December 3, 2009, www
     .nytimes.com/2008/12/04/science/earth/04meat.html.

243 *According to a* New York Times *essay*: Mark Bittman, "Rethinking the Meat-
     Guzzler," *New York Times*, January 27, 2008, www.nytimes.com/2008/01/27/week
     inreview/27bittman.html.

244 *Even the United Nations' Nobel Prize–winning scientific panel*: "Lifestyle Changes
     Can Curb Climate Change: IPCC Chief," Agence France-Presse, January 15, 2008,
     http://afp.google.com/article/ALeqM5iIVBkZpOUA9Hz3Xc2u-61mDlrwoQ.

246 *It's known that slaughterhouse workers may develop acute and chronic lung disease*: For
     these and more details on factory farming, see Wikipedia, "Factory Farming,"
     http://en.wikipedia.org/wiki/Factory_farming.

246 *Mad cow disease that causes variant Creutzfeldt-Jakob disease (vCJD)*: For more on
     this, see Kathy Freston, "How Factory Farms Are Pumping Americans Full of
     Deadly Bacteria and Pathogens," AlterNet, January 12, 2010, www.alternet.org
     /story/145068/how_factory_farms_are_pumping_americans_full_of_deadly_bacteria
     _and_pathogens.

246 *Millions of Americans are infected and thousands die each year*: For more on this, see

the Farm Sanctuary website, "Factory Farming," www.farmsanctuary.org/learn/factory-farming.

248 *In an all-too-brief April 2013 interview in the* New York Times *titled "Temple Grandin":* Andrew Goldman, "Temple Grandin on Autism, Death, Celibacy and Cows," *New York Times Magazine,* April 12, 2013, www.nytimes.com/2013/04/14/magazine/temple-grandin-on-autism-death-celibacy-and-cows.html.

248 *Years ago, here's what she wrote about this stairway:* This quote is from Ben Wolfson, "Kosher Slaughter," *Mishpahah* 364 (August 30, 1998): 16–17, www.grandin.com/ritual/kosher.slaughter.html.

249 *I first addressed this in a February 2010 essay called:* Marc Bekoff, "Going to Slaughter: Should Animals Hope to Meet Temple Grandin," *Psychology Today,* February 6, 2010, www.psychologytoday.com/blog/animal-emotions/201002/going-slaughter-should-animals-hope-meet-temple-grand.

252 *During the past six months I've been fortunate to go to a number of wonderful:* National Conference to End Factory Farming, October 27–29, 2011, http://conference.farmsanctuary.org/.

252 *For example, according to Farm Sanctuary, "the quantity of waste":* See the "Environmental Impact" page on the Farm Sanctuary website, www.nofoiegras.org/issues/factoryfarming/environment.

255 *As reported by Farm Sanctuary, recent research using functional magnetic resonance imaging:* Nick Cooney, "The Caring Vegetarian," Farm Sanctuary blog, July 12, 2012, http://ccc.farmsanctuary.org/the-caring-vegetarian. In the quote, I could not find the reference to Preyo and Arkiwawa, 2008, but the 2010 essay is from Massimo Filippi et al., "The Brain Functional Networks Associated to Human and Animal Suffering Differ Among Omnivores, Vegetarians and Vegans," PLOS ONE (May 26, 2010), doi: 10.1371/journal.pone.0010847.

256 *I just read an interview called "Killer Cuisine":* Twilight Greenaway, "Killer Cuisine: Can Hunting Help Us Make Better Food Choices," Grist.com, March 15, 2012, http://grist.org/food/girl-hunter-hunting-help-us-make-better-food-choices.

258 *There's even scientific research that shows that pigs can be optimists or pessimists:* "Can You Ask a Pig If His Glass Is Half Full?" *Science Daily,* July 28, 2010, www.sciencedaily.com/releases/2010/07/100727201515.htm.

259 *Paul McCartney once said, "If slaughterhouses had glass walls":* For Paul McCartney's quote, see the PETA "Glass Walls" video, http://action.peta.org.uk/ea-campaign/clientcampaign.do?ea.client.id=5&ea.campaign.id=5133.

260 *Carrie Packwood Freeman, who teaches at Georgia State University, points this out:* Carrie Packwood Freeman, "This Little Piggy Went to Press: The American News Media's Construction of Animals in Agriculture," *Communication Review* 12, no. 1 (2009): 78–103, doi: 10.1080/10714420902717764.

262 *Just today I learned about the cancellation of a dog-eating festival:* Wen Ya and Xu Tianran, "Dog Slaughter Continues," *Global Times,* October 17, 2011, www.globaltimes.cn/NEWS/tabid/99/ID/679495/Dog-slaughter-continues.aspx. See also Bo Gu, "Chinese Activists Rescue Dogs Destined for Dinner Table," NBC News, April 19, 2011, http://behindthewall.nbcnews.com/_news/2011/04/19/6496746-chinese-activists-rescue-dogs-destined-for-dinner-table.

263 *However, Christopher Cox disagrees, and in an April 2010* Slate *essay, he tries to argue that*: Christopher Cox, "Consider the Oyster," *Slate*, April 7, 2010, www.slate.com /articles/life/food/2010/04/consider_the_oyster.html.

264 *Braithwaite concludes, "I have argued that there is as much evidence"*: Victoria Braithwaite, *Do Fish Feel Pain?* (New York: Oxford University Press, 2010), 153.

Part 10. Who Lives, Who Dies, and Why:
Redecorating Nature, Peaceful Coexistence, and Compassionate Conservation

271 *a new publication called "Living with Wild Neighbors in Urban and Suburban Communities"*: For a copy of this pamphlet, visit the Humane Society of the United States website, www.humanesociety.org/animals/wild_neighbors/register_community _leaders_wildlife_guide.html.

272 *there's no dearth of information available for how to coexist humanely and ethically*: For more information, visit the Humane Society of the United States, "Wild Neighbors," www.humanesociety.org/animals/wild_neighbors/; read John Hadidian, *Wild Neighbors: The Humane Approach to Living with Wildlife* (Washington, DC: The Humane Society of the United States, 2007); and visit the Project Coyote website, www.projectcoyote.org.

275 *As human activity increases with soaring overpopulation and an increasing number of vehicles*: For the sources for this paragraph's statements, see Mark Matthew Braunstein, "Driving Animals to Their Graves," *Culture Change*, no. 8 (Spring 1996), www.culturechange.org/issue8/roadkill.htm; Richard T. T. Forman and Lauren Alexander, "Roads and Their Major Ecological Effects," *Annual Review of Ecology and Systematics* 29 (November 1998), doi: 10.1146/annurev .ecolsys.29.1.207; and Richard T. T. Forman et al., *Road Ecology: Science and Solutions* (Washington, DC: Island Press, 2003).

275 *Automobiles are a "development of eye consciousness rather than foot consciousness"*: Quote is from James Hillman, *A Blue Fire* (New York: HarperPerennial, 1989).

276 *around three thousand deer are killed annually*: This detail is from Jeff Peterson, Colorado Department of Transportation, personal communication.

276 *The detrimental impact of roads on Colorado's wildlife populations has been documented by Kevin Crooks and his colleagues*: Kevin Crooks et al., "Roads and Connectivity in Colorado: Animal-Vehicle Collisions, Wildlife Mitigation Structures, and Lynx-Roadway Interactions," Report No. CDOT-2008-4, Colorado Department of Transportation, Research Branch, March 2008, http://arc-solutions.org/wp-content /uploads/2012/03/Crooks-et-al.-2008-Roads-and-Connectivity-of-Colorado.pdf.

276 *the passage of a law called the Wildlife Crossing Zones Traffic Safety Law*: for text of this law, visit www.scribd.com/doc/28524137/Colorado-House-Bill-1238-highway -wildlife-crossing.

280 *A friend of mine just alerted me to a* Slate *essay in which author Jackson Landers*: Jackson Landers, "Why Kill Animals That Attack Humans?" *Slate*, July 11, 2012, www.slate. com/articles/health_and_science/science/2012/07/an_alligator_ate_my_arm _should_we_kill_it_.single.html#comments.

283 *From time to time I've written about the many horrific and heartless ways in which*

Wildlife Services: Tom Knudson, "Federal Agency Kills 7,800 Animals by Mistake in Steel Body-Grip Traps," *Sacramento Bee*, April 29, 2012, www.sacbee .com/2012/04/28/4450684/federal-agency-kills-7800-animals.html. See also Marc Bekoff, "Bella, a Husky, Miraculously Survives Illegal Government Snare, Dismissed as an 'Act of God,'" *Psychology Today*, February 22, 2012, www.psychologytoday .com/blog/animal-emotions/201202/bella-husky-miraculously-survives-illegal -government-snare-dismissed-act; and Marc Bekoff, "Dog Killed by Wildlife Services: The Horrific War on Wildlife Knows No Bounds or Decency," *Psychology Today*, April 20, 2011, www.psychologytoday.com/blog/animal-emotions/201104 /dog-killed-wildlife-services-the-horrific-war-wildlife-knows-no-bounds-0.

283   *Now, a three-part series by Tom Knudson of the* Sacramento Bee *on the clandestine activities*: The three-part report is as follows: Tom Knudson, "The Killing Agency: Wildlife Services' Brutal Methods Leave a Trail of Animal Death," *Sacramento Bee*, April 29, 2012, www.sacbee.com/2012/04/28/4450678/the-killing -agency-wildlife-services.html; Tom Knudson, "Wildlife Services' Deadly Force Opens Pandora's Box of Environmental Problems," *Sacramento Bee*, April 30, 2012, www.sacbee.com/2012/04/30/4452212/wildllife-services-deadly-force.html; and Tom Knudson, "Suggestions in Changing Wildlife Services Range from New Practices to Outright Bans," *Sacramento Bee*, May 6, 2012, www.sacbee.com /2012/05/06/4469067/suggestions-in-changing-wildlife.html.

283   *You can also preview the 2012 documentary* Wild Things: Daniel Hinerfeld, "Wildlife Services: You've Read the Exposé, Now Watch the Movie," NRDC Switchboard blog, May 3, 2012, http://switchboard.nrdc.org/blogs/dhinerfeld/wildlife_services _youve_read_t.html.

For more on ranchers who choose more humane ways to deal with potential predators, see Peter Fimrite, "Ranchers Shift from Traps to Dogs to Fight Coyotes," *San Francisco Chronicle*, April 27, 2012, www.sfgate.com/science/article/Ranchers -shift-from-traps-to-dogs-to-fight-coyotes-3514405.php.

284   *Here is a summary of some of Wildlife Services' egregious activities*: see Knudson, "The Killing Agency."

285   *According to WildEarth Guardians (www.wildearthguardians.org), between 2004 and 2010*: See "Ending the War on Wildlife," WildEarth Guardians, www.wildearth guardians.org/site/PageServer?pagename=priorities_wildlife_war_wildlife# .UZZGGBxdah8.

285   *WildEarth Guardians has sued Wildlife Services*: Tom Knudson, "Environmental Group Sues to Halt Killing Practices of Federal Wildlife Agency," *Sacramento Bee*, May 2, 2012, www.sacbee.com/2012/05/02/4458430/environmental-group-sues-to -halt.html.

286   *The US Fish & Wildlife Service keeps track of the number of people who hunt and fish*: US Fish & Wildlife Service, Wildlife & Sport Fish Restoration Program, 2011 National Survey, http://wsfrprograms.fws.gov/Subpages/NationalSurvey/2011_Survey.htm.

286   *One example of this egregious activity that made the news in 2012*: Marc Bekoff, "Trumping Wildlife: Heinous Trophy Hunting, Not Conservation," *Psychology Today*, March 14, 2012, www.psychologytoday.com/blog/animal-emotions/201203 /trumping-wildlife-heinous-trophy-hunting-not-conservation.

286 *Hunting for food or clothing that aren't needed really amounts to sport hunting*: For more on this issue, see "Why Sport Hunting Is Cruel and Unnecessary," PETA press release, www.peta.org/issues/wildlife/why-sport-hunting-is-cruel-and-unnecessary.aspx.

286 *or species more appropriately called "out of place species," according to my Australian colleague Dr. Rod Bennison*: Rod Bennison, "An Inclusive Re-engagement with Our Nonhuman Animal Kin: Considering Human Interrelationships with Nonhuman Animals," *Animals* 1, no. 1 (2011): 40–55, doi: 10.3390/ani1010040.

287 *For example, this is happening with the iconic kangaroo*: Marc Bekoff, "Kangaroos: These Iconic Animals Are Relentlessly Slaughtered Throughout Australia and They Shouldn't Be," *Psychology Today*, December 12, 2010, www.psychology today.com/blog/animal-emotions/201012/kangaroos-these-iconic-animals -are-relentlessly-slaughtered-throughout-a. For more information, visit the website for Thinkk, http://thinkkangaroos.uts.edu.au.

287 *In some instances the animals are tortured in the most egregious ways*: For more information on these incidents, see Marc Bekoff, "Trapped Wolf Used for Target Practice," *Psychology Today*, March 29, 2012, www.psychologytoday.com /blog/animal-emotions/201203/trapped-wolf-used-target-practice; Lauren Toney, "Protestors Decry Predator Master Convention; Group Says They're Misunderstood," *Las Cruces Sun-News*, February 9, 2013, www.lcsun-news.comlas_cruces -news/ci_22557936/protesters-decry-predator-masters-convention-group-says -theyre?source=most_emailed; Cheryl Hanna, "Upstate N.Y. Fire Department to Host 'Hazzard County Squirrel Slam,'" Examiner.com, February 5, 2013, www .examiner.com/article/upstate-n-y-fire-department-to-host-hazzard-county -squirrel-slam.

287 *Some call pig dogging "arguably the cruellest and most brutal form of hunting"*: See "Stop Savage 'Pig Dogging' in Australia," Animals Australia, www.animalsaustralia .org/take_action/stop-pig-dogging/. See also Dan Proudman, "Pig Dogging Supporter Speaks Out," *Newcastle Herald*, October 27, 2012, www.theherald.com.au /story/424341/pig-dogging-supporter-speaks-out/.

288 *For compassionate conservation, the first premise is "First do no harm"*: Marc Bekoff, "Conservation and Compassion: First Do No Harm," *New Scientist* (September 1, 2010), www.newscientist.com/article/mg20727750.100-conservation-and-compassion -first-do-no-harm.html.

289 *In a previous essay I wrote about the plight of captive-bred pandas*: Marc Bekoff, "Pandas: Do We Really Need Another Cute 'Ambassador'?" *Psychology Today*, September 17, 2012, www.psychologytoday.com/blog/animal-emotions/201209/pandas-do-we -really-need-another-cute-ambassador. See also Marc Bekoff, "Baby Panda Dies at National Zoo, Mother Grieves," *Psychology Today*, September 23, 2012, www .psychologytoday.com/blog/animal-emotions/201209/baby-panda-dies-national -zoo-mother-grieves.

289 *one video of a baby panda sneezing*: See "The Sneezing Baby Panda," YouTube, posted November 6, 2006, www.youtube.com/watch?v=FzRH3iTQPrk.

289 *This past Friday (February 22, 2013) giant pandas once again appeared in major news media*: Kate Snow, "Are Giant Pandas Worth Saving?" Rock Center with

Brian Williams, *NBC News*, February 21, 2013, http://rockcenter.nbcnews.com/_news/2013/02/21/16964074-are-giant-pandas-worth-saving?lite.

289 *Similarly, noted conservation psychologist and* Psychology Today *blogger Susan Clayton writes*: Susan Clayton, "The Panda Page," May 31, 2011, http://sustainability.scotblogs.wooster.edu/2011/05/31/the-panda-page/.

290 *In an essay called "Another Inconvenient Truth"*: Elizabeth Bennett, "Another Inconvenient Truth: The Failure of Enforcement Systems to Save Charismatic Species," *Oryx* 45, no. 4 (October 2011): 476–79, doi: 10.1017/S0030605311000178X. See also David Malakoff, "Another Inconvenient Truth," *Conservation*, June 24, 2011, www.conservationmagazine.org/2011/06/another-inconvenient-truth.

290 *In an Internet survey conducted by the Univeristy of York's Murray Rudd*: Murray Rudd, "Scientists' Opinions on the Global Status and Management of Biological Diversity," *Conservation Biology* 25, no. 6 (December 2011): 1,165–75, doi: 10.1111/j.1523-1739.2011.01772.x. See also "Is It Time to Let Some Species Go Extinct?" *New Scientist*, no. 2838 (November 12, 2011), www.newscientist.com/article/mg21228383.800-is-it-time-to-let-some-species-go-extinct.html.

294 *A study published in 2006 in the prestigious peer-reviewed journal* Science: "Even Mice Show Empathy for Each Other," *New Scientist*, no. 2559 (July 6, 2006), www.newscientist.com/article/mg19125595.400-even-mice-show-empathy-for-each-other.html.

295 *It has been estimated that when only released surviving ferrets are considered*: See Karl Hess Jr., "Saving the Black-Footed Ferret: Policy Reforms and Private Sector Incentives," research paper no. 32, Thoreau Institute, www.ti.org/bffhess.html.

295 *Biologists John Vucetich and Michael Nelson argue in their excellent paper titled*: John Vucetich and Michael Nelson, "What Are 60 Warblers Worth? Killing in the Name of Conservation," *Oikos* 116, no. 8 (August 2007): 1,267–78, doi: 10.1111/j.00301299.2007.15536.x.

296 *We suggest that the guiding principles for conservation projects*: For more on this, see Marc Bekoff, "The Importance of Ethics in Conservation Biology: Let's Be Ethicists Not Ostriches," *Endangered Species Update*, March 1, 2002, www.thefreelibrary.com/The+importance+of+ethics+in+conservation+biology:+let's+be+ethicists...-a087426650.

298 *VINE, a sanctuary near GMC, has offered to have them live there for free*: See "Action Alert: Act Now to Save Bill and Lou!" *VINE Sanctuary News*, October 9, 2012, http://blog.bravebirds.org/archives/709.

301 *it's been estimated by the ASPCA (www.aspca.org) that "approximately 5 million"*: This quote is from the ASPCA website, FAQ, "Pet Statistics," www.aspca.org/about-us/faq/pet-statistics.aspx.

301 *In the United Kingdom alone, more than 120,000 stray dogs*: Robin Knowles, "Number of Stray Dogs Is on the Rise, Says Dogs Trust," *BBC Radio Newsbeat*, September 5, 2011, www.bbc.co.uk/newsbeat/14754304.

301 *In Detroit, Michigan, there are at least 50,000 stray dogs*: Marc Binelli, "City of Strays: Detroit's Epidemic of 50,000 Abandoned Dogs," *Rolling Stone*, March 20, 2012, www.rollingstone.com/culture/news/city-of-strays-detroits-epidemic-of-50-000-wild-dogs-20120320.

303 *Compassionate conservation is a rapidly growing interdisciplinary and international*

movement: For information on these events, see Marc Bekoff, "Compassionate Conservation Finally Comes of Age: Killing in the Name of Conservation Doesn't Work," *Psychology Today*, August 20, 2010, www.psychologytoday.com/blog/animal-emotions/201008/compassionate-conservation-finally-comes-age-killing-in-the-name-conserv; Compassionate Conservation International Symposium, University of Oxford, September 1–3, 2010, www.bornfree.org.uk/comp/compconsymp2010.html; Marc Bekoff, "Animal Protection and Conservation in Asia: Animal Emotions Matter," *Psychology Today*, June 16, 2011, www.psychologytoday.com/blog/animal-emotions/201106/animal-protection-and-conservation-in-asia-animal-emotions-matter; and Lori Marino, "Compassionate Conservation Needs to Be Based on Rights," Kimmela Center for Animal Advocacy blog, December 7, 2012, www.kimmela.org/compassionate-conservation-needs-to-be-based-on-rights/.

303 *The gathering in Sydney was called "Compassionate Conservation"*: For further information and interviews, visit "Is Recreational Hunting Defensible?" A Question of Balance website, www.aqob.com.au/details.php?p_id=151&listid=616&slistid=&menuid=category_id_16&submenuid. Transcripts and video of the talks can be found on the University of Technology Sydney: Science website, www.science.uts.edu.au/science-in-focus/compassionate-conservation.html and www.science.uts.edu.au/multimedia/flash-media/transcripts/in-focus/compassionate-conservation.html.

Part 11. Rewilding Our Hearts:
The Importance of Kindness, Empathy, and Compassion for All Beings

309 *This essay, called the "Twelve Millennial Mantras"*: Marc Bekoff and Jane Goodall, "Twelve Millenial Mantras," http://animalliberty.com/articles/marc-bekoff/marc-13.html. This essay first appeared in the Boulder, Colorado, *Daily Camera*, December 19, 1999.

312 *We've learned that it's natural to be good, cooperative, kind, empathic, and compassionate*: see also Christopher Bergland, "The Evolutionary Biology of Altruism," *Psychology Today*, December 25, 2012, www.psychologytoday.com/blog/the-athletes-way/201212/the-evolutionary-biology-altruism.

312 *A free online book called* Kids & Animals: Marc Bekoff, *Kids & Animals: Drawings from the Hands and Hearts of Children and Youth* (Boulder, CO: Children, Youth & Environments Center, University of Colorado, 2011); download a copy of this book at www.ucdenver.edu/academics/colleges/ArchitecturePlanning/discover/centers/CYE/Publications/Pages/Books.aspx.

313 *We know that being positive and hopeful are important for getting people to care and to act*: Michael Slezak, "How to Convince Climate Change Sceptics to be Pro-environment," *New Scientist* (June 17, 2012), www.newscientist.com/article/dn21932-how-to-convince-climate-sceptics-to-be-proenvironment.html.

314 *A July 2102 essay in the* New York Times *called "Compassion Made Easy"*: David DeSteno, "Compassion Made Easy," *New York Times Sunday Review*, July 14, 2012, www.nytimes.com/2012/07/15/opinion/sunday/the-science-of-compassion.html.

316 *as ethologist Peter Verbeek calls it, a "peace ethology"*: Peter Verbeek, "Peace Ethology," *Behaviour* 145, no. 11 (2008): 1,497–1,524, doi:10.1163/156853908786131270.

317 *reminded me of a very interesting and important* New York Times *essay concerning*: Daniel B. Smith, "Is There an Ecological Unconscious?" *New York Times Magazine*, January 27, 2010, www.nytimes.com/2010/01/31/magazine/31ecopsych-t.html. For more on the concept of solastalgia, see Emily Loose, "Solastalgia — Homesick for the Wilderness," The Wild Foundation blog, February 1, 2010, www.wild.org /blog/solastalgia-homesick-for-the-wilderness, and "What Is Solastalgia?" *Seed*, May 20, 2013, http://seedmagazine.com/content/article/what_is_solastalgia.

317 *Years ago I discovered the following quotation by the renowned author Henry Miller*: Henry Miller, *Big Sur and the Oranges of Hieronymus Bosch* (New York: New Directions, 1957), 93.

320 *One report on the conference said, "The results reveal that, on average"*: "IUCN Study Confirms Vertebrate Extinction Crisis," Arkive.com blog, October 27, 2010, http:// blog.arkive.org/2010/10/iucn-study-confirms-vertebrate-extinction-crisis.

322 *Robert Berry fears we're simply "running out of world"*: Robert Berry, *God's Book of Works* (London: Continuum, 2003).

322 *two well-known conservation biologists, Michael Soulé and Reed Noss, wrote a now-classic paper called*: Michael Soulé and Reed Noss, "Rewilding and Biodiversity: Complementary Goals for Continental Conservation," *Wild Earth* 8 (Fall 1998): 18–28.

324 *Erle Ellis, who works in the Department of Geography and Environmental Systems*: Erle C. Ellis, "Forget Mother Nature: This Is a World of Our Making," *New Scientist*, no. 2816 (June 14, 2011), www.newscientist.com/article/mg21028165.700-forget -mother-nature-this-is-a-world-of-our-making.html.

326 *When I need an "upper," I find myself revisiting another essay I wrote*: Marc Bekoff, "Animals and Us: Maintaining Hope and Keeping Our Dreams Alive in Difficult Times," *Psychology Today*, December 12, 2009, www.psychologytoday.com/blog /animal-emotions/200912/animals-and-us-maintaining-hope-and-keeping-our -dreams-alive-in-difficul.

BIBLIOGRAPHY

Aitken, Gill. *A New Approach to Conservation*. Hants, England: Ashgate Publishing, 2004.

Balcombe, Jonathan. *Second Nature: The Inner Lives of Animals*. Hampshire, England: Palgrave Macmillan, 2010.

Baur, Gene. *Farm Sanctuary: Changing Hearts and Minds About Animals and Food*. New York: Touchstone, 2008.

Beatley, Timothy, and Peter Newman. *Green Urbanism Down Under: Learning from Sustainable Communities in Australia*. Washington, DC: Island Press, 2008.

Becker, Marty. *The Healing Power of Pets*. New York: Hyperion, 2003.

Bekoff, Marc, ed. *The Smile of a Dolphin: Remarkable Accounts of Animal Emotions*. New York: Random House/Discovery Books, 2000.

————. *Minding Animals: Awareness, Emotions, and Heart*. New York: Oxford University Press, 2003.

————. *Animal Passions and Beastly Virtues: Reflections on Redecorating Nature*. Philadelphia: Temple University Press, 2005.

————. *Animals Matter*. Boston: Shambhala, 2007.

————. *The Emotional Lives of Animals*. Novato, CA: New World Library, 2007.

————. *Animals at Play: Rules of the Game*. Philadelphia: Temple University Press, 2008.

————. *The Animal Manifesto: Six Reason for Expanding Our Compassion Footprint*. Novato, CA: New World Library, 2010.

————, ed. *Ignoring Nature No More: The Case for Compassionate Conservation*. Chicago: University of Chicago Press, 2013.

Bekoff, Marc, and Cara Blessley Lowe, eds. *Listening to Cougar*. Boulder: University Press of Colorado, 2008.

Bekoff, Marc, and Jessica Pierce. *Wild Justice: The Moral Lives of Animals*. Chicago: University of Chicago Press, 2010.

Berger, John. *About Looking*. New York: Pantheon Books, 1980.

Bexell, Sarah, and Zhang Zhihe. *Giant Pandas: Born Survivors*. New York: Penguin Global, 2013.

Blumstein, Daniel, and Esteban Fernandez-Juricic. *A Primer of Conservation Behavior*. Sunderland, MA: Sinauer Associates, 2010.

Boesch-Ackerman, Christophe, and Hedwige Boesch-Ackerman. *The Chimpanzees of the Taï Forest*. New York: Oxford University Press, 2000.

Bradshaw, Gay. *Elephants on the Edge*. New Haven, CT: Yale University Press, 2010.

Braithwaite, Victoria. *Do Fish Feel Pain?* New York: Oxford University Press, 2010.

Burghardt, Gordon M. *The Genesis of Animal Play*. Cambridge, MA: MIT Press, 2005.

Burton, Neel. *Hide & Seek: The Psychology of Self-Deception*. Oxford, England: Acheron Press, 2012.

Cerulli, Tovar. *The Mindful Carnivore: A Vegetarian's Hunt for Sustenance*. New York: Pegasus, 2012.

Chance, Michael R. A., and Ray R. Larsen. *Social Structure of Attention*. Hoboken, NJ: John Wiley & Sons, 1976.

Chappell, Paul K. *Peaceful Revolution: How We Can Create the Future Needed for Humanity's Survival*. Westport, CT: Easton Studio Press, 2012.

Clayton, Susan, ed. *The Oxford Handbook of Environmental and Conservation Psychology*. New York: Oxford University Press, 2012.

Clayton, Susan, and Gene Myers. *Conservation Psychology: Understanding and Promoting Human Care for Nature*. Hoboken, NJ: Wiley-Blackwell, 2009.

Coetzee, J. M. *The Lives of Animals*. Princeton, NJ: Princeton University Press, 1999.

Cooney, Nick. *Change of Heart: What Psychology Can Teach Us About Spreading Social Change*. New York: Lantern Books, 2011.

Corballis, Michael. *The Recursive Mind*. Princeton, NJ: Princeton University Press, 2011.

Darwin, Charles. *On the Origin of Species*. New York: Signet Classics, 1859/1958.

———. *The Descent of Man and Selection in Relation to Sex*. New York: Random House, 1871/1936.

Dawkins, Marian. *Why Animals Matter: Animal Consciousness, Animal Welfare, and Human Well-being*. New York: Oxford University Press, 2012.

Derr, Mark. *Dog's Best Friend*. Chicago: University of Chicago Press, 1997/2004.

———. *A Dog's History of America*. New York: North Point Press, 2004.

———. *How the Dog Became the Dog*. New York: Overlook Press, 2011.

de Waal, Frans. *The Age of Empathy: Nature's Lessons for a Kinder Society*. New York: Broadway, 2010.

Dugatkin, Lee Alan. *Principles of Animal Behavior*, 3rd ed. New York: W. W. Norton & Co., 2013.

Dunlap, Julie, and Stephen Kellert, eds. *Companions in Wonder: Children and Adults Exploring Nature Together*. Cambridge, MA: MIT Press, 2012.

Ehrlich, Paul, *A World of Wounds: Ecologists and the Human Dilemma*. Oldendorf/Luhe, Germany: Ecology Institute, 1997.

Foreman, Dave. *Rewilding North America: A Vision for Conservation in the 21st Century*. Washington, DC: Island Press, 2004.

Forman, Richard T. T., et al. *Road Ecology: Science and Solutions*. Washington, DC: Island Press, 2003.

Fraser, Caroline. *Rewilding the World: Dispatches from the Conservation Revolution*. New York: Henry Holt & Co., 2009.

Fry, Douglas. *Beyond War: The Human Potential for Peace*. New York: Oxford University Press, 2009.

————, ed. *War, Peace, and Human Nature: The Convergence of Evolutionary and Cultural Views*. New York: Oxford University Press, 2012.

Gigliotti, Carol, ed. *Leonardo's Choice: Genetic Technologies and Animals*. New York: Springer, 2010.

Goodall, Jane. *The Chimpanzees of Gombe*. Cambridge, MA: Belknap Press, 1986.

Goodall, Jane, and Marc Bekoff. *The Ten Trusts: What We Must Do to Care for the Animals We Love*. San Francisco: HarperCollins, 2002.

Goldstein, Joshua. *Winning the War on War*. New York: Dutton, 2011.

Grandin, Temple, with Richard Panek. *The Autistic Brain: Thinking Across the Spectrum*. New York: Houghton Mifflin Harcourt, 2013.

Greek, Ray, and Niall Shanks. *FAQs About the Use of Animals in Science*. Millburn, NJ: University Press of America, 2009.

Greger, Michael. *Bird Flu: A Virus of Our Own Hatching*. New York: Lantern Books, 2006.

Gruen, Lori. *Ethics and Animals: An Introduction*. New York: Cambridge University Press, 2011.

Gullone, Eleonora. *Animal Cruelty, Antisocial Behaviour, and Aggression: More than a Link*. Hampshire, England: Palgrave Macmillan, 2012.

Hadidian, John. *Wild Neighbors: The Humane Approach to Living with Wildlife*. Washington, DC: The Humane Society of the United States, 2007.

Hare, Brian, and Vanessa Woods. *The Genius of Dogs: How Dogs Are Smarter Than You Think*. New York: Dutton, 2013.

Heinrich, Bernd. *Life Everlasting: The Animal Way of Death*. New York: Houghton Mifflin Harcourt, 2012.

Herzog, Hal. *Some We Love, Some We Hate, Some We Eat*. New York: HarperCollins, 2010.

Hillman, James. *A Blue Fire*. New York: HarperPerennial, 1989.

Horgan, John. *The End of War*. San Francisco: McSweeney's, 2012.

Horowitz, Alexandra. *Inside of a Dog: What Dogs See, Smell, and Know*. New York: Scribner, 2009.

Imhoff, Daniel, ed., *CAFO: The Tragedy of Industrial Animal Factories*. San Rafael, CA: Earth Aware Editions, 2010.

Irvine, Leslie. *If You Tame Me: Understanding Our Connections with Animals*. Philadelphia: Temple University Press, 2004.

————. *My Dog Always Eats First: Homeless People and Their Animals*. Boulder, CO: Lynne Rienner Publishers, 2013.

Keltner, Dacher. *Born to Be Good*. New York: W. W. Norton, 2009.

Kirby, David. *Death at SeaWorld: Shamu and the Dark Side of Killer Whales in Captivity*. New York: St. Martin's Press, 2012.

Landers, Jackson. *Eating Aliens: One Man's Adventures Hunting Invasive Animal Species*. North Adams, MA: Storey Publishing, 2012.

Levine, Peter. *Waking the Tiger: Healing Trauma*. Berkeley, CA: North Atlantic Books, 1997.

Louv, Richard. *Last Child in the Woods*. Chapel Hill, NC: Algonquin Books, 2005.

Marzluff, John, and Tony Angell. *Gifts of the Crow: How Perception, Emotion, and Thought Allow Smart Birds to Behave Like Humans*. New York: Free Press, 2012.

Masson, Jeffrey Moussaieff, and Susan McCarthy. *When Elephants Weep: The Emotional Lives of Animals*. New York: Delacorte Press, 1995.

McConnell, Patricia. *For the Love of a Dog*. New York: Ballantine Books, 2007.

Nowak, Martin, and Roger Highfield. *Super Cooperators: Altruism, Evolution, and Why We Need Each Other to Succeed*. New York: Free Press, 2011.

Olmert, Meg Daley. *Made for Each Other: The Biology of the Human-Animal Bond*. Cambridge, MA: Da Capo Press, 2009.

Palmer, Chris. *Shooting in the Wild: An Insider's Account of Making Movies in the Animal Kingdom*. San Francisco: Sierra Club Books, 2010.

Payne, Katy. *Silent Thunder: In the Presence of Elephants*. New York: Penguin Books, 1999.

Pellegrini, Georgia. *Girl Hunter: Revolutionizing the Way We Eat, One Hunt at a Time*. Cambridge, MA: Da Capo Lifelong Books, 2011.

Pellis, Sergio, and Vivien Pellis. *The Playful Brain: Venturing to the Limits of Neuroscience*. London: Oneworld Publication, 2010.

Peterson, Dale. *Elephant Reflections*. Berkeley: University of California Press, 2009.

————. *The Moral Lives of Animals*. New York: Bloomsbury Press, 2011.

Rachels, James. *Created from Animals: The Moral Implications of Darwinism*. New York: Oxford University Press, 1990.

Regan, Tom. *The Case for Animal Rights*. Berkeley: University of California Press, 1983.

Restak, Richard, and Scott Kim. *The Playful Brain*. New York: Riverhead Books, 2010.

Rivera, Michelle. *On Dogs and Dying*. West Lafayette, IN: Purdue University Press, 2010.

Robbins, Martha, and Christophe Boesch. *Among African Apes*. Berkeley: University of California Press, 2011.

Robinson, Jill, and Marc Bekoff. *Jasper's Story: Saving Moon Bears*. Chelsea, MI: Sleeping Bear Press, 2013.

Ryan, Thomas. *Animals and Social Work: A Moral Introduction*. Hampshire, England: Palgrave Macmillan, 2011.

Sahn, Jennifer, ed. *Thirty-Year Plan: Thirty Writers on What We Need to Build a Better Future*. Great Barrington, MA: Orion, 2012.

Schoen, Allen. *Kindred Spirits: How the Remarkable Bond Between Humans and Animals Can Change the Way We Live*. New York: Broadway, 2002.

Sharpe, Lynne, *Creatures Like Us?* Exeter, England: Imprint Academci, 2005.

Shumaker, Robert, Kristina Walkup, Benjamin Beck, and Gordon Burghardt. *Animal Tool Behavior: The Use and Manufacture of Tools by Animals*. Baltimore, MD: Johns Hopkins University Press, 2011.

Singer, Peter, ed. *In Defense of Animals*. New York: Basil Blackwell, 1985.

Sussman, Robert W., and C. Robert Cloninger, eds. *Origins of Altruism and Cooperation*. New York: Springer, 2011.

Tobias, Michael, and Jane Morrison, *Donkey: The Mystique of Equus Asinus*. Tulsa, OK: Council Oak Books, 2006.

————. *The Bonobo and the Athiest: In Search of Humanism Among the Primates*. New York: W. W. Norton & Co, 2013.

Williams, Erin, and Margo DeMello. *Why Animals Matter: The Case for Animal Protection*. Amherst, NY: Prometheus Books, 2007.

Wilson, Edward O. *Biophilia*. Cambridge: Harvard University Press, 1984.

Wise, Steven. *Rattling the Cage: Toward Legal Rights for Animals*. New York: Perseus Publishing, 2001.

————. *Drawing the Line: Science and the Case for Animal Rights*. New York: Basic Books, 2003.

INDEX

In Defense of Animals, 106
Indiana Coyote Rescue Center, 196
individual exceptionalism, 44, 87
Inside of a Dog (Horowitz), 79, 87
Institute for Human-Animal Connection
 (Denver University), 10, 317
Interactive Futures meeting (Vancouver,
 BC), 65–66
interconnectedness, 278
International Congress for Conservation
 Biology, 303
International Homeless Animals Day, 302
interrelationships, 1–2
 See also human-animal bond
interspecies cooperation, 176–77
intimidation, training techniques based on,
 104–6
Invictus (film), 326
iPads, orangutan use of, 133
Irvine, Leslie, 74–75
Isle Royale National Park, 102
Iyal (cognitively impaired boy), 76–77

Jaicks, Hannah, 215
Jamestown (CO), *272*, 272–73
Jamieson, Dale, 122, 171, 220
Jasper (moon bear), 25–28, 312–13
Jasper's Story (Bekoff and Robinson), 313
Jaws (film), 280
jellyfish, 150
Jethro (dog), 26, 30–31, 72, 88–89, 112,
 120–21, 124, 189–90, 191
Jevbratt, Lisa, 66
Jewel (elephant), 221
Jinhua (Zhejiang Province, China), 262
Joe (coyote), 165
Joe (homeless man), 74
Journal of Experimental Biology, 156
joy, 86, 160
justice, sense of, 196
juvenilization, 95–96

kangaroos, 287
Kanzi (bonobo), 127–28, 129
Karisoke Research Center (Rwanda), 162
Katz, Elliot, 106
Kaufman, F., 191

Kean University, 12
Kellert, Stephen, 274
Kelley, Lee Charles, 102, 103, 335n103
Keltner, Dacher, 202
Kentucky Derby (2008), 230
Kesho (gorilla), 160
Kids & Animals (online book; Bekoff), 18,
 312
Kindness Ranch, 258
Kindred Spirits (Schoen), 12
King, Barbara J., 49–50
Kirby, David, 215, 223–24
Knudson, Tom, 283
Kotler, Steven, 143
Krajnc, Anita, 258
Krause-Parello, Cheryl, 12
Kyoto University (Japan), 183

Lahvis, Garet, 182
Lambert, CeAnn, 196–97
Landers, Jackson, 280–81
Langdale, Kaleb, 281
language, 46, 141, 152, 260
Lantin, Maria, 65
Larsen, Ray, 101
Last Child in the Woods (Louv), 17–18
lateralization, 141–42
laughing, 46
LeDoux, Joseph, 114
Leeuwen, Edwin van, 160
Leonardo's Choice (ed. Gigliotti), 65, 66
leopards, 280
Levine, Peter, 166
Lewis, D., 191
Libby (cat), 196
Library Journal, 223
Lieff, Jon, 151–55, 340n155
Lilly (dog), 177
Linn, Susan, 18
lions, 235, 280
Lisbon Treaty (2009), 113, 117–18
Lives of Animals, The (Coetzee), 36–37
"Living with Wild Neighbors in Urban
 and Suburban Communities" (Humane
 Society), 271–72
lizards, 135–36, 270
Lobster (dog), 28–29

ABOUT THE AUTHOR

MARC BEKOFF IS professor emeritus of ecology and evolutionary biology at the University of Colorado, Boulder, and a former Guggenheim Fellow. In 2000 he was awarded the Exemplar Award from the Animal Behavior Society for major long-term contributions to the field of animal behavior, and in 2009 he was presented with the Saint Francis of Assisi Award by the Auckland (New Zealand) SPCA. Marc has published more than 800 scientific and popular essays and twenty-five books, including *Minding Animals*, *The Ten Trusts* (with Jane Goodall), *The Emotional Lives of Animals*, *Animals Matter*, *Animals at Play: Rules of the Game*, *Wild Justice: The Moral Lives of Animals*, *The Animal Manifesto: Six Reasons for Expanding Our Compassion Footprint*, *Ignoring Nature No More: The Case for Compassionate Conservation*, *Jasper's Story: Saving Moon Bears*, the *Encyclopedia of Animal Rights and Animal Welfare*, the *Encyclopedia of Animal Behavior*, and the *Encyclopedia of Human-Animal Relationships*. In 2005 Marc was presented with the Bank One Faculty Community Service Award for the work he has done with children, senior citizens, and prisoners as part of Jane Goodall's Roots & Shoots program. His websites are www.marcbekoff.com and, with Jane Goodall, www.ethologicalethics.org.